Social Structure and Political Theory

WILLIAM E. CONNOLLY
GLEN GORDON
University of Massachusetts, Amherst

Social Structure and Political Theory

D. C. HEATH AND COMPANY
Lexington, Massachusetts Toronto London

Published simultaneously in Canada.

Printed in the United States of America.

International Standard Book Number: 0–669–83923–X

Library of Congress Catalog Card Number: 73–9233

PREFACE

Philosophy, political science, and sociology as academic disciplines intersect at many points in social inquiry. Our purpose in this volume is to identify such points of intersection and to indicate how work within each can illuminate dark areas in the others. We shall examine and compare alternative theories of social structure and politics, theories advanced by social theorists who recognize that the attempt to render intelligible the broadest dimensions of social and political life requires a perspective broader than that offered by any single academic discipline.

Essays by Kingsley Davis and Wilbert Moore, Gerhard Lenski, and C. Wright Mills,* placed at the center of this volume, stake out alternative positions on the central question we seek to probe; the other essays revolve around the arguments of these authors, preparing the reader to compare the positions reflectively and exposing problems in each view that require critical attention.

Each of the core authors attempts to explain a perennial feature of social life: the nature and causes of social inequality. Inequalities in power, prestige, opportunities for satisfying social relationships, income, and property, each of these writers agrees, are persistent features of modern industrial society. Yet despite the ubiquity of social inequality, there remains a variety of interpretations as to which of its dimensions are the most important, what factors explain the persistence of the important dimensions, and to what extent politics can or should provide a vehicle for reducing the important inequalities. These variations in interpretation, in turn, reflect more fundamental theoretical differences, which are seldom explored carefully by the proponents of each theory. Identification of the basic assumptions, the conceptual contours, and the normative priorities of each theoretical perspective enables us to translate underlying disagreements into explicit issues subject to critical reflection and judgment.

We are grateful to those who participated in our graduate and undergraduate seminars at the University of Massachusetts from 1970 to 1972, both for con-

* To conform to conditions established by the original publishers of the selections from Mills, we have listed them as three separate readings (8, 9, 10). The intent of our volume, however, is best fulfilled if each selection is read as part of a single perspective or essay which diverges at several points from views advanced by Davis and Moore and Lenski, respectively.

tributing to our understanding of the pertinent issues and for suggesting selections for this volume that help to clarify those issues.

A final note of thanks is due to Beverly Labbee for her outstanding clerical assistance and to Pat Rector and Mary K. Lewis for their competence in handling other matters associated with the volume.

CONTENTS

IV. Theoretical Conflict and Critical Choice

Social Structure and Political Theory

INTRODUCTION

POWER, HUMAN NATURE, AND SOCIAL INEQUALITY

Though most investigators agree about many of the "facts" of inequality, the importance of these facts depends to a large extent upon the perspective one brings to the question. Let us take the present situation in the United States as an example. When Alexis de Tocqueville traveled in the United States before the Civil War, he was struck by the relative economic equality of Americans, which he judged to be remarkable compared to the situation in Europe. However, with the coming of rapid industrialization after the Civil War, considerable disparities in the distribution of wealth and income developed. While scant statistical data is available for this period, there seems little doubt that the period of industrialization, reaching its climax in the last decades of the nineteenth century, created a new class of great wealth and increased the gap between rich and poor in American society generally.

Probably the most seminal and most frequently cited study of income distribution in the twentieth century is Gabriel Kolko's *Wealth and Power in America,* published in 1962. Kolko has amassed impressive statistical evidence suggesting that the distribution of income in America since 1910 is marked by considerable and persistent inequalities. According to Kolko, in 1910, the bottom 20% of the population received 8.3% of the national personal income; by 1959 that segment's share had actually declined to 4%. Meanwhile, in 1910, the top 10% of the population received 33% of the national personal income; their share declined modestly to 28.9% by 1959.[1]

More recent studies of income distribution corroborate Kolko's findings. Frank Ackerman et al.,[2] in an article published in 1972, argue that during the postwar period in America, the poorest 20% have consistently received less

[1] Gabriel Kolko, *Wealth and Power in America* (New York: Praeger Publishers, 1962), p. 14. Of course the distribution of income represents but one dimension of inequality. Kolko also provides considerable data on the distribution of wealth (that is, stocks and bonds, real estate, savings) and finds it to be even more concentrated than income. See Ibid., pp. 46–54.

[2] Frank Ackerman, Howard Birnbaum, James Wetzler, and Andrew Simbalist, "The Extent of Income Inequality in the United States," in *The Capitalist System,* ed. Richard C. Edwards, Michael Reich, and Thomas E. Weisskopf (Englewood Cliffs, New Jersey: Prentice-Hall, Inc., 1972), pp. 208–209.

than 6% of total personal income, while the top 20% have received over 40% (see Table 1). In 1969, for example, the top 5% received 14.7% of total

TABLE 1. Distribution of Before-Tax Family Income

	1969	*1964*	*1960*	*1956*	*1950*	*1947*
Poorest Fifth	5.6%	5.2%	4.9%	5.0%	4.5%	5.0%
Second Fifth	12.3%	12.0%	12.0%	12.4%	12.0%	11.8%
Middle Fifth	17.6%	17.7%	17.6%	17.8%	17.4%	17.0%
Fourth Fifth	23.4%	24.0%	23.6%	23.7%	23.5%	23.1%
Richest Fifth	41.0%	41.1%	42.0%	41.2%	42.6%	43.0%
Richest 5%	14.7%	15.7%	16.8%	16.3%	17.0%	17.2%

Source: U.S. Census Bureau, *Current Population Reports,* Series P-60, No. 75, Table 11, p. 26.

family income—more than twice as much as the entire bottom 20%. Ackerman argues further that the decline in the share of top-income groups, reflected in Table 1, results from the exclusion from Census Bureau data of capital gains. If the increase in the value of assets is included in the calculation, the relative position of the top fifth has been constant during the twenty-year period.

All of the data presented above refer to income *before taxes.* Since we presumably have a "progressive" income tax system, the distribution of income *after taxes* should manifest less inequality. Yet, as the data in Table 2 indicate, the share of the top fifth of the population is only about two percentage points lower after taxes.

TABLE 2. Income Distribution Before and After the Federal Income Tax, 1962

	Poorest Fifth	*Second Fifth*	*Middle Fifth*	*Fourth Fifth*	*Richest Fifth*	*Richest 5%*
Before Tax	4.6%	10.9%	16.3%	22.7%	45.5%	19.6%
After Tax	4.9%	11.5%	16.8%	23.1%	43.7%	17.7%

Source: Edward C. Budd, *Inequality and Poverty* (New York: W. W. Norton, 1967), pp. xiii, xvi.

Clearly, there are a number of features in the tax laws that give the income of certain individuals and groups special treatment and therefore reduce the effectiveness of the tax system to promote equality. Thus, as Table 3 indicates, the percentage of income paid in taxes differs very little whether a family earns $6,000 or $50,000. It is also important to recognize that less than 40%

of all taxes collected are based upon the progressive income tax system. An almost equal amount is collected in property and sales taxes, forms of taxation that most experts agree fall more heavily on the poor than the rich.

TABLE 3. Taxes and Taxes Less Transfers as Per Cent of Income, 1968

Income	*Taxes*	*Taxes Less Transfers**
$ 0–2,000	40.3%	−24.7%
2,000–4,000	32.8	− 5.6
4,000–6,000	30.8	14.9
6,000–8,000	30.5	23.5
8,000–10,000	29.8	25.4
10,000–15,000	30.5	27.3
15,000–25,000	30.6	28.2
25,000–50,000	33.2	31.6
50,000 and over	45.3	44.9

* Minus indicates transfer payments from federal, state, and local governments exceeded amounts paid in taxes.

Source: C. Peter Magrath, Elmer E. Cornwell, Jr., and Jay S. Goodman, *The American Democracy*, 2nd ed. (New York: The Macmillan Company, 1973), p. 53; data from *Counterbudget, A Blueprint for Changing National Priorities 1971–1976*, ed. Robert S. Benson and Harold Wolman (New York: Praeger Publishers, 1971) © 1971 by the National Urban Coalition.

As Frank Parkin points out in a recent study of social stratification, inequalities in the distribution of income are correlated roughly with inequalities along other dimensions.[3] We can consider occupational categories to form a hierarchy in which professional and managerial positions receive the highest income, followed by semi-professional, routine white collar, skilled manual, semi-skilled manual, and unskilled manual. And, as Parkin shows, the inequalities in income among these positions are matched by other inequalities of reward as well. For example, managerial employees are more likely than manual employees to have (or to have more fully) sick pay schemes, adequate pension plans, long-term economic security, clean and safe working environments, freedom to plan their own work schedules and routines, a voice in decision-making in their firm, and so on.[4] When inequalities are cumulatively attached to occupational categories in this manner, we can speak meaningfully of a stratification system and of the stratified occupational categories as the "backbone" of the social structure.

If inequalities of income and reward attached to occupational positions are

[3] Frank Parkin, *Class Inequality and Political Order* (New York: Praeger Publishers, 1971), p. 19.

[4] Ibid., p. 25.

TABLE 4. Median Income of Civilians (25 years and older) with Year-round, Full-time Jobs, 1968

Years of Schooling		*Male Income*	*Female Income*	*Ratio*
Elementary — less than	8	$ 5,300	$3,300	.62
	8	$ 6,600	$3,600	.55
High School	1–3	$ 7,300	$3,900	.53
	4	$ 8,300	$4,800	.58
College	1–3	$ 9,300	$5,500	.59
	4	$11,800	$6,700	.57
	5 or more	$12,800	$8,300	.64
	Total	$ 8,100	$4,700	.58

Source: U.S. Census Bureau, *Current Population Reports,* Series P-60, No. 66, Table 41, p. 98.

significant, has the school system equalized *opportunities* among strata of the society to attain the more privileged positions? While it is true that better-educated people earn higher incomes, it is also true that children who come from wealthier families receive more education. Table 4 indicates the linkage between level of education and income. Table 5 suggests that college education is closely correlated with family income and also indicates that a high

TABLE 5. College Attendance of High School Graduates by Income, 1966

Family Income in 1965	*Percentage of 1966 High School Graduates Who Started College by February, 1967*
Under $3,000	19.8
$3,000–$4,000	32.3
$4,000–$6,000	36.9
$6,000–$7,000	41.1
$7,500–$10,000	51.0
$10,000–$15,000	61.3
Over $15,000	86.7
Total, all incomes	46.9%

Source: U.S. Census Bureau, *Current Population Reports,* Series P-20, No. 185, Table 8.

school senior from the top-income group is over four times as likely to enter college as a senior from the bottom group. One might be tempted to conclude that the data in Table 5 simply reflect unequal scholastic ability in high school and do not reflect any additional inequalities related to the process of college admission. Yet, as Samuel Bowles has shown, although children from upper-income groups whose parents have received advanced education perform substantially better on national standardized tests, access to college is unequal even for children of the same academic ability. Thus, the data in Table 6 indicate that high school students in the top quartile of ability are twice as likely to go to college if they come from the highest income group than if they come from the lowest. Bowles concludes his analysis by asserting that "on balance, the available data suggest that the number of years of schooling which the average

TABLE 6. Probability of College Entry for a Male Who Has Reached Grade 11*

		*Socioeconomic Quartiles**			
		Low 1	*2*	*3*	*High 4*
	Low 1	.06	.12	.13	.26
Ability	2	.13	.15	.29	.36
Quartiles	3	.25	.34	.45	.65
	High 4	.48	.70	.73	.87

* Based on a large sample of U.S. high school students as reported in John C. Flannagan and William W. Cooley, *Project* TALENT, *One-Year Follow-Up Studies,* Cooperative Research Project No. 2333, School of Education, University of Pittsburgh, 1966.

† The socioeconomic index is a composite measure including family income, father's occupation and education, mother's education, and so on. The ability scale is a composite of tests measuring general academic aptitude.

Source: Samuel Bowles, "Unequal Education and the Reproduction of the Hierarchical Division of Labor," in *The Capitalist System,* ed. Richard C. Edwards, Michael Reich, and Thomas E. Weisskopf (Englewood Cliffs, N.J.: Prentice-Hall, Inc., 1972), p.217.

child attains depends at least as much upon the social class of his father as it did fifty years ago." [5]

The facts suggest, then, that inequality remains a persistent feature of American social life. Despite the general increase in prosperity since the years of the Great Depression, the basic distribution of wealth and income in the United States remains essentially the same now as it was in 1939 or even in 1910. Clearly, although the real wages of low-income groups have risen during this period, their relative percentage of the national income has not changed significantly.

Yet even if we were to accept these facts as more or less accurate, their presentation represents only the barest beginnings of analysis. Their proper interpretation requires an answer to a whole host of very difficult questions. Why are burdens and benefits distributed unequally in modern industrial so-

[5] Samuel Bowles, "Unequal Education and the Reproduction of the Hierarchical Division of Labor," in *The Capitalist System,* ed. Richard C. Edwards, Michael Reich, and Thomas E. Weisskopf (Englewood Cliffs, New Jersey: Prentice-Hall, Inc., 1972), p. 226.

cieties? Is inequality along these dimensions perceived as a problem or as a reflection of the functional requirements of modern industrial society? What standard shall we use to decide whether inequalities in the United States are "substantial" or "insignificant"? Shall we compare the United States today with the United States of fifty years ago and celebrate the increase in real wages, or shall we compare the United States with other modern industrial societies (for example, Sweden) and bemoan the fact that poverty remains so widespread in the midst of such phenomenal affluence? Does the complex division of labor apparently induced by advanced technology extend these inequalities or diminish them? To what extent do inequalities in some spheres (such as income, security, educational opportunity, chances for fulfilling work) arise from disparities in the distribution of power? If these inequalities do flow in part from power disparities, how are the latter to be explained, and to what extent are they remediable through politics? If remediable, what are the costs of "taking the remedy"?

In considering alternative responses to these questions, a host of problems emerge. For example, social theorists do not concur fully on what to count as a "burden" and what as a "benefit" in distribution systems. We cannot, for instance, ascertain whether anomie is a burden distributed unequally between workers and managers until we have decided whether the theory of anomie itself is valid. And judgments about the degree to which members of different classes are susceptible to mental illness might depend in part upon whose definition of "mental illness" is to be accepted.

Several other difficult and controversial issues arise in this context. Is our study of inequality more appropriately geared to analysis of the extent to which *opportunities* for advancement are distributed unequally among different segments of society? Or should we study the extent to which the *positions* to be filled are graded by inequalities of status, income, and opportunities for personal fulfillment? Answers to these two questions do not necessarily flow in the same direction. Equality of opportunity might operate in a system where only a few privileged positions are available and where the benefits attached to those top positions are significantly greater than those attached to positions at the bottom of the system. Conversely, a system with inequalities of opportunity might stratify income and other benefits narrowly, so that the top positions carry only two or three times more income than those at the bottom.

Finally, we must decide which lines of differentiation are to be given the most weight in the study of inequality. Are inequalities between classes more or less important than those between generations, genders, races, or nations? Do women in the lower class have more in common with upper-class women than with lower-class males? Do lower-class males of twenty, say, have more in common with lower-class males of seventy than they do with middle-class males of twenty? Questions about the appropriate units of analysis, the definition of burdens and benefits, the relative importance of equality of opportunity and equality of condition, and the relationships between inequality, social function, and power must be confronted in the process of developing a theory of social inequality. And before such a theory can proceed very far, one is forced to turn to fundamental questions about the relationships between human nature and social organization.

Our purpose in this volume, then, goes beyond providing substantive material on the dynamics of inequality and social malaise. Our further intent is to explore a set of methodological considerations (in the broadest sense) that enable students to subject the core theories advanced in Part III by Davis and Moore, Lenski, and Mills to the most careful kinds of critical scrutiny. Our most general objective is to contribute to a broader understanding of the theoretical dimensions of social and political inquiry.

Perhaps we can exemplify at least one aspect of this objective a bit more concretely. In his essay on power and privilege, Gerhard Lenski explicitly *assumes* that most people in all societies are primarily motivated by considerations of self-interest and that, partially as a result of these motivations, as the surplus of a society expands, inequalities in privilege and status will increase. Those assumptions seem to fit his study of hunting and gathering, horticultural, and agricultural societies; but as he points out, the range of inequality in advanced industrial societies is less than his assumptions would lead one to expect. His problem now becomes to *explain* why inequalities in industrial societies are not greater. He must either adopt an explanation that preserves his initial assumptions about human nature or conclude that his explanation of inequality in the nonindustrial societies is faulty. Since he believes his theory of human nature is well supported by empirical evidence, he opts for the former course. But what is an anomaly to be explained for Lenski is for C. Wright Mills an expectation flowing from his most fundamental assumptions. Mills's assumptions about human nature make it possible to *expect* less inequality in a society with a large surplus; he has to *explain* why the prevailing inequalities are as great as they are. For Mills rejects Lenski's view that "human nature" is basically the same in all societies. The motivational systems dominant in any society, according to Mills, are explicable in terms of the socialization processes of that society. People are not always and everywhere aggressive and self-serving:

> it is *not* true . . . that "man's chief enemy and danger is his own unruly nature" . . . ; on the contrary: man's chief danger today lies in the unruly form of contemporary society itself, with its alienating methods of production, its enveloping techniques of political domination, its international anarchy—in a word, its pervasive transformations of the very "nature" of man and the conditions and aims of his life.[6]

Adopting different images of human nature, Mills and Lenski are led to opposing interpretations of social inequality.

[6] C. Wright Mills, "Troubles in Mass Society," in this volume, p. 162.

Davis and Moore find both these explanatory theories to be defective. In their view, Mills and Lenski both overestimate the role power normally plays in maintaining modern stratification systems. As they state their view, "a position does not bring power and prestige *because* it draws a high income. Rather it draws a high income because it is functionally important." [7] Power is less important in explaining stratification than either Mills or Lenski imagines; for "every society . . . must differentiate persons in terms of both prestige and esteem, and must therefore possess a certain amount of institutionalized inequality." [8]

Mills, Lenski, and Davis and Moore, then, confront many of the same facts about inequality in modern society. But since they draw upon different assumptions, each accounts for those facts in a way somewhat opposed to the accounts of the others. What is to be expected, from the vantage point of assumptions accepted by one theorist, are phenomena to be explained, given the corollary assumptions of the other. And each theorist believes he has independent arguments to support these basic assumptions. The task of theoretical judgment then becomes complicated. If the independent evidence available is insufficient to establish any single set of assumptions authoritatively, then those trying to assess the comparative strengths and weaknesses of each theory are placed in a quandary.

The lead essays by Charles Taylor and William Connolly are intended to clarify issues of this sort. Taken together, they seek to clarify *connections* between a particular set of assumptions and the explanatory theory it supports, to elucidate the *normative implications* of accepting one such explanatory framework over others, and to explore possible routes to *rational judgment* among competing theories when the most basic assumptions dividing them are not currently amenable to empirical resolution.

Taylor argues that acceptance of an explanatory theory goes some distance toward implicating one in a corollary set of normative judgments. No explanation of any complexity can be offered, Taylor contends, in the absence of a theoretical framework. Yet to adopt an explanatory theory is to adopt, first, a schedule of human needs, wants, and purposes and, second, to lay out the alternative ways in which these needs, wants, and purposes can be met or frustrated. To adopt a particular theory, then, is to maintain that certain ideals cherished by some are simply unattainable, that other ideals would impose heavy costs on wide segments of the society if implemented, and that still others are attainable in ways that are at least moderately fulfilling to most of the inhabitants. And, as Taylor argues in the last section of his essay, once such "dimensions of variation" in a theory are married to those rules of normative discourse tacitly understood by all investigators, the theory itself

[7] Kingsley Davis and Wilbert Moore, "Some Principles of Stratification," in this volume, p. 119.

[8] Ibid., p. 114.

can be seen to generate a set of normative commitments. There are qualifications noted by Taylor to this general thesis, but they do not undermine its central point.

It is not therefore coincidental, Taylor argues, that one who accepts the explanatory theory of western democracy advanced by, say, Seymour Martin Lipset, will also support the elitist ideal of democracy Lipset advances. For according to Lipset's interpretation (a) a classless, conflict-free society is unattainable; (b) a democracy of widespread participation promotes disorder and tends to lead to autocracy; (c) a democracy of open elections and competition among diverse elites within a general consensus promises to protect freedom in a context of social stability. When one appraises these alternative possibilities from the moral point of view, it becomes clear that one could hardly accept as correct the interpretation of alternatives while rejecting the *concept* and *ideal* of democracy (c) advanced by Lipset. If Taylor's argument is valid, similar connections between explanatory theory and prescriptive judgment can be discerned in the work of Lenski, Davis and Moore, and Mills. These latter essays can be viewed both as a test and an illustration of Taylor's thesis.

It is important to see here that Taylor is not simply arguing that the biases one brings to inquiry infiltrate into one's explanatory theory. More fundamentally, he contends that the results of any empirical inquiry that purports to explain always carry normative import. This nexus between "fact" and "value" helps to explain, if true, just why the debates between proponents of opposing explanatory theories are often so intense; it reveals further just what turns on the judgment to adopt one theoretical framework and to reject others.

William Connolly's essay on theoretical self-consciousness builds on Taylor's argument. Exploring the connections *within* a theory among its set of basic assumptions, its conceptual system, and its test procedures, he argues that proponents of a given explanatory/normative theory can draw upon impressive resources to protect their cherished theory from defeat. But the very availability of such resources introduces serious complications into efforts to adjudicate *between* opposing theories. Advocates of opposing theories are likely to construe key concepts such as "power" or "class" in somewhat different ways and to weigh the importance of available test procedures differently. These subtle differences make it easy for the proponents of one theory to misconstrue central points in other theories; such differences also make it difficult for students comparing these theories critically to adduce evidence which can effectively adjudicate between them. But these difficulties, according to Connolly, do not force a retreat to complete skepticism. For as one becomes more fully aware of the presuppositions and conceptual contours of his own theory, and as he becomes better able to view opposing theories as alternatives worthy of consideration, he opens himself to new arguments and forms of evidence previously beyond his reach.

If the essays in Part I lay the groundwork for examining the basic assumptions and normative implications of alternative theories, those in Part II exemplify the importance and difficulty of the enterprise. For Hobbes, Marx, and Durkheim agree that the theory of human nature one adopts profoundly shapes one's understanding of social and political life, but each opts for a theory of human nature and society fundamentally opposed to that of the other two.

Hobbes sketches an image of the abstract individual who is motivated primarily by desires for security, glory, and happiness, whose motivational system is basically the same in all societies, and whose fixed characteristics provide the basis from which social explanation and evaluation must proceed. In Hobbes' view, and in the view of other individualists as well, we can explain the sources of order and disorder in society and evaluate rationally the desirability of alternative social ideals only after we have faced up to the fixed motivational structure programmed into all human beings in every society.

Both Marx and Durkheim repudiate all versions of the theory of abstract individualism. They agree that the image of the abstract individual is, in the words of Marx, "as great an absurdity as the idea of the development of language without individuals living together and talking to one another." [9] In Durkheim's view, the Hobbesian individual is not a universal phenomenon, but a particular historical type that emerges when the ties of community break down. The restless egoist, "in a perpetual state of discontent," [10] suffers from anomie. Lacking a socially defined station with clearly stated rules, expectations, and rights attached to it, detached from a rich tradition that can give meaning and purpose to life, people in such circumstances will *take on* the characteristics of Hobbesian individuals. And when an entire society becomes anomic, from "top to bottom of the ladder, greed is aroused without knowing where to find the ultimate foothold. Nothing can calm it, since its goal is far beyond all it can attain." [11]

Since Durkheim does not trace this restless egoism to the innate and invariant characteristics of all human beings, but to particular forms of social life, his response to this pattern is quite unlike that of Hobbes. The postulate of the restless egoist does not explain social organization; rather, a particular form of social organization explains the restless egoist. Anomie will be resolved, then, by a form of social life that nurtures solidarity and authority; persons socialized to particular roles in such a hierarchical sytem will come to define themselves in terms of their station and to view their socially defined roles as morally legitimate. Shaped and developed by the roles they internalize, they will adapt their purposes to socially legitimate aspirations within their reach. Perhaps the elimination of anomie will require the maintenance of inequalities in material rewards, authority, and prestige, but this is a small price to pay for the

[9] Quoted in Steven Lukes, *Individualism* (Oxford: Basil Blackwell, 1973), p. 76.

[10] Emile Durkheim, "On Anomie," in this volume, p. 76.

[11] Ibid., p. 83.

benefits of life in an organic community where each knows his place and his role in the whole system.

Marx agrees that an individualistic view of human nature cannot be invoked to explain social organization; he agrees too that the restless egoist is a particular type peculiar to a historically specific system best described as "bourgeois society." "Activity and mind," he says, "are social in their content as well as in their *origin;* they are *social* activity and *social* mind." [12] The individual in bourgeois society, socialized primarly through the division of labor, is alienated from his species life. "In general, the statement that man is alienated from his species life means that each man is alienated from others, and that each of the others is likewise alienated from human life." [13]

But though Marx joins Durkheim in his critique of Hobbesian individualism, his understanding of and response to the specific historical conditions that produce such individualism is rather different from Durkheim's. "Species life" for Marx involves less the adjustment to established social roles and more the active involvement by persons in shaping and defining those roles; it involves less an acceptance of narrow specialization on the part of role bearers and more the development of broad and diverse interests on the part of citizens; it involves less an appreciative understanding of stable arrangements and more the development of a critical consciousness with respect to prevailing arrangements. Conditions postulated by Durkheim to resolve anomie will, in Marx's view, sustain alienation; and Marx's unalienated persons will suffer, in Durkheim's view, from at least a mild case of anomie.

Through comparing the classic images of human nature and society offered by Hobbes, Durkheim, and Marx to the contemporary theories of social organization offered by Lenski, Davis and Moore, and Mills, one can see what role an image of human nature plays in explanatory and normative theory. The former theorists illuminate ideas that play a central but less explicit role in the thought of their contemporary counterparts. It is too simple to say that Lenski adopts Hobbesian individualism, Davis and Moore the theory of anomie, and Mills the theory of alienation; for none of these contemporary theorists can be fitted neatly or completely into any single classical framework. Nevertheless, there are definite connections here, and attention to similarities and differences at this basic level exposes a dimension of social theory that has been pushed into the background of contemporary studies. Comparisons between the classical and contemporary theories help one to come to grips with the underlying dimensions of contemporary perspectives in ways that the proponents themselves do not always do.

Part IV consists of essays that sharpen the issues posed previously. Fred Dallmayr sketches three alternative "images of man" that, he argues, are implicitly built into contemporary research in the social sciences. He shows

[12] Karl Marx, "On Alienation," in this volume, p. 109.

[13] Ibid., p. 103.

meticulously how the images of *homo sociologicus, homo economicus,* and *homo politicus* enter into alternative explanatory theories, revealing as well the extent to which the role of such assumptions is ignored by many of the very theorists whose work leans on them so thoroughly. Dallmayr's message is clear: the theoretical issues posed by these alternative images can be confronted squarely only after their role in contemporary explanatory theories is acknowledged and explored.

Steven Lukes builds on the insights of Dallmayr's essay. He dissects the theories of alienation and anomie to identify their points of congruence and divergence. He argues that these theories embody "quite opposite and incompatible ideals . . . of critical and normative thinking about society." [14] Moreover, though Marx and Durkheim, like many of their contemporary followers, "*thought* that they had found empirical ground upon which to base statements about human nature," [15] in fact their respective theories cannot be assessed *fully* by appeal to empirical evidence.

The last three essays approach these issues from a slightly different angle. Each selects a key concept in the literature of social stratification and politics and examines it in some detail. P. H. Partridge examines the concept of power, appraising alternative definitions adopted by contemporary social theorists. He argues that the definition of power one accepts is intimately connected to one's ideas about freedom. He further suggests that, when appraised from this perspective, several definitions of the concept prevalent in social science are deficient. William Connolly explores four alternative definitions of interests advanced in the contemporary literature. Rejecting definitions commonly advanced by theorists of pluralism, as well as those of quasi-individualists such as Lenski, he proposes a definition that would allow us to explore the interests we have as essentially social beings and that would make it possible to identify interests of various parties, even when they themselves do not presently recognize or acknowledge them. Finally, Stanislaw Ossowski examines the concepts of class prevalent in contemporary theory, seeking to show how different explications of this notion reflect and affect the explanatory theory within which they are embedded. Ossowski represents all of the authors of these latter essays when he says that disputes surrounding such concepts as power, class, and interests are "usually a symptom of differences which reach into the core of the matter." [16] Taken together, these essays seek to show why judgment on *conceptual* issues must be self-conscious and critical if theoretical judgment itself is to be informed.

The methodological principle underlying this collection of essays is simple enough: The comparison of the explanatory assumptions, evidential support,

[14] Steven Lukes, "Alienation and Anomie," in this volume, p. 211.

[15] Ibid., p. 204.

[16] Stanislaw Ossowski, *Class Structure in the Social Consciousness* (New York: The Free Press, 1963), p. 160.

and normative implications of alternative theories is the most promising route to that intellectual self-awareness which informs reflective theoretical judgment. But comparison of theories along multiple dimensions is a difficult, arduous task. To make it somewhat more feasible, we have telescoped complex, lengthy theoretical arguments into shorter statements that highlight, we think, the basic dimensions of each orientation. With such skeletal statements, the concrete detail, nuance, and qualification that enhance the plausibility of *each* theory is sacrificed. If the sacrifice is justified initially, it must later be rectified. In that sense, we present these essays as an essential preliminary to a larger enterprise. For reflective theoretical judgment, essential as it is to thoughtful political involvement, is a process never completed. We must act on the best considerations available to us now, while remembering that there are always new considerations to bring to bear on that theory we presently accept, always new alternatives in front of us capable of deepening and altering current orientations.

Perhaps several of the essays included here will challenge methodological commitments widely held in contemporary social science. But this cannot be avoided. While there is no doubt that evidence can and must play a central role in clearing away our most grievous errors and prejudices, we must also recognize that profound differences among theories and theorists persist even after the data available to any one generation has settled. The quest for a truer vision of our social world must continue, but it must proceed with a heightened awareness of pitfalls and possibilities that accompany the study of a creature who is able to affect his world by thinking about it.

I
The Challenge of Competing Perspectives

1

Neutrality in Political Science

Charles Taylor

I

A few years ago one heard it frequently said that political philosophy was dead, that it had been killed by the growth of science, the growth of positivism, the end of ideology, or some combination of these forces, but that, whatever the cause, it was dead.

It is not my intention to rake over the coals of this old issue once more. I am simply using this as a starting point for a reflection on the relation between political science and political philosophy. For behind the view that political philosophy was dead, behind any view which holds that it *can* die, lies the belief that its fate can be separated from that of political science; for no one would claim that the science of politics is dead, however one might disapprove of this or that manner of carrying it on. It remains a perpetually possible, and indeed important enterprise.

The view was indeed that political science has come of age in freeing itself finally of the incubus of political philosophy. No more would its scope be narrowed and its work prejudiced by some value position which operated as an initial weight holding back the whole enterprise. The belief was that political science had freed itself from philosophy in becoming value free and in adopting the scientific method. These two moves were felt to be closely connected; indeed, the second contains the first. For scientific method is, if nothing else, a dispassionate study of the facts as they are, without metaphysical presuppositions, and without value biases.

As Vernon van Dyke puts it: "*science* and *scientific,* then, are words that relate to only one kind of knowledge, i.e., to knowledge of what is observable, and not to any other kinds of knowledge that may exist. They do not relate to alleged knowledge of the normative—knowledge of what ought to be. Science

Source: Peter Laslett and W. G. Runciman, eds., *Philosophy, Politics and Society* (Oxford: Basil Blackwell and Mott Ltd., 1967); reprinted with permission of the author.

concerns what has been, is, or will be, regardless of the 'oughts' of the situation." [1]

Those who could hold that political philosophy was dead, therefore, were those who held to a conception of the social sciences as *wertfrei;* like natural science, political science must dispassionately study the facts. This position received support from the views of the logical empiricists who had, for philosophers, an extraordinarily wide influence among scientists in general, and among the sciences of man in particular. Emboldened by their teaching, some orthodox political scientists tended to claim that the business of normative theory, making recommendations and evaluating different courses of action, could be entirely separated from the study of the facts, from the theoretical attempt to account for them.

Many, of course, had doubts, and these doubts seem to be growing today among political scientists. But they do not touch the thesis of the logical separation between fact and value. They center rather around the possibility of setting one's values to one side when one undertakes the study of politics. The relation between factual study and normative beliefs is therefore thought of in the same traditional positivist way: that the relationship if any is from value to fact, not from fact to value. Thus, scientific findings are held to be neutral: that is, the facts as we discover them do not help to establish or give support to any set of values; we cannot move from fact to value. It is, however, often admitted that our values can influence our findings. This can be thought of as a vicious interference, as when we approach our work with bias which obscures the truth, or as something anodyne and inevitable, as when our values select for us the area of research on which we wish to embark. Or it can be thought of as a factor whose ill effects can be compensated by a clear consciousness of it: thus many theorists today recommend that one set out one's value position in detail at the beginning of a work so as to set the reader (and perhaps also the writer) on guard.

Value beliefs remain therefore as unfounded on scientific fact for the new generation of more cautious theorists as they were for the thinkers of the heyday of "value freedom." They arise, as it were, from outside factual study; they spring from deep choices which are independent of the facts. Thus David Easton, who goes on to attempt to show that "whatever effort is exerted, in undertaking research we cannot shed our values in the way we remove our coats," [2] nevertheless states his acceptance at the outset of the "working assumption" which is "generally adopted today in the social sciences," and which "holds that values can ultimately be reduced to emotional responses conditioned by the individual's total life-experiences." [3] Thus there is no ques-

[1] Vernon van Dyke, *Political Science: A Philosophical Analysis* (Stanford: Stanford University Press, 1960), p. 192.

[2] David Easton, *The Political System* (New York: Alfred A. Knopf, 1953), p. 225.

[3] Ibid., p. 221.

tion of founding values on scientific findings. Emotional responses can be explained by life experience, but not justified or shown to be appropriate by the facts about society: "The moral aspect of a proposition . . . expresses only the emotional response of an individual to a state of real or presumed facts. . . . Although we can say that the aspect of a proposition referring to a fact can be true or false, it is meaningless to characterize the value aspect of a proposition in this way." [4] The import of these words is clear. For, if value positions could be supported or undermined by the findings of science, then they could not simply be characterized as emotional responses, and we could not say simply that it was *meaningless* (although it might be misleading) to speak of them as true or false.

Political philosophy, therefore, as reasoned argument about fundamental political values, can be entirely separated from political science, even on the mitigated positivist view which is now gaining ground among political scientists. "Values" steer, as it were, the process of discovery, but they do not gain or lose plausibility by it. Thus although values may be somehow ineradicable from political science, reasoned argument concerning them would seem easily separable (though theorists may differ as to whether this is wise or not: cf. Easton, *The Political System*). Indeed, it is hard to see in what such reasoned argument could consist. The findings of science will be relevant to our values, of course, in this sense, that they will tell us how to realize the goals we set ourselves. We can reconstruct political science in the mold of a "policy science," like engineering and medicine, which shows us how to attain our goals. But the goals and values still come from somewhere else; they are founded on choices whose basis remains obscure.

The aim of this paper is to call into question this notion of the relation of factual findings in politics to value positions, and thus the implied relation between political science and political philosophy. In particular my aim is to call into question the view that the findings of political science leave us, as it were, as free as before, that they do not go some way to establishing particular sets of values and undermining others. If this view is shown to be mistaken, then we will have to recognize a convergence between science and normative theory in the field of politics.

It is usual for philosophers, when discussing this question, to leave the realms of the sciences of man and launch into a study of "good," or commending, or emotive meaning, and so on. I propose to follow another course here, and to discuss the question first in connection with the disciplines in terms of which I have raised it, namely, political philosophy and political science. When we have some understanding of the relations between these two on the ground, as it were, it will be time to see if these are considered possible in the heaven of philosophy.

The thesis that political science is value neutral has maximum plausibility

[4] Easton, *The Political System,* p. 221.

when we look at some of its detailed findings. That French workers tend to vote Communist may be judged deplorable or encouraging, but it does not itself determine us to accept either of these judgments. It stands as a fact, neutral between them.

If this were all there is to political science, the debate would end here. But it is no more capable than any other science of proceeding by the random collection of facts. At one time it was believed that science was just concerned with the correlation of observable phenomena—the observables concerned being presumed to lie unproblematically before our gaze. But this position, the offshoot of a more primitive empiricism, is abandoned now by almost everyone, even those in the empiricist tradition.

For the number of features which any given range of phenomena may exhibit, and which can thus figure in correlations, is indefinite; and this because the phenomena themselves can be classified in an indefinite number of ways. Any physical object can be classified according to shape, color, size, function, aesthetic properties, relation to some process, etc.; when we come to realities as complex as political society, the case is no different. But among these features only a limited range will yield correlations which have some explanatory force.

Nor are these necessarily the most obtrusive. The crucial features, laws or correlations concerning which will explain or help to explain phenomena of the range in question, may at a given stage of the science concerned be only vaguely discerned if not frankly unsuspected. The conceptual resources necessary to pick them out may not yet have been elaborated. It is said, for instance, that the modern physical concept of mass was unknown to the ancients, and only slowly and painfully evolved through the searchings of the later Middle Ages. And yet it is an essential variable in the modern science. A number of more obtrusive features may be irrelevant; that is, they may not be such that they can be linked in functions explanatory of the phenomena. Obvious distinctions may be irrelevant, or have an entirely different relevance from that attributed to them, such as the distinction between Aristotle's "light" and "heavy" bodies.

Thus when we wish to go beyond certain immediate low-level correlations whose relevance to the political process is fairly evident, such as the one mentioned above; when we want to explain why French workers vote Communist, or why McCarthyism arises in the United States in the late forties, or why the level of abstentionism varies from election to election, or why new African regimes are liable to military take-over, the features by reference to which we can explain these results are not immediately in evidence. Not only is there a wide difference of opinion about them, but we are not even sure that we have as yet the conceptual resources necessary to pick them out. We may easily argue that certain more obtrusive features, those pertaining, say, to the institutional structure, are not relevant, while others less obtrusive, say, the character structure prevalent in certain strata of the society, will yield the real explanation. We may, for instance, refuse to account for McCarthyism in terms of the struggle between executive and legislature, and look rather to the development of a certain personality structure among certain sections of the American population. Or else we may reject both these explanations and look to the role of a new status group in American society, newly rich but excluded from the eastern establishment. Or we may reject this, and see it as a result of the new position of the United States in the world.

The task of theory in political science, one which cannot be foregone if we are to elaborate any explanations worth the name, is to discover what are the kinds of features to which we should look for explanations of this kind. In which of the above dimensions are we to find an explanation for McCarthyism? Or rather, since all of these dimensions obviously have relevance, how are we to relate them in explaining the political phenomena? The task of theory is to delineate the relevant features in the different dimensions and their relation so that we have some idea of what can be the cause of what, of how character affects political process, or social structure affects character, or economic relations affect social structure, or political process affects economic relations, or vice versa; how ideological divisions affect party systems, or history affects ideological divisions, or culture affects history, or party systems affect culture, or vice versa. Before we have made some at least tentative steps in this direction we don't even have an idea where to look for our explanations; we don't know which facts to gather.

It is not surprising, then, that political science should be the field in which a great and growing number of "theoretical frameworks" compete to answer these questions. Besides the Marxist approach, and the interest-group theory associated with the name of Bentley, we have seen the recent growth of "structural-functional" approaches under the influence of systems theory; there have been approaches which have attempted to relate the psychological dimension to political behavior (e.g., Lasswell), different applications of sociological concepts and methods (e.g., Lipset and Almond), applications of game theory (e.g., Downs and Riker), and so on.

These different approaches are frequently rivals, since they offer different accounts of the features crucial for explanation and the causal relations which hold. We can speak of them, along with their analogues in other sciences, as "conceptual structures" or "theoretical frameworks," because they claim to delimit the area in which scientific enquiry will be fruitful. A framework does not give us at once all the variables which will be relevant and the laws which will be true, but it tells us what needs to be explained, and roughly by what kinds of factors. For instance, if we accept the principle of inertia, certain ways of conceiving bodies and therefore certain questions are beyond the pale. To pursue them is fruitless, as was the search for what kept the cannonball moving in pre-Galilean physics. Similarly an orthodox Marxist approach cannot allow that McCarthyism can be explained in terms of early upbringing and the resultant personality structure.

But we can also see a theoretical framework as setting the crucial dimensions through which the phenomena can vary. For it sets out the essential functional relations by which they can be explained, while at the same time ruling out other functional relations belonging to other, rival frameworks. But the given set of functional relations defines certain dimensions in which the phenomena can vary; a given framework therefore affirms some dimensions of variation and denies others. Thus for a Marxist, capitalist societies do not vary as to who wields power, no matter what the constitution or the party in office; supposed variations in these dimensions, which are central to a great many theories, are sham; the crucial dimension is that concerning class structure.

In the more exact sciences theoretical discovery may be couched in the form of laws and be called principles, such as, e.g., of inertia, or the rectilinear propagation of light. But in the less exact, such as politics, it may consist simply of a general description of the phenomena couched in the crucial concepts. Or it may be implicit in a series of distinctions which a given theory makes (e.g., Aristotle's classification of the types of polity), or in a story of how the phenomena came to be (e.g., the myth of the social contract), or in a general statement of causal relations (e.g., Marx's Preface to *A Contribution to the Critique of Political Economy*).

But, however expressed, theoretical discovery can be seen as the delineating of the important dimensions of variation for the range of phenomena concerned.

Theoretical discovery of this kind is thus one of the concerns of modern political science, as we have seen. But it also is a traditional concern of what we call political philosophy, that is, normative political theory. It is not hard to see why. Normative theorists of the tradition have also been concerned with delineating crucial dimensions of variation—of course, they were looking for the dimensions which were significant for judging of the value of polities and policies rather than for explaining them. But the two types of research were in fact closely interwoven so that in pursuing the first they were also led to pursue the second.

Aristotle, for instance, is credited with a revision of Plato's threefold classification of political society which enhanced its explanatory value. He substituted for the number criterion a class criterion which gives a more revealing classification of the differences, and allows us to account for more: it made clear what was at stake between democracy and oligarchy; it opened up the whole range of explanations based on class composition, including the one for which Aristotle is known in history, the balancing role of the middle class.

But this revision was not unconnected with differences in the normative theory of the two thinkers. Plato attempted to achieve a society devoid of class struggle, either in the perfect harmony of the Republic, or in the single class state of the Laws. Aristotle is not above weaving the dream of the ideal state in one section of the Politics, but there is little connection between this and the political theory of the rest of the work. This latter is solidly based on the understanding that class differences, and hence divergence of interest and tension, are here to stay. In the light of this theory, Plato's idea in the *Republic* of overcoming class tension by discipline, education, a superior constitution, and so on, is so much pie in the sky (not even very tasty pie in Aristotle's view, as he makes clear in Book II, but that is for other reasons).

Aristotle's insight in political science is incompatible with Plato's normative theory, at least in the *Republic,* and the *Politics* therefore takes a quite different line (for other reasons as well, of course). The difference on this score might perhaps be expressed in this way: both Plato and Aristotle held that social harmony was of crucial importance as a value. But Plato saw this harmony as achieved in the ending of all class conflict; Aristotle saw it as arising from the domestication of this conflict. But crucial to this dispute is the question of the causal relevance of class tension: is it an eradicable blot on social harmony, in the sense that one can say, for instance, that the violent forms of this conflict are? Or is it ineradicable and ever present, only varying in its forms? In the first case one of the crucial dimensions of variation of our explanatory theory is that concerning the presence or absence of class conflict. In the second case, this dimension is not even recognized as having a basis in fact. If this is so, then the normative theory collapses, or rather is shifted from the realm of political philosophy to that we call Utopia building. For the idea of a society without class conflict would be one to which we cannot even approach. Moreover, the attempt to approach it would have all the dangerous consequences attendant on large-scale political changes based on illusory hopes.

Thus Plato's theory of the *Republic,* considered as the thesis that a certain dimension of variation is normatively significant, contains claims concerning the dimensions of variation which are relevant for explanation, for it is only compatible with those frameworks which concede the reality of the normatively crucial dimension. It is incompatible with any views of politics as the striving of different classes, or interest groups, or individuals against one another.

It is clear that this is true of any normative theory, that it is linked with certain explanatory theory or theories, and incompatible with others. Aristotle's dimension whereby different constitutions were seen as expressing and molding different forms of life disappears in the atomistic conception of Hobbes. Rousseau's crucial dimension of the *Social Contract,* marking a sharp discontinuity between popular sovereignty and states of dependence of one form or another, could not survive the validation of the theories of Mosca, or Michels or Pareto.

Traditional political philosophy was thus forced to engage in the theoretical function that we have seen to be essential to modern political science; and the more elaborate and comprehensive the normative theory, the more complete and defined the conceptual framework which accompanied it. That is why political science can learn something still from the works of Aristotle, Hobbes, Hegel, Marx, and so on. In the tradition one form of enquiry is virtually inseparable from the other.

II

This is not a surprising result. Everyone recognized that political philosophers of the tradition were engaged in elaborating on, at least embryonic, political science. But, one might say, that is just the trouble; that is why political science was so long in getting started. Its framework was always set in the interests of some normative theory. In order to progress science must be liberated from all *parti pris* and be value neutral. Thus if normative theory requires political science and cannot be carried on without it, the reverse is not the case; political science can and should be separated from the older discipline. Let us examine some modern attempts to elaborate a science of politics to see if this is true.

Let us look first at S. M. Lipset's *Political Man.* In this work Lipset sets out the conditions for modern democracy. He sees societies as existing in two dimensions—conflict and consensus. Both are equally necessary for democracy. They are not mere opposites as a simple-minded view might assume. Conflict here is not seen as a simple divergence of interest, or the existence of objective relations of exploitation, but as the actual working out of these through the struggle for power and over policy.

> Surprising as it may sound, a stable democracy requires the manifestation of conflict or cleavage so that there will be struggle over ruling positions, challenges to parties in power, and shifts of parties in office; but without consensus—a political system allowing the peaceful "play" of power, the adherence by the "outs" to decisions made by the "ins", and the recognition by the "ins" of the rights of the "outs"—there can be no democracy. The study of the conditions encouraging democracy must therefore focus on the sources of both cleavage and consensus.[5]

And again,

> Cleavage—where it is legitimate—contributes to the integration of societies and organizations.[6]

The absence of such conflict, such as where a given group has taken over, or an all-powerful state can produce unanimity, or at least prevent diversity from expressing itself, is a sign that the society is not a free one. De Tocque-

[5] S. M. Lipset, *Political Man* (New York: Doubleday, 1960), p. 21.
[6] Ibid.

ville feared [7] that the power of the state would produce apathy and thus do away even with consensus.

> Democracy in a complex society may be defined as a political system which supplies regular constitutional opportunities for changing the governing officials, and a social mechanism which permits the largest possible part of the population to influence major decisions by choosing among contenders for political office.[8]

Such a society requires the organization of group interests to fight for their own goals—provided that this is done in a peaceful way, within the rules of the game, and with the acceptance of the arbiter in the form of elections by universal suffrage. If groups are not organized, they have no real part, their interests are neglected, and they cannot have their share of power; they become alienated from the system.

Now this view can at once be seen to conflict with a Rousseauian view which disapproves of the organization of "factions," and which sees consensus as arising out of isolated individuals. It also goes against the modern conservative view that to organize people on a class basis gratuitously divides the society. In face of Rousseau, Lipset holds that the absence of close agreement among all concerning the general will is not a sign that something has gone wrong. There are ineradicable basic divergences of interest; they have to be adjusted. If we get to some kind of conflictless state, this can only be because some of the parties have been somehow done down and prevented from competing. For Lipset, absence of conflict is a sure sign that some groups are being excluded from the public thing.

This difference closely parallels the one mentioned above between Plato and Aristotle. Indeed, Lipset points out on several occasions the similarity between his position and that of Aristotle. And it is clear that it is a difference of the same kind, one in which a normative theory is undermined because the reality of its crucial dimension of variation is challenged. A similar point can be made concerning the difference with conservatives who allow for divergence in the state, but resist class parties. Here the belief is that the divergence is gratuitous, that the real differences lie elsewhere, either in narrower or in broader interests, and that these are obfuscated and made more difficult of rational adjustment by class divisions. More, the state can be torn apart if these divisions are played up. Conservatives tend to feel about class in politics as liberals do about race in politics. Once again, Lipset's view would undermine the position, for he holds that class differences are at the center of politics, and cannot be removed except by reducing the number of players, as it were. They are therefore the very stuff of democratic politics, provided they are moderately and peacefully expressed. The struggle

[7] Ibid., p. 27.

[8] Ibid., p. 45.

between rich and poor is ineradicable; it can take different forms, that's all.

Attempts to break outside of this range are thus irrational and dysfunctional. Irrational, because based on false premises; and dysfunctional, because the goal of conflictlessness or absence of class tension can only be achieved at the expense of features of the system which most will accept as valuable; by oppressing some segment of the population, or by its apathy and lack of organization. This is, of course, the usual fate of theories with a false factual base in politics; as was remarked above, they are not just erroneous, but positively dangerous.

It can be seen that the value consequences of Lipset's theory are fairly widespread even restricting ourselves to the alternatives which it negates or undermines. An examination of some of the factors which tend to strengthen democracy according to the theory will increase this list of rejected alternatives. Lipset holds that economic development is conducive to the health of democracy, in that, *inter alia,* it narrows gaps in wealth and living standards, tends to create a large middle class, and increases the "cross pressures" working to damp down class conflict. For a society cannot function properly as a democracy unless, along with an articulation of class differences, there is some consensus which straddles them. Now Lipset's "cross pressures"—typically exercised by religious affiliation, for instance, which cuts across class barriers—are the "opiates" of a strict Marxist. For they are integrators which prevent the system coming apart at the social seam, and thus prevent the class war from coming to a head. But we are not dealing here simply with two value judgments about the same facts understood in the same way. The crucial difference is that for Lipset the stage beyond the class struggle doesn't and cannot exist; the abolition of the conflict in unanimity is impossible; his view is: "the rich ye have always with you." But in this case the integrating factors cease to be "opiates," breeding false consciousness and hiding the great revolutionary potentiality. There is nothing there to hide. Lipset's view therefore negates revolutionary Marxism in a direct way—in the same way as it negates the views above—by denying that the crucial dimensions of variation have reality.

But if we examine this last example a little more closely, we can see even wider normative consequences of Lipset's view. For if we rule out the transformation to the classless society, then we are left with the choice between different kinds of class conflict: a violent kind which so divides society that it can only survive under some form of tyranny, or one which can reach accommodations in peace. This choice, set out in these terms, virtually makes itself for us. We may point out that this does not cover the range of possibility, since there are also cases in which the class conflict is latent, owing to the relative absence of one party. But this is the result of underdevelopment, of a lack of education, or knowledge, or initiative on the part of the underprivileged. Moreover, it unfailingly leads to a worsening of their position relative to the privileged. As Lipset says in the statement of his political position which forms the introduction to the Anchor Edition of *Political Man,* "I believe with Marx that all privileged classes seek to maintain and *enhance* their advantages against the desire of the underprivileged to reduce them." [9]

Thus, for Lipset, the important dimension of variation for political societies can be seen as L-shaped, as it were. On one end lies societies where the divisions are articulated but are so deep that they cannot be contained without violence, suppression of liberty and despotic rule; on the other end lie societies which are peaceful but oligarchic and which are therefore run to secure the good of a minority ruling group. At the angle are the societies whose differences are articulated but which are capable of accommodating them in a peaceful way, and which therefore are characterized by a high degree of individual liberty and political organization.

Faced with this choice, it is hard to opt for anywhere else but the angle. For to do so is either to choose violence and despotism and suppression over peace, rule by consent and liberty, or to choose a society run more for the benefit of a minority over a society run more for the benefit of all, a society which exploits and/or manipulates over a society which tends to secure the common good as determined by the majority. Only in the angle can we have a society really run for the common good, for at one end is oligarchy based on an unorganized mass, at the other despotism.

Lipset himself makes this option explicit: "A basic premise of this book is that democracy is not only or even primarily a means through which different groups can attain their ends or seek the good society; it is the good society itself in operation. Only the give and take of a free society's internal struggles offers some guarantee that the products of the society will not accumulate in the hands of a few power holders, and that men may develop and bring up their children without fear of persecution." [10]

This is a succinct statement of the value position implicit in *Political Man,* but it is wrongly characterized as a "premise." The use of this term shows the influence of the theory of value neutrality, but it is misplaced. It would be less misleading to say "upshot," for the value position flows out of the analysis of the book. Once we accept Lipset's analysis concerning the fundamental role of class in politics, that it always operates even when division is not overt, and that it can never be surmounted in unanimity, then we have no choice but to accept democracy as he defines it, as a society in which most men are doers, take their fate in their own hands, or have a hand in determining it, and at least reduce the degree to which injustice is done to them, or their interests are unfavorably handled by others, as the good society.

But now we have gone far beyond the merely negative consequences noted above for Marxism, conservatism or Rousseau's general will. We are saying that the crucial dimensions of variation of Lipset's theory not only negate

[9] Ibid., p. xxii.

[10] Ibid., p. 403.

dimensions crucial to other normative theories but support one of their own, which is implicit in the theory itself. But this conclusion, if true, goes against the supposed neutrality of scientific fact. Let us examine it a bit more closely.

We have said above that faced with the choice between a regime based on violence and suppression, and one based on consent, between regimes which serve the interests more or less of all versus regimes which serve the interests only of a minority, the choice is clear. Is this simply a rhetorical flourish, playing on generally accepted values among readers? Or is the connection more solid?

Granted that we wish to apply "better" and "worse" to regimes characterized along this dimension, can one conceive of reversing what seemed above to be the only possible judgment? Can one say: yes, a regime based on minority rule with violent suppression of the majority is better than one based on general consensus, where all have a chance to have their interests looked to? Certainly this is not a logically absurd position in itself. But if someone accepted the framework of Lipset and proceeded to make this judgment, surely we would expect him to go on and mention some other considerations which led him to this astounding conclusion. We might expect him to say, that only minorities are creative, that violence is necessary to keep men from stagnating, or something of this kind. But supposing he said nothing of the sort? Supposing he just maintained that violence was better than its opposite, not qua stimulus to creativity, or essential element in progress, but just qua violence; that it was better that only the minority interest be served, not because the minority would be more creative but just because it was a minority? A position of this kind would be unintelligible. We could understand that the man was dedicating himself to the furtherance of such a society, but the use of the words "good" or "better" would be totally inappropriate here, for there would be no visible grounds for applying them. The question would remain open whether the man had understood these terms, whether, e.g., he hadn't confused "good" with "something which gives me a kick," or "aesthetically pleasing."

But, it might be argued, this is not a fair example. Supposing our unorthodox thinker did adduce other grounds for preferring violence and majority rule? Surely, then, he would be permitted to differ from us? Yes, but then it is very dubious whether he could still accept Lipset's framework. Suppose, for instance, that one believed (as Hegel did about war) that violence was morally necessary from time to time for the well-being of the state. This would not be without effect on one's conception of political science; the range of possible regimes would be different from that which Lipset gives us; for peaceful democratic regimes would suffer a process of stagnation which would render them less viable; they would not in fact be able to maintain themselves, and thus the spectrum of possible regimes would be different from the one Lipset presents us with; the most viable regime would be one which was able to ration violence and maintain it at a non-disruptive level without falling over into stagnation and decay.

But why need this change of values bring along with it a change in explanatory framework? We seem to be assuming that the evils of internal peace must be such as to have a political effect, to undermine the viability of the political society. Is this assumption justified? Normally, of course, we would expect someone putting forward a theory of this kind to hold that inner violence is good because it contributes to the dynamism, or creativity of people, or progress of the society, or something of the kind which would make peaceful societies less viable. But supposing he chose some other benefits of violence which had nothing to do with the survival or health of political society? Let us say that he held that violence was good for art, that only in societies rent by internal violence could great literature, music, painting be produced? The position, for instance, of Harry Lime in *The Third Man*?

This certainly is a possible case. But let us examine it more closely. Our hypothetical objector has totally forsaken the ground of politics, and is making his judgment on extraneous (here aesthetic) grounds. He cannot deny that, setting these grounds aside, the normal order of preference is valid. He is saying in effect that, although it is better abstracting from aesthetic considerations that society be peaceful, nevertheless this must be overridden in the interests of art.

This distinction is important. We must distinguish between two kinds of objection to a given valuation. It may be that the valuation is accepted, but that its verdict for our actual choices is overridden, as it were, by other more important valuations. Thus we may think that freedom of speech is always a good, while reluctantly conceding that it must be curtailed in an emergency because of the great risks it would entail here. We are in this case self-consciously curtailing a good. The other kind of objection is the one which undermines the valuation itself, seeks to deprive the putative good of its status. This is what Lipset does, for instance, to spiritual followers of Rousseau in showing that their harmony can only be the silence of minority rule.[11] In one case we are conceding that the thing in question does really have the properties which its proponents attribute to it (e.g., that free speech does contribute to justice, progress, human development, or whatever), but we are adding that it also has other properties which force us to proceed against it (e.g., it is potentially disruptive) temporarily or permanently. In the other case, we are denying the condition in question the very properties by which it is judged good (e.g., that the legislation of the society without cleavage emanates from the free conscious will of all its citizens). Let us call these two objections respectively overriding and undermining.

Now what is being claimed here is that an objection which undermines the

[11] Of course, Rousseau's general will may remain a value in the hypothetical world he casts for it, but that concerns Utopia building, not political philosophy.

values which seem to arise out of a given framework must alter the framework; that in this sense the framework is inextricably connected to a certain set of values; and that if we can reverse the valuation without touching the framework, then we are dealing with an overriding.

To go back to the example above. In order to undermine the judgment against violence we would have to show that it does not have the property claimed for it. Now obviously, violence has the property of killing and maiming which goes some way towards putting it in the list of undesirables, one might think irrevocably; so that it could only be overridden. But here we are not dealing with a judgment about violence per se, but rather with one concerning the alternatives of peace and violence; and the judgment rests on the ground that violence has properties which peace has not, that the evils obviously attributed to violence are effectively avoided by peace. But if one can show that peace leads to stagnation, and thus to breakdown (and hence eventual chaos or violence) or foreign conquest, then the supposed gap between the two narrows. On the contrary, one is presented with a new alternative, that between more or less controlled violence and the destructive uncontrolled kind associated with internal breakdown or foreign conquest. What the undermining job has done is to destroy the alternative on which the original judgment was based, and thus deprive the previously preferred alternative of its differential property for which it was valued.

But any undermining of this kind is bound to alter the explanatory framework of which the original alternative was an essential part. If we cannot maintain a peaceful polity, then the gamut of possibilities is very different, and Lipset is guilty of neglecting a whole host of factors, to do with the gamut tension-stagnation.

To take the other example, let our objector make a case for rule by the minority. Let him claim that only the minority are creative, that if they are not given preference, then they will not produce, and then everyone will suffer. Thus the supposed difference between rule for the minority and that for all, viz., that the ordinary bloke gets something out of the second that he doesn't out of the first, is set aside; rather the opposite turns out to be the case. The value is undermined. But so is the political framework altered, for now we have an elitist thesis about the importance of minority rule; another variable has entered the picture which was not present in the previous framework and which cuts across it, in so far as the previous framework presented the possibility of good progressive societies run for all.

Let us hold, however, that violence or elite rule is good for painting, and we have an overruling; for it remains the case that it would be better to have no violence and everybody getting a square deal, but alas. . . .

Thus the framework does secrete a certain value position, albeit one that can be overridden. In general we can see this arising in the following way: the framework gives us as it were the geography of the range of phenomena in question, it tells us how they can vary, what are the major dimensions of variation. But since we are dealing with matters which are of great importance to human beings, a given map will have, as it were, its own built-in value slope. That is to say, a given dimension of variation will usually determine for itself how we are to judge of good and bad, because of its relation to obvious human wants and needs.

Now this may seem a somewhat startling result, since it is well known that there are wide differences over what human needs, desires and purposes are. Not that there is not a wide area of agreement over basic things like life; but this clearly breaks down when one tries to extend the list. There can thus be great disagreement over the putative human need for self-expression or for autonomous development, both of which can and do play important parts in debates and conflicts over political theory.

Does this mean, therefore, that we can reject the previous result and imagine a state of affairs where we could accept the framework of explanation of a given theory, and yet refuse the value judgments it secretes, because we took a different view of the schedule of human needs? [12] Or, to put it another way, does this mean that the step between accepting a framework of explanation and accepting a certain notion of the political good is mediated by a premise concerning human needs, which may be widely enough held to go unnoticed, but which nevertheless can be challenged, thus breaking the connection?

The answer is no. For the connection between a given framework of explanation and a certain notion of the schedule of needs, wants and purposes which seems to mediate the inference to value theory is not fortuitous. If one adopted a quite different view of human need, one would upset the framework. Thus to pursue another example from Lipset, stable democracies are judged better than stable oligarchies, since the latter can only exist where the majority is so uneducated and tradition bound or narrowed that it has not yet learned to demand its rights. But suppose we tried to upset this judgment by holding that underdevelopment is good for men, that they are happier when they are led by some unquestioned norms, don't have to think for themselves, and so on? One would then be reversing the value judgment. But at the same time one would be changing the framework. For we are introducing a notion of anomie here, and we cannot suppose this factor to exist without having some important effect on the working of political society. If anomie is the result of the development of education and the breakdown of tradition, then it will affect the stability of the societies which promote this kind of development. They will be subject to constant danger of being undermined

[12] This could involve either an undermining or an overriding of the value judgment. For we can deny something, a condition or outcome, the property by which it is judged good not only by denying it a property by which it fulfils certain human needs, wants or purposes, but also by denying that these needs, wants or purposes exist. And we can override the judgment that it is good by pointing to other needs, wants or purposes that it frustrates.

as their citizens, suffering from anomie, look for havens of certainty. If men are made unhappy by democracy, then undoubtedly it is not as good as its protagonists make out, but it is not so viable either.

The view above that we could accept the framework of explanation and reject the value conclusion by positing a different schedule of needs cannot be sustained. For a given framework is linked to a given conception of the schedule of human needs, wants and purposes, such that, if the schedule turns out to have been mistaken in some significant way, the framework itself cannot be maintained. This is for the fairly obvious reason that human needs, wants and purposes have an important bearing on the way people act, and that therefore one has to have a notion of the schedule which is not too wildly inaccurate if one is to establish the framework for any science of human behavior, that of politics not excepted. A conception of human needs thus enters into a given political theory, and cannot be considered something extraneous which we later add to the framework to yield a set of value judgments.

This is not to say that there cannot be needs or purposes which we might add to those implicit in any framework, and which would not alter the framework since their effect on political events might be marginal. But this would at most give us the ground of an overruling, not for an undermining. In order to undermine the valuation we would have to show that the putative need fulfilled was not a need, or that what looked like fulfilling a need, or a want or a human purpose was really not so, or really did the opposite. Now even an overruling might destroy the framework, if a new need were introduced which was important enough motivationally to dictate quite different behavior. But certainly an undermining, which implies that one has misidentified the schedule of needs, would do so. . . .

III

The thesis we have been defending, however plausible it may appear in the context of a discussion of the different theories of political science, is unacceptable to an important school of philosophy today. Throughout the foregoing analysis, philosophers will have felt uneasy. For this conclusion tells against the well-entrenched doctrine according to which questions of value are independent of questions of fact; the view which holds that before any set of facts we are free to adopt an indefinite number of value positions. According to the view defended here, on the other hand, a given framework of explanation in political science tends to support an associated value position, secretes its own norms for the assessment of polities and policies.

It is of course this philosophical belief which, because of its immense influence among scientists in general and political scientists as well, has contributed to the cult of neutrality in political science, and the belief that genuine science gives no guidance as to right and wrong.

It is time, therefore, to come to grips with this philosophical view.

There are two points about the use of "good" which are overlooked or negated by the standard "non-naturalist" view: (1) to apply "good" may or may not be to commend, but it is always to claim that there are reasons for commending whatever it is applied to, (2) to say of something that it fulfils human needs, wants or purposes always constitutes a prima facie reason for calling it "good," that is, for applying the term in the absence of overriding considerations.[13]

Now the nonnaturalist view, as expressed, for instance, by Hare or Stevenson, denies both these propositions. Its starting point is the casting of moral argument in deductive form—all the arguments against the so-called "naturalistic fallacy" have turned on the validity of deductive inference. The ordinary man may think that he is moving from a factual consideration about something to a judgment that it is good or bad, but in fact one cannot deduce a statement concerning the goodness or badness of something from a statement attributing some descriptive property to it. Thus the ordinary man's argument is really an enthymeme: he is assuming some major premise: when he moves from "X will make men happy" to "X is good," he is operating with the suppressed premise "What makes men happy is good," for only by adding this can one derive the conclusion by valid inference.

To put the point in another way: the ordinary man sees "X will make men happy" as the reason for his favorable verdict on it. But on the nonnaturalist view, it is a reason only because he accepts the suppressed major premise. For one could, logically, reject this premise, and then the conclusion wouldn't follow at all. Hence, that something is a reason for judging X good depends on what values the man who judges holds. Of course, one can find reasons for holding these values. That is, facts from which we could derive the major premise, but only by adopting a higher major which would allow us to derive our first major as a valid conclusion. Ultimately, we have to decide beyond all reasons, as it were, what our values are. For at each stage where we adduce a reason, we have already to have accepted some value (enshrined in a major premise) in virtue of which this reason is valid. But then our ultimate major premises stand without reasons; they are the fruit of a pure choice.

Proposition (1) above, then, is immediately denied by nonnaturalism. For in the highest major premises "good" is applied to commend without the claim that there are reasons for this commendation. And (2) also is rejected, for nothing can claim always to constitute a reason for calling something good. Whether it does or not depends on the decisions a man has made about his values, and it is not logically impossible that he should decide to consider

[13] We might also speak of "interests" here, but this can be seen as included in "wants" and "needs." Interest may deviate from want, but can only be explicited in terms of such concepts as "satisfaction," "happiness," "unhappiness," etc., the criteria for whose application are ultimately to be found in what we want.

human needs, wants and purposes irrelevant to judgments about good and bad. A reason is always a reason-for-somebody, and has this status because of the values he has accepted.

The question at issue, then, is first whether "good" can be used where there are no reasons, either evident or which can be cited for its application.[14] Consider the following case: [15] There are two segregationists who disapprove of miscegenation. The first claims that mixing races will produce general unhappiness, a declince in the intellectual capacity and moral standards of the race, the abolition of a creative tension, and so on. The second, however, refuses to assent to any of these beliefs: the race will not deteriorate, men may even be happier; in any case they will be just as intelligent, moral, etc. But, he insists, miscegenation is bad. When challenged to produce some substitute reason for this judgment, he simply replies: "I have no reasons; everyone is entitled, indeed has to accept some higher major premise and stop the search for reasons somewhere. I have chosen to stop here, rather than seeking grounds in such fashionable quarters, as human happiness, moral stature, etc." Or supposing he looked at us in puzzlement and said: "Reasons? why do you ask for reasons? Miscegenation is just bad."

Now no one would question that the first segregationist was making the judgment "miscegenation is bad." But in the case of the second, a difficulty arises. This can be seen as soon as we ask the question: how can we tell whether the man is really making a judgment about the badness of miscegenation and not just, say, giving vent to a strongly felt repulsion, or a neurotic phobia against sexual relations between people of different races? Now it is essential to the notions "good" and "bad" as we use them in judgments that there be a distinction of this kind between these judgments and expressions of horror, delight, liking, disliking and so on. It is essential that we be able, e.g., to correct a speaker by saying: "What you want to say would be better put as 'miscegenation horrifies me,' or 'miscegenation makes me go all creepy inside.' " Because it is an essential part of the grammar of "good" and "bad" that they claim more than is claimed by expressions of delight, horror, etc. For we set aside someone's judgment that X is good when we say: "All you're saying is that you *like* X." To which the man can hotly reply: "I don't like X any more than you do, but I recognize that it's good."

There must therefore be criteria of distinction between these two cases if "good" and "bad" are to have the grammar that they have. But if we allow that our second segregationist is making the judgment "miscegenation is bad,"

[14] In what follows I am indebted to the arguments of Mrs. P. Foot, e.g., to her "When Is a Principle a Moral Principle?" in *Supplementary Vol. of Aristotelian Society,* 1954, and her "Moral Arguments" in *Mind,* 1958, although I do not know whether she would agree with the conclusions I draw from them.

[15] Borrowed with changes from Hare's *Freedom and Reason.*

then no such distinction can be made. A judgment that I like something doesn't need grounds. That is, the absence of grounds doesn't undermine the claim "I like X" (though other things, e.g., in my behavior, may undermine it). But unless we adduce reasons for it (and moreover reasons of a certain kind as we shall see below) we cannot show that our claim that X is good says more than "I like X." Thus a man can only defend himself against the charge that all he's saying is that he likes X by giving his grounds. If there are no grounds, then judgment becomes indistinguishable from expression; which means that there are no more judgments of good and bad, since the distinction is essential to them as we have seen.

Those who believe in the fact-value dichotomy have naturally tried to avoid this conclusion; they have tried to distinguish the two cases by fastening on the use made of judgments of good and bad in commending, prescribing, expressing approval and so on. Thus, no matter what a man's grounds, if any, we could know that he was making a judgment of good and bad by the fact that he was commending, prescribing or committing himself to pursue the thing in question, or something of the kind. But this begs the question, for we can raise the query: what constitutes commending, or prescribing, or committing myself, or expressing approval, or whatever? How does one tell whether a man is doing one of these things as against just giving vent to his feelings?

If we can say that we can tell by what the man accepts as following from his stand—whether he accepts that he should strive to realize the thing in question—then the same problem breaks out afresh: how do we distinguish his accepting the proposition that he should seek the end and his just being hell-bent on seeking this end? Presumably, both our segregationists would agree that they should fight miscegenation, but this would still leave us just as puzzled and uncertain about the position of the second. Perhaps we can tell by whether they are willing to universalize their prescription? But here again we have no touchstone, for both segregationists would assent that everyone should seek racial purity, but the question would remain open whether this had a different meaning in the two cases. Perhaps the second one just means that he can't stand interracial mating, whether done by himself or by anyone else. Similarly, a compulsive may keep his hands scrupulously clean and feel disgust at the uncleanliness of others, even plead with them to follow his example; but we still want to distinguish his case from one who had judged that cleanliness was good.

Can we fall back on behavioral criteria, meaning by "behavior" what a man does in contrast to how he thinks about what he does? But there is no reason why a man with a neurotic phobia against X shouldn't do all the things which the man who judges X is bad does, i.e., avoiding X himself, trying to stop others from doing it, and so on.

Thus the nonnaturalists would leave us with no criteria except what the man was willing to say. But then we would have no way of knowing whether the words were correctly applied or not, which is to say that they would have no meaning. All that we achieve by trying to mark the distinction by what follows from the judgment is that the same question which we raised about "X is bad" as against "X makes me shudder" can be raised about the complex "X is bad, I/you shouldn't do X" as against the complex "X makes me shudder, please I/you don't do X." We simply appeal from what the man is willing to say on the first question to what he is willing to say on the second. The distinction can only be properly drawn if we look to the reasons for the judgment, and this is why a judgment without reasons cannot be allowed, for it can no longer be distinguished from an expression of feeling.[16]

This analysis may sound plausible for "miscegenation is bad," but how about "anything conducive to human happiness is good"? What can we say here, if asked to give grounds for this affirmation? The answer is that we can say nothing, but also we need say nothing. For that something conduces to human happiness is already an adequate ground for judging it good—adequate, that is, in the absence of countervailing considerations. We come, then to the second point at issue, the claim that to say of something that it fulfils human needs, wants or purposes always constitutes a prima facie reason for calling it "good."

For in fact it is not just necessary that there be grounds for the affirmation if we are to take it at its face value as an attribution of good or bad, they must also be grounds of a certain kind. They must be grounds which relate in some intelligible way to what men need, desire or seek after. This may become clearer if we look at another example. Suppose a man says: "To make medical care available to more people is good"; suppose, then, that another man wishes to deny this. We could, of course, imagine reasons for this: world population will grow too fast, there are other more urgent claims on scarce resources, the goal can only be obtained by objectionable social policies, such as socialized medicine, and so on. The espousal of any of these would make the opposition to the above judgment intelligible, even if not acceptable, and make it clear that it was *this* judgment that was being denied, and not just, say, an emotional reaction which was being countered with another. If, how-

16 We may use behavior, of course, to judge which of the two constructions to put on a man's words, but the two are not distinguished by behavioral criteria alone, but also by what a man thinks and feels. It is possible, of course, to challenge a man's even sincere belief that he is judging of good and bad, and to disvalue it on the grounds that one holds it to be based largely on irrational prejudice or unavowed ambitions or fears. Thus our first segregationist may be judged as not too different from our second. For there is some evidence that segregationist ideas can at least partly be assimilated to neurotic phobias in their psychological roots. But this is just why many people look on the judgments of segregationists as self-deception and unconscious sham. "Really," they are just expressions of horror. But this respects the logic of "good" as we have outlined it: for it concludes that if the rational base is mere show, then the judgment is mere show. Segregationists, for their part, rarely are of the second type, and pay homage to the logic of "good" by casting about for all sorts of specious reasons for the correct form.

ever, our objector said nothing, and claimed to have nothing to say, his position would be unintelligible, as we have seen; or else we would construe his words as expressing some feeling of distaste or horror or sadness at the thought.

But supposing he was willing to give grounds for his position, but none of the above or their like, saying instead, for instance, "There would be too many doctors," or "Too many people would be dressed in white"? We would remain in doubt as to how to take his opposition, for we would be led to ask of his opposition to the increase of doctors, say, whether he was making a judgment concerning good and bad or simply expressing a dislike. And we would decide this question by looking at the grounds he adduced for *this* position. And if he claimed to have nothing to say, his position would be unintelligible in exactly the same way as if he had decided to remain silent at the outset and leave his original statement unsupported. "What's this?" we would say, "You are against an increase in medical services, because it would increase the number of doctors? But are you just expressing the feelings of dislike that doctors evoke in you or are you really trying to tell us that the increase is bad?" In the absence of any defence on his part, we would take the first interpretation.

It is clear that the problem would remain unsolved, if our opponent grounded his opposition to doctors on the fact that they generally wore dark suits, or washed their hands frequently. We might at this point suspect him of having us on. So that the length or elaboration of the reasoning has nothing to do with the question one way or another.

What would make his position intelligible, and intelligible as a judgment of good and bad, would be his telling us some story about the evil influence doctors exercise on society, or the sinister plot they were hatching to take over and exploit the rest of mankind, or something of the kind. For this would relate the increase of doctors in an intelligible way to the interests, needs or purposes of men. In the absence of such a relation, we remain in the dark, and are tempted to assume the worst.

What is meant by "intelligibility" here is that we can understand the judgment as a use of "good" and "bad." It is now widely agreed that a word gets its meaning from its place in the skein of discourse; we can give its meaning, for instance, by making clear its relations to other words. But this is not to say that we can give the meaning in a set of logical relations of equivalence, entailment, and so on, that an earlier positivism saw as the content of philosophical endeavor. For the relation to other terms may pass through a certain context. Thus, there is a relation between "good" and commending, expressing approval, and so on. But this is not to say that we can construe "X is good," for instance, as *meaning* "I commend X." [17] Rather, we can say that "good" can be used for commending, that to apply the word involves being

[17] Cf. John Searle's "Meaning and Speech Acts," *Philosophical Review*, October 1962.

ready to commend in certain circumstances, for if you aren't then you are shown to have been unserious in your application of it, and so on.[18]

The relation between "good" and commending, expressing approval, persuading, and so on, has been stressed by nonnaturalist theorists of ethics (though not always adequately understood, because of the narrow concentration on logical relations), but the term has another set of relations, to the grounds of its predication, as we have tried to show. These two aspects correspond respectively to what has often been called the evaluative, emotive or prescriptive meaning on one hand (depending on the theory) and the "descriptive" meaning on the other. For half a century an immense barrage of dialectical artillery has been trained on the so-called "naturalistic fallacy" in an effort to prize "good" loose from any set range of descriptive meanings. But this immense effort has been beside the point, for it has concentrated on the nonexistence of logical relations between descriptive predicates and evaluative terms. But the fact that one cannot find equivalences, make valid deductive argument, and so on, may show nothing about the relation between a given concept and others.

Just as with the "evaluative" meaning above, so with the "descriptive" meaning: "good" doesn't *mean* "conducive to the fulfilment of human wants, needs or purposes"; but its use is unintelligible outside of any relationship to wants, needs and purposes, as we saw above. For if we abstract from this relation, then we cannot tell whether a man is using "good" to make a judgment, or simply express some feeling; and it is an essential part of the meaning of the term that such a distinction can be made. The "descriptive" [19] aspects of "good's" meaning can rather be shown in this way: "good" is used in evaluating, commending, persuading and so on by a race of beings who are such that through their needs, desires, and so on, they are not indifferent to the various outcomes of the world process. A race of inactive, godless angels, as really disinterested spectators, would have no use for it, could not make use of it, except in the context of cultural anthropology, just as human anthropologists use "mana." It is because "good" has this use, and can only have

[18] Thus, if I say, "This is a good car," and then my friend comes along and says, "Help me choose a car," I have to eat my words if I am not willing to commend the car to him, *unless* I can adduce some other countervailing factor such as price, my friend's proclivity to dangerous driving, or whatever. But this complex relationship cannot be expressed in an equivalence, e.g., "This is a good car" entails "If you are choosing a car, take this."

[19] The terms "descriptive meaning" and "evaluative meaning" can be seen to be seriously misleading, as is evident from the discussion. For they carry the implication that the meaning is "contained" in the word, and can be "unpacked" in statements of logical equivalence. There is rather a descriptive aspect and an evaluative aspect of its role or use, which are, moreover, connected, for we cannot see whether a use of the term carries the evaluation force of "good" unless we can also see whether it enters into the skein of relations which constitute the descriptive dimension of its meaning.

meaning because there is this role to fill in human life, that it becomes unintelligible when abstracted from this role. Because its having a use arises from the fact that we are not indifferent, its use cannot be understood where we cannot see what there is to be not indifferent about, as in the strange "grounds" quoted by our imaginary opponent above. Moreover, its role is such that it is supposed to be predicated on general grounds, and not just according to the likes and dislikes or feelings of individuals. This distinction is essential since (among other things) the race concerned spends a great deal of effort achieving and maintaining consensus within larger or smaller groups, without which it would not survive. But where we cannot see what the grounds could be, we are tempted to go on treating the use of "good" as an expression of partiality, only of the more trivial, individual kind.

We can thus see why, for instance, "anything conducive to human happiness is good" doesn't need any further grounds to be adduced on its behalf. In human happiness, which by definition men desire, we have an adequate ground. This doesn't mean that all argument is foreclosed. We can try to show that men degenerate in various ways if they seek only happiness, and that certain things which also make men unhappy are necessary for their development. Or we can try to show that there is a higher and a lower happiness, that most men seek under this title only pleasure, and that this turns them away from genuine fulfilment; and so on. But unless we can bring up some countervailing consideration, we cannot deny a thesis of this kind. The fact that we can always bring up such countervailing considerations means that we can never say that "good" *means* "conducive to human happiness," as Moore saw. But that something is conducive to human happiness, or in general to the fulfilment of human needs, wants and purposes, is a prima facie reason for calling it good, which stands unless countered.

Thus the nonneutrality of the theoretical findings of political science need not surprise us. In setting out a given framework, a theorist is also setting out the gamut of possible polities and policies. But a *political* framework cannot fail to contain some, even implicit, conception of human needs, wants and purposes. The context of this conception will determine the value slope of the gamut, unless we can introduce countervailing considerations. If these countervailing factors are motivationally marginal enough not to have too much relevance to political behavior, then we can speak of the original valuation as being only overridden. For that part of the gamut of possibilities which we originally valued still has the property we attributed to it and thus remains valuable for us in one aspect, even if we have to give it low marks in another. For instance, we still will believe that having a peaceful polity is a good, even if it results in bad art. But if the countervailing factor is significant for political behavior, then it will lead us to revise our framework and hence our views about the gamut of possible polities and policies; this in turn will lead to new valuations. The basis of the old values will be undermined.

Thus, if we believe that an absence of violence will lead to stagnation and foreign conquest or breakdown, then we change the gamut of possibility: the choice no longer lies between peace and violence, but between, say, controlled violence and greater uncontrolled violence. Peace ceases to figure on the register: it is not a good we can attain.

Of course, the countervailing factor may not revise our gamut of choices so dramatically. It may simply show that the values of our originally preferred regime cannot be integrally fulfilled or that they will be under threat from a previously unsuspected quarter, or that they will be attended with dangers or disadvantages or disvalues not previously taken into account, so that we have to make a choice as in the peace-versus-good-art case above. Thus not all alterations of the framework will undermine the original values. But we can see that the converse does hold, and all undermining will involve a change in the framework. For if we leave the original framework standing, then the values of its preferred regime will remain as fully realizable goods, even if they are attended with certain evils which force on us a difficult choice, such as that between peace and good art, or progress and psychic harmony, or whatever.

In this sense we can say that a given explanatory framework secretes a notion of good, and a set of valuations, which cannot be done away with—though they can be overridden—unless we do away with the framework. Of course, because the values can be overridden, we can only say that the framework tends to support them, not that it establishes their validity. But this is enough to show that the neutrality of the findings of political science is not what it was thought to be. For establishing a given framework restricts the range of value positions which can be defensibly adopted. For in the light of the framework certain goods can be accepted as such without further argument, whereas other rival ones cannot be adopted without adducing overriding considerations. The framework can be said to distribute the onus of argument in a certain way. It is thus not neutral.

The only way to avoid this while doing political science would be to stick to the narrow-gauge discoveries which, just because they are, taken alone, compatible with a great number of political frameworks, can bathe in an atmosphere of value neutrality. That Catholics in Detroit tend to vote Democrat can consort with almost anyone's conceptual scheme, and thus with almost anyone's set of political values. But to the extent that political science cannot dispense with theory, with the search for a framework, to that extent it cannot stop developing normative theory.

Nor need this have the vicious results usually attributed to it. There is nothing to stop us making the greatest attempts to avoid bias and achieve objectivity. Of course, it is hard, almost impossible, and precisely because our values are also at stake. But it helps, rather than hinders, the cause to be aware of this.

2

Theoretical Self-Consciousness

William E. Connolly

An explanatory theory, Charles Taylor argues persuasively, sustains a set of prima facie normative conclusions.[1] That thesis carries profound implications for the intellectual responsibilities of the social scientist. For now it is not permissible to construe the most difficult and challenging questions of social inquiry as "the task of ethics as a separate enterprise."[2] The investigator can no longer be content merely to present his empirical findings for public assessment; he has a corollary responsibility to elaborate the normative import of his work and to present these findings to the wider intellectual community for critical scrutiny.

And yet, if sufficient means were available to bring competing explanatory theories of social structure and politics to impersonal test, the thesis posed by Taylor would simply extend the *scope* of the social scientist's assignment. His established methods and approach would remain untouched. What if, though, the explanatory theory one adopts inevitably stretches beyond the reach of available evidence? To put the query more sharply, *What if the available evidence is compatible with more than one theory?* If this is chronically the situation in social science, the Taylor thesis can be seen to infect the very "logic" of social inquiry. For a weakly supported explanatory theory supports problematic normative judgments. And when more than one explanatory theory is compatible with the available evidence, the investigator lacks secure and neutral ground from which to assess his moral commitments; it becomes essentially contestable whether his theoretical posture reflects more the constraints of evidence or his *previous* attachment to normative priorities congruent with that posture.

Classical issues of theoretical judgment assume renewed urgency when the

[1] Charles Taylor, "Neutrality in Political Science," in this volume, pp. 16–39.

[2] Heinz Eulau, "Tradition and Innovation: On the Tension Between Ancient and Modern Ways in the Study of Politics," in *Behavioralism in Political Science*, ed. Heinz Eulau (New York: Atherton Press, 1969), 11–12. For a generally supportive argument see Kurt Baier, *The Moral Point of View* (New York: Random House, 1965).

contemporary mind is exposed to the connection between explanation and evaluation: How can I become more fully aware of the extent to which my theoretical commitments reflect either the constraints of evidence or the pull of my moral aspirations? How can I subject my favored interpretation, and the norms it sustains, to the most challenging critique? As the foundations of my theoretical judgment become more susceptible to my conscious scrutiny, how should I proceed when available evidence is insufficient to control the theoretical choices before me?

THEORETICAL ASSESSMENT AND THE NATURAL SCIENCES

To lay the groundwork for assessing these questions, I will draw briefly on the recent work of Thomas Kuhn and Stephen Toulmin in the philosophy of the natural sciences. Because their work has been so widely and diversely used by social theorists recently, I must offer a few caveats. I do not interpret either Kuhn or Toulmin to hold an extreme "relativist" or "historicist" view of science.[3] Neither am I concerned here to decide whether theoretical change in the natural sciences follows an evolutionary course (Toulmin), occurs in revolutionary bursts (Kuhn), or follows neither pattern consistently. Finally, I will not be concerned here to define more precisely Kuhn's idea of a "paradigm," nor to argue that perspectives, as I shall call their cousins in the social sciences, are either as precise or as well developed as paradigms are in the natural sciences. My purpose here is to provide some pointers for the exploration of depth connections among the assumptions, conceptual contours, and test procedures in a theory of politics or society. Starting in an area both more precise and less complicated than social theory renders that task a bit more manageable.

Every scientific theory, according to Stephen Toulmin, reflects an "ideal of natural order," a set of theoretical recommendations about how the objects and processes studied will behave when disturbing forces are not at work. Events that conform to these fundamental expectations *need no further ex-*

[3] In this respect I disagree with the interesting article by Eugene F. Miller, "Positivism, Historicism, and Political Inquiry," *American Political Science Review* (September 1972), 796–818; and I would therefore deny that the Kuhn-Toulmin position generates the "absurd" consequences attributed to it by David Braybrooke and Alexander Rosenberg in their reply to Miller. Ibid., 818–826. Kuhn and Toulmin point to *barriers* to communication across theories, but do not assert that it is impossible; they probe strong *tendencies* within theoretical communities to remain unaware of disconfirming evidence, but do not conclude that such tendencies cannot be reduced; they speak of *nonrational* influence in theoretical decision, but do not celebrate these influences or argue that they cannot be further reduced. Their objective of course is to expose such barriers, tendencies, and nonrational influences in order to probe means of reducing their influence. These points are too often ignored by some social scientists seeking to celebrate a purely subjectivist view of their disciplines and by others seeking to debunk efforts to revise the behavioral orthodoxy in political inquiry.

planation; they are, within that theoretical system, "self-explanatory." Only events that deviate from these expectations (that is, "phenomena") require explanation, and they are adequately explained only as they are rendered compatible with the "ideal of natural order," the basis of the explanatory theory. A scientist working with such an "ideal," Toulmin argues, "begins with the conviction that things are not just happening but rather that some fixed set of laws or patterns or mechanisms account for Nature's following the course it does, and his understanding of these should guide his expectations." [4]

Consider alternative "ideals" of bodies in motion scientists have accepted at various times in the history of mechanics. For Aristotle, the "natural" or paradigm case, that is, the condition when no disturbing forces intervene, was a body at rest. A body at rest required no further explanation. Bodies in motion were "phenomena" to be explained by discovering the forces acting upon them. Galileo modified this model. He assumed a paradigm case in which bodies in motion followed a circular orbit. Objects at rest (contra Aristotle), objects that changed their rate of motion, and objects that deviated from a circular orbit became "phenomena" to be explained. For Newton, finally, a body either at rest or moving at a uniform rate of speed in a straight line was "self-explanatory"; only deviations from this paradigm required explanation.

In each case, then, the "ideal of natural order" establishes certain happenings as self-explanatory and marks off others as phenomena in need of explanation. In each case, too, the phenomena are not explained until they are made congruent somehow with the basic paradigm adopted. Since the ideals of natural order vary significantly among the theories of Aristotle, Galileo, and Newton, events that are phenomena to be explained within one framework provide in alternative frameworks the starting point to which explanation must refer. Newton, but not Galileo, must *explain* why a body follows a circular orbit; Galileo, but not Newton, must *explain* why a body follows a straight line. The ideal or paradigm at the base of a theory, then, plays a fundamental role in explanation: It identifies "those happenings in the world around us which do require explanation by contrasting them with 'the natural course of events' —those which do not." [5]

How, though, should the scientist *test* the ideal of natural order he accepts? According to the conventional wisdom among social scientists, theories in the natural sciences are tested by searching systematically for facts that would disconfirm them. To be testable in principle, a theory must be incompatible with a set of conceivable observations. And if a thorough search is then made

[4] Stephen Toulmin, *Foresight and Understanding* (New York: Harper and Row, 1961), p. 45.

[5] Ibid., p. 79.

for disconfirming facts and none are found, the theory can be said to be corroborated.[6]

Revisionists in the philosophy of science have challenged this view. It is not attacked as wholly untenable, but it is said to underplay seriously the extent to which a given theory itself helps to constitute and demarcate the "facts" that its practitioners can observe. For example, in the middle of the eighteenth century, the phlogiston theory of combustion was widely accepted by the scientific community. Oxygen, of course, was an active element in the very experiments thought to confirm the phlogiston theory, but experiments could not be controlled for its presence. *Without access to modern chemical theory, experimenters lacked the theoretical basis to make those observations which could most thoroughly discredit phlogiston theory.* The commitment to phlogiston theory, and to the test procedures tied to it, was "simultaneously a commitment to the nonexistence of gases that could behave as oxygen did." [7]

The general point is this: Natural science requires a rather elaborate and precise conceptual system to locate and explain phenomena. That conceptual system necessarily structures observation; it tends to limit the range of unexpected phenomena available for observation and to inhibit the investigator in his exploration of alternative conceptual schemes. The concepts we employ at once focus and limit observation. "We see the world through them to such an extent that we forget what it would be like without them: Our very commitment to them tends to blind us to other possibilities." [8]

The conceptual system one adopts reflects the "ideal of natural order" or the paradigm orienting inquiry; and because that conceptual system in turn limits the kinds and range of phenomena available for inspection, *an immense complication is introduced into efforts to devise neutral tests that can adjudicate between alternative theories.* The tests themselves are theory imbued. "Men who accept different paradigms have really no common theoretical terms in which to discuss their problems fruitfully. They will not even have the same problem: events which are 'phenomena' in one man's eyes will be passed over by the other as 'perfectly natural.' " [9]

Since our brief discussion of these issues anticipates the exploration of

[6] For the most authoritative elaboration of the falsification thesis, see Karl Popper, *The Logic of Scientific Discovery* (Basic Books, 1959). The debate between revisionists and supporters of the Popper thesis is effectively presented in Imre Lakatos and Alan Musgrave, eds., *Criticism and the Growth of Knowledge* (London: Cambridge University Press, 1970). See especially the essays by Thomas Kuhn, P. H. Feyerabend, and Imre Lakatos in that volume.

[7] Thomas Kuhn, *The Structure of Scientific Revolutions* (Chicago: University of Chicago Press, 1962), p. 60.

[8] Toulmin, *Foresight and Understanding,* p. 101. Kuhn's conclusion is similar. A paradigm, he says, "restricts the phenomenological field accessible for scientific investigation at any time." Kuhn, *Structure of Scientific Revolutions,* pp. 60–61.

[9] Toulmin, *Foresight and Understanding,* p. 57.

parallel problems in social inquiry, we might review also the methodological responses recommended by philosophers of natural science. Thomas Kuhn, a methodological conservative, emphasizes the importance of retaining and perfecting established theoretical schemes. By articulating the established theory more fully, by specifying more closely what observations are to be expected, researchers pave the way for the proliferation of anomalies that will eventually force rejection of the theory. Anomalies or unexpected observations, he emphasizes, appear "only against the background provided by a paradigm"; and a well-articulated paradigm provides the precise observational expectations that enable scientists to "recognize that something has gone wrong" when those expectations are not met.[10] Methodological conservatism, then, pursued patiently, will eventually create massive pressures for a thorough overhaul of the established theory. The proliferation of ad hoc adjustments to save the old shell will finally become too much for a new generation of scientists to tolerate.

P. K. Feyerabend accepts the analysis of Kuhn and Toulmin in broad outline, but he rejects Kuhn's methodological response to the problems posed. Given the extent to which a particular theory construes certain happenings as self-explanatory, and given the extent to which a theoretical framework blinds the investigator to possible observations in conflict with theoretical expectations, Feyerabend concludes that theoretical pluralism is a precondition of good empiricism. Researchers working within a single theoretical framework are unlikely to be aware of the subtle ways in which it structures and limits inquiry, but exposure to competing theories heightens that awareness and increases the likelihood that a reigning theory will be confronted with new and discomforting facts. For "however closely a theory seems to reflect the facts its factual adequacy can be asserted only *after* it has been confronted with alternatives *whose invention and detailed development must therefore precede any final assertion of practical success and factual adequacy.* Such a pluralism allows for a much sharper criticism of accepted ideas than does the comparison with a domain of 'facts' which are supposed to sit there independently of theoretical considerations."[11]

THE PERSPECTIVE IN SOCIAL INQUIRY

Now there is a difference of some import between inquiry into inert nature and inquiry into social and political life. For in society the "phenomena" are constituted in part by the concepts and beliefs the beings studied have themselves developed through social interaction; and changes in those concepts and

[10] Kuhn, *Structure of Scientific Revolutions,* p. 65.

[11] "How To Be a Good Empiricist—A Plea for Tolerance in Matters Epistemological," in *The Philosophy of Science,* ed. P. H. Nidditch (New York: Oxford University Press, 1968), pp. 14–15.

beliefs can go some distance toward reconstituting the social context of human conduct.[12] But this feature of social life means that its inquiry is more, not less, complicated than inquiry in the natural sciences.

We begin with a simple fact: Human beings, including social scientists, do not and cannot approach the study of society with a blank slate. Each evolves, in conjunction with those others with whom he interacts in the course of his life, a *perspective* that organizes his awareness and understanding of social life.[13] The perspective, comparable to Toulmin's "ideal of natural order" in significant respects, involves a set of fundamental *assumptions* or *expectations* about the "normal" operation of society and politics and a relatively integrated set of *concepts* within which interpretations of society are constructed. The connections between expectations and conceptual system provide the justification for considering both as component parts of a larger perspective: the expectations help to shape the contours of the conceptual system, and the concepts in turn are the medium through which deviations from those expectations are confronted.

The role of language communities in shaping and sustaining the perspective is central. For, as G. H. Mead has shown in his impressive study of how the self and mind emerge out of social transactions, it is the set of rich, subtle distinctions and expectations of language that sustains coherence and stable purpose in life. "A person learns a new language and, as we say, gets a new soul. He puts himself into the attitude of those that make use of that language. He cannot read its literature, cannot converse with those that belong to that community, without taking on its peculiar attitudes. He becomes in that sense a different individual." [14]

The perspective one brings to inquiry both predisposes one to interpret the society in a particular way and marshalls impressive resources to protect the favored interpretive scheme. These protective mechanisms work more tacitly than explicitly, assimilating "phenomena" to the basic theoretical system and directing research observations to those aspects of the sociopolitical world most congenial to that basic framework.

[12] Social scientists have often tried to capture this phenomenon under the rubric of "self-fulfilling prophecy" or "bandwagon effect." These approaches seem insufficient to me. I have been influenced on these points by Alasdair MacIntyre, *Against the Self-Images of the Age* (New York: Schocken Books, 1971), Chs. 18–23; Charles Taylor, "Interpretation and the Sciences of Man," *Review of Metaphysics* (Fall 1971), pp. 4–51; Peter Winch, *The Idea of a Social Science* (New York: Humanities Press, 1958).

[13] For a more detailed discussion of the perspective and its role in inquiry, see William E. Connolly, *Political Science and Ideology* (New York: Atherton Press, 1967). That work, in turn, is indebted to Karl Mannheim, from whom the term "perspective" is borrowed, and G. H. Mead. See Karl Mannheim, *Ideology and Utopia* (New York: Harcourt, Brace and World, 1936) and Anselm Straus, ed., *The Social Psychology of G. H. Mead: Selected Writings of an American Pragmatist* (Chicago: University of Chicago Press, 1934).

[14] Straus, *The Social Psychology of G. H. Mead*, p. 270.

Perspectives on Social Structure and Politics

Several contemporary social theorists have suggested that two discernible frameworks or perspectives, the "consensus" and "conflict" perspectives, have competed historically for the honor of serving as *the* interpretive framework for the study of society.[15] This overstates a partial truth: While several versions of these two frameworks have competed for acceptance, they do not together exhaust the logical or historical alternatives. Nonetheless, for purposes of explication we will construct highly abbreviated versions of these two orientations, labelling them, in accord with conventional usage, the "consensus" and "conflict" perspectives.

The Consensus Perspective

Durkheim exemplifies this perspective in its classic form. In contemporary social science, Talcott Parsons, Kingsley Davis and Wilbert Moore, Thomas Berger and Peter Luckmann, and William Kornhauser, while disagreeing with one another in matters of some importance, share most of the assumptions and research priorities involved in this perspective.[16] The perspective is characterized by a set of presumptions or expectations, that is, conditions assumed to hold in particular settings unless and until strong countervailing evidence is confronted:

1. Human beings are highly adaptable creatures who typically adjust to established social roles with a minimum of friction. Since the human being has "no species-specific environment, no environment firmly structured by his own instinctual organization," he can be socialized readily to those norms and roles established in his society.[17]
2. It is fruitful to view social relations as analogous to the relations among the parts of a complex organism. Each part contributes to

[15] Ralf Dahrendorf, *Class and Class Conflict in Industrial Society* (Stanford University Press, 1959), Ch. 5; John Horton, "Order and Conflict Theories of Social Problems as Competing Ideologies," *American Journal of Sociology* (May 1966), pp. 701–713; Gerhard Lenski, *Power and Privilege* (New York: McGraw-Hill, 1966), Chs. 1 and 2, and the excerpts from that book in this volume, pp. 124–145; Michael Mann, "The Social Cohesion of Liberal Democracy," *American Sociological Review* (June 1970), 423–439; P. L. Van den Berghe, "Dialectic and Functionalism: Toward a Theoretical Synthesis," *American Sociological Review* (June 1963), pp. 695–705.

[16] See Durkheim, "On Anomie" in this volume, pp. 75–96; Talcott Parsons, *Essays in Sociological Theory* (Glencoe, Ill.: Free Press, 1964); Kingsley Davis and Wilbert Moore, "Some Principles of Stratification," in this volume, pp. 112–123; Thomas Berger and Peter Luckmann, *The Social Construction of Reality* (New York: Doubleday and Co., 1966); William Kornhauser, *The Politics of Mass Society* (Glencoe, Ill.: Free Press, 1959).

[17] The quotation is from Berger and Luckman, *The Social Construction of Reality,* p. 45. The role this assumption plays in contemporary social theory is examined lucidly by Fred Dallmayr, "Empirical Theory and Images of Man," in this volume, pp. 168–191.

the maintenance of the entire system, and the "parts" are adequately understood when their functions in the system are grasped.

3. When the parts are thus viewed functionally, the extent to which existing inequalities of privilege, wealth, and power work to the advantage of the whole community is highlighted. Extreme inequality may be exploitative, but the presumption is that traditionally established inequalities generally help to maintain a system which is quite advantageous to each and all.
4. Social stability rests predominantly upon a set of shared beliefs and mutual expectations (a consensus) whereby each accepts his socially defined tasks and rights as appropriate and each internalizes established views about how those above, beside, and below him should behave. Coercion, the threat of force, and manipulation normally play a marginal role in maintaining order.

Given such presumptions about the plasticity of human nature and the consensual basis of order and inequality, a central problem tends to dominate research: Why, in any particular setting, does such extensive social conflict exist, and how can established authorities cope with this conflict while maintaining the ongoing system?[18] In this perspective, then, consensus is to be *expected,* while conflict and coercion, when they are perceived, are to be *explained.* And the preferred explanation, as we shall see shortly, introduces auxiliary hypotheses that either square the unexpected deviations with basic theoretical presumptions or require a minimal adjustment of them.

The perspective also generates normative implications. Its tendency is to justify established inequalities as conducive to the general welfare and as a reflection of social consensus more than elite coercion. Its view that "all social reality is precarious; all societies are constructions in the face of chaos," provides a rationale for defending the delicate fabric of an existing equilibrium against pressure for significant change. Those pressures could generate unanticipated dislocations and insecurities, destroying the precarious balance.

The Conflict Perspective

Rousseau and Marx express variants of this perspective in their interpretations of actual societies, although each projects a contrast model in which inequality, conflict, and coercion are displaced by egalitarian community.

[18] That this question receives highest priority is often denied by its adherents. David Easton's comments on the limits and biases of his own approach are therefore refreshing: "It is true that entirely different kinds of questions could have been posed and these would certainly have led to the construction of a conceptual framework quite remote from, although not entirely alien to the one that has been presented. . . . To put it in colloquial . . . terms, a systems approach draws us away from a discussion of the way in which the political pie is cut up and how it happens to get cut up in one way rather than another." *A Systems Analysis of Political Life* (New York: John Wiley, 1965), pp. 473–474, 475.

C. Wright Mills, Herbert Marcuse, Peter Bachrach, and Thomas Bottomore reflect this perspective to varying degrees in their contemporary interpretive schemes.[19] Characteristic presumptions are

1. Human beings have certain "needs" that can be fulfilled through social life, but that are in fact often frustrated by the constraints of social organization and political power.[20]
2. Simmering beneath the surface of officially sanctioned relations are conflicts of interest among various segments of society, and each "party" or unit of society is adequately understood only when its basic interests are grasped. Those participants who do not perceive that what is to the interest of one unit is often to the disadvantage of others have not attained true consciousness.
3. Given prevailing socialization processes and the power resources accruing to those in privileged positions, elites act more at the expense of subordinates than on their behalf. The interests of the under classes are often sacrificed to the interests (or at least the desires) of the upper classes.[21]
4. Coercion, the threat of coercion, and manipulation are important instruments by which overt conflict is minimized. The reduction of inequalities protected by these instruments requires efforts by the under classes and their allies to increase the scope and intensity of overt social conflict.

Researchers operating with these presumptions do not need to explain further the conflict, dissension, and unrest in an inegalitarian society. Such a society, though, with minimal overt conflict and apparent consensus, is a "phenomenon" in need of explanation: How are existing inequalities main-

[19] See Marx, "On Alienation" in this volume, pp. 97–99; C. Wright Mills, "The Structure of Power in American Society," in this volume, pp. 147–158; Herbert Marcuse, *One Dimensional Man* (Boston: Beacon Press, 1964); Peter Bachrach, *The Theory of Democratic Elitism: A Critique* (Boston: Little, Brown and Co., 1967); Thomas Bottomore, *Elites and Society* (Baltimore: Penguin, 1964).

[20] The most specific application of the vocabulary "needs" in this context is Christian Bay, "Politics and Pseudo-politics, A Critique of Some Behavioral Literature," *American Political Science Review* (March 1965). It seems clear to me, though, that the vocabulary of needs is not sufficient to cover the theory of human nature assumed in this perspective. See my "On Interests in Politics," in this volume, pp. 228–248.

[21] George Simmel reflects the conflict perspective perfectly on these points: "In every hierarchy, a new pressure or imposition moves along the line of least resistance which, though not in its first stage, usually and eventually, runs in a descending direction. This is the tragedy of whoever is lowest in any social order. He not only has to suffer from the deprivations, efforts, and discriminations which, taken together, characterize his position; in addition, every new pressure on any point whatever in the superordinate layers is, if technically possible at all, transmitted downward and stops only at him." Kurt H. Wolff, ed., *The Sociology of Georg Simmel* (Free Press, 1950), pp. 236–237.

tained with the minimal use of explicit sanctions? How are the underlying conflicts contained and the most deprived groups suppressed? And, once again, the task undertaken is to provide answers congruent with the fundamental presumptions of the perspective.

The normative import of this perspective should be clear enough: Established inequalities are viewed critically; the legitimacy of those in authority is seen as marginal; dissident activists are viewed presumptively as creative catalysts of needed social change.

Theoretical Perspectives and Conceptual Systems

Note that the two perspectives presented in such abbreviated and idealized form do not merely ask different questions about social structure and politics—though such differences do emerge. They are not simply two complementary "faces of society." For each theory incorporates presumptions about the organization of society that are quite incompatible with those adopted by the other. Neither is it the case that one perspective pays attention to "conflict" while the other deals only with "consensus." Each deals with both, but within the framework of its own assumptions and expectations.

Because of its characteristic presumptions, each perspective gives highest priority to a particular set of questions that the other tends to treat either as less fundamental or self-explanatory. And when those immersed in one perspective do turn to the highest priority questions of the other, they tend to redefine them in subtle ways and to anticipate answers compatible with presumptions already accepted. These tendencies are not typically perceived by the investigators themselves as biases or prejudices; they operate well below the level of conscious awareness. For not only do opposing perspectives differ in the questions given highest priority and in the answers anticipated to the questions; they differ too in the very concepts brought to the study of politics. *The concepts employed reflect the presumptions of the perspective and tacitly gear perceptions to fit these presumptions.* In the study of society, as in the natural sciences, when we habituate ourselves to a set of concepts we "see the world through them to such an extent that we forget what it would be like without them: our very commitment to them tends to blind us to other possibilities." [22] This fact, in social inquiry as in the study of nature, renders communication across opposing theoretical perspectives difficult and misleading, and it profoundly complicates efforts to bring opposing theories to impersonal test.

The consensus perspective, for instance, will discourage interpretive perceptions of citizen discontent, resentment, or vague anxiety, while the conflict perspective encourages such interpretations. And to the extent that he does

[22] Toulmin, *Foresight and Understanding,* p. 57.

perceive widespread anxiety, the consensus theorist tends to interpret it as "anomie"—a rupture in societal roles that disorients citizens by depriving them of socially defined purpose. Persons whose status is "inconsistent" (for example, high status in one's capacity as a physician, low status as a black) will suffer from this condition in a stable society. Their troubles are rooted in the peculiar conditions of their personal biographies, and their deviations from established role expectations reflect personal maladjustment. Less often, perhaps during periods of rapid social change, this sense of disorientation will infect the lives of broad segments of society. In such circumstances consensus theorists will speak of the structural basis of personal troubles and will explore possibilities of structural change. But even here, the very precariousness of social order requires cautious gradualism; and one important aspect of the response needed is to lower the expectations of those whose current aspirations outstrip the society's capacity to deliver.[23]

The conflict theorist is likely to perceive discontent and vague anxiety where none is seen by adherents of the opposing view. And the tendency is not to trace the troubles perceived to individual idiosyncracies, but to emphasize the extent to which the troubles of some are shared by others and to locate their common source in the structural arrangements of the society. Even where citizens are apparently content, the proponent of this second perspective will identify social and political constraints on their development unbeknown to them. He will, that is, see theirs as a condition of "alienation"—a form of repressive social organization that limits unnecessarily the development of the highest human potential or "species being."

The consensus theorist, then, brings the concept of anomie to the study of social malaise, while the conflict theorist comprehends these "same" situations as expressions of alienation. These concepts in turn reflect opposing theoretical assumptions about the direction human development can take, the linkages between human development and social organization, and the extent to which a reconstitution of social life could encourage that development.[24]

To illuminate further the problems of testing and communicating across opposing perspectives, consider the different interpretation devotees of the consensus and of the conflict perspectives might place on the following hypothesis: "In American society, the upper class rules in its own interests." [25]

[23] These sentiments are well expressed by Durkheim: "But those who only have the void above them are almost bound to lose themselves in it, if there is not force to hold them back," and "We know only too well what a laborious work it is to erect this society where each individual will have the place he merits . . . , where everybody . . . will work for the good of all and each." "On Anomie," in this volume, pp. 75–96.

[24] These issues are explored with skill and clarity by Stephen Lukes, "Alienation and Anomie," in this volume, pp. 192–211.

[25] The example picked is not purely fanciful. In his study of community power Nelson Polsby attributes the following view to "stratification theorists": "The upper-class power elite rules in its own interests." *Community Power and Political Theory* (New Haven: Yale University Press, 1963), p. 11. He then translates that hypothesis into a position

Before the hypothesis can be tested, it must be understood; before it is fully understood, several component concepts require clarification, including especially the concepts "power," "class," and "interests." For, as several analysts have noted,[26] to share the same vocabulary is not necessarily to share *exactly* the same set of concepts. And in fact these shared terms tend to mark significant differences among perspectives in the definitions tacitly followed.

Suppose, for example, that proponents of our first perspective were to define class in terms of subjectively defined status in the community, to view power as the ability to achieve *intended* goals even against the will of others, and to construe an agent's interests to be those public policies he favors—whatever they might be. Now the hypothesis to be tested becomes: "Those elements of society who view themselves and are viewed by others to have the highest status, are consistently able to enact policies they prefer over the opposition of groups who oppose their passage." Indeed this translation of the initial hypothesis is not far removed from that rendered by a recent critic of ruling elite theories: "A ruling elite, then, is . . . a minority of individuals whose preferences regularly prevail in cases of differences in preferences on key political issues." [27]

While the preceding translation is abbreviated, it is not implausible to expect one immersed in the consensus perspective to adopt one quite similar. For *assuming* that a broad consensus provides the fundamental basis of social order, he wants to *know* how effectively overt conflicts are handled by the institutions of government, how such institutions manage conflicts so as to maintain the consensual basis of order. But overt conflicts arise only when the preferences or demands of one faction are opposed to the preferences of another; and one side can be said to "win" such conflicts when it achieves its intended objectives. In other words, given the fundamental presumptions and corollary set of high-priority questions built into this perspective, it is not implausible for its proponents to construe interest as policy preference and power as the ability to gain intended objectives.[28] And this will seem to them to be the obvious or natural way to think about power and interests.

---

few "stratification theorists" would recognize as their own and offers a critique of the translated hypothesis. For a discussion, that connects Polsby's effort to the larger themes argued here, see William Connolly and Felix Oppenheim, "The Language of Political Inquiry: Problems of Clarification," in *The Handbook of Political Science,* ed. Fred Greenstein and Nelson Polsby (Reading, Mass.: Addison-Wesley, forthcoming).

[26] See Stanislaw Ossowski, "Conceptions of Class," William E. Connolly, "On Interests in Politics," and P. H. Partridge, "Some Notes on the Concept 'Power,'" all in this volume. For lucid discussions of the basis and import of this feature of language, see W. B. Gallie, "Essentially Disputed Concepts," in *The Importance of Language,* ed. Max Black (Prentice-Hall, 1962), pp. 121–146, and William Alston, *The Philosophy of Language* (Englewood Cliffs, N.J.: Prentice-Hall, 1964), Ch. 5.

[27] Robert Dahl, "A Critique of the Ruling Elite Model," *American Political Science Review* (June 1957), p. 464.

[28] Such construing of these two concepts is most likely to be adopted by consensus theorists during times of social quiescence. For qualifications of the statement above as it

Unfortunately, though, such a translation of the initial hypothesis will impede communication with those immersed in the conflict perspective (who are likely to have advanced the hypothesis in the first place) and imperil efforts to devise neutral observational tests of the opposing theories. For those implicated in the latter perspective are quite likely to understand the hypothesis differently. The proponent of conflict theory *assumes* that those who exert control over the means of production are likely to have the resources to promote their objectives inside and outside of government. He *anticipates* that, as these agents go about their business, they will intentionally and unintentionally limit the life chances of those in other social locations. He *expects* that the policy preferences of the under classes, shaped by the narrow range of experience and limited information available to them, will often be at odds with policies that would in fact benefit them.

Thus, to abbreviate again, he construes class in terms of the relationship people have to the means of production; he views the interests of an agent as those possible outcomes of social action that will in fact improve his opportunities for development, whether or not he presently favors those outcomes; he defines power as the ability both to gain intended objectives and to generate unintended results of importance for the life chances of other segments of society. Finally, he looks not only to the politics of governmental choice but construes the policy choices of corporate elites in their corporate capacities as part of politics.

In this way, consensus and conflict theorists adopt different interpretations of the initial hypothesis, and the resulting translation effect impedes understanding across perspectives.

It is not that the investigator's conceptual system, linked as it is to the presumptions he brings to inquiry, forecloses the very possibility of making observations discrepant with those presumptions. But his system does open him to those aspects of the environment most congruent with those expectations. Since the rules covering the use of these concepts are typically more tacit than explicit—that is, we understand and use such concepts in something like the way we understand how to ride a bike or to use our native language—those immersed in opposing perspectives will not easily comprehend the discrepancies we have noted. Here, as in natural science, those "who accept different paradigms have no common theoretical terms in which to discuss their problems fruitfully." [29]

The line of influence from presumptions to conceptual scheme continues further, for the test procedures one accepts are affected by these previous commitments. The consensus theorist is more comfortable with survey analysis—identifying the class location of citizens in part by asking them

applies to "interests," see Connolly, "On Interests in Politics," in this volume, pp. 228–248.

[29] Toulmin, *Foresight and Understanding*, p. 57.

where they belong, locating the interests citizens have by questionnaires about their policy preferences, studying power by observing participants in the policy process and asking them the extent to which their objectives were promoted or thwarted.[30] The conflict theorist is naturally wary of these tests; he finds other test procedures more plausible. He identifies classes by looking for external evidence about the amount of control segments of society have over the means of production. He assesses the interests of citizens in various locations by tracing the effects of governmental policies and corporate decisions on their life chances. He adopts the "position test" of power,[31] seeking to trace, for example, the unintentional effects for workers produced by decisions of corporate elites to increase work efficiency and corporate profits through introduction of the assembly line.

The preceding comments only begin to capture the subtle connections between perspective and test procedures. Further complications in this relationship flow from the fact, to be considered shortly, that the tacit acceptance of a theoretical perspective by those whose conduct the theory purports to explain, becomes a source of evidence in support of that theory. But we have sufficiently explored the line of influence from presumptions through conceptual systems to test procedures to point to the need for theoretical self-consciousness among students of politics and society. Table 1 summarizes concisely these connections.

To illustrate the way in which a conceptual system reflects the presumptions of an underlying perspective, we have simplified matters a bit. The following caveats will redress that imbalance.

First, to share the same conceptual system is not *necessarily* to share the same interpretation. Two people might mean the same thing by "unicorn," while one affirms and the other denies that such a being exists. I might, accordingly, accept the concepts "power," "elite," and "interest" as employed by C. Wright Mills and still reject important aspects of his theory of the power elite. Understanding his theory perfectly, I might simply think that the evidence against it is strong. It is useful to remember this point so long as two related points are not forgotten: First, one cannot even begin to assess an

[30] For a nice example of this tendency at work, see Robert Lane, "The Politics of Consensus in an Age of Affluence," *American Political Science Review* (December 1965), pp. 874–895. Lane makes it clear that his surveys are to be taken as refutations of theories held by "alienists such as C. Wright Mills and Erich Fromm. "I have long suspected that they reflected their own discontent with society rather more than any mass discontent. . . . Partly too, I think, their views reflect their own alienation from the field of endeavor where there is a true *élan,* the field of science" (pp. 879–880).

[31] This test is variously appraised and compared to other proposed tests in Robert Dahl, *Modern Political Analysis* (Englewood Cliffs, N.J.: Prentice-Hall, 1963), Ch. 5; Peter Bachrach and Morton Daratz, "The Two Faces of Power," *American Political Science Review* (December 1962), 947–952; and William Connolly, *Political Science and Ideology,* Ch. 2.

TABLE 1. Perspectives and Theoretical Systems*

CONSENSUS	*CONFLICT*
PRESUMPTIONS	
Individuals shaped by social roles. Each unit of society tends to benefit whole. Inequalities supportive of order and necessary. Consensual basis of order.	Universal human needs. Some roles more fulfilling than others. Mutual opposition of interests among units. Inequalities unnecessarily exploitative of lower units. Coercive basis of order.
CONCEPTUAL SYSTEMS	
Anomie-Alienation	
E.g., maladjustment to role requirements.	E.g., rebellion based on recognition of repressive social roles.
Political Power	
Ability to gain intended objectives through government.	Includes unintended effects of elite activity for under classes and some decisions made outside of government as well as inside.
Class	
Mix of subjective location in status hierarchy and identification by income level.	Control or noncontrol of means of production.
Interests	
Policy preferences or the goals one explicitly defines.	Effects of policies on chances for development, where development provides standard for appraising existing wants.
NORMATIVE IMPORT	
Justifies existing inequalities and cautions against massive change.	Critical of existing inequalities and calls for structural change.

* The table is offered only to *illustrate* connections among presumptions, concepts, theory, test procedures, and normative conclusions. It cannot, of course, either exhaust the range of possible perspectives or capture the rich variety of expressions within the two orientations outlined.

EXPLANATORY THEORY	
E.g., existing inequalities help to maintain the consensual basis of order and upper class is constrained by that consensus.	E.g., upper class has great power employed against the interests of under classes to maintain inequalities.

TEST PROCEDURES	
("The upper class rules in its own interests.")	
Emphasis on survey analysis of political participants (power), polls of citizen policy preferences (interests), and self-location in society (class).	Emphasis on tracing effects of policies for life chances via indices of distribution of mental health problems, work-life opportunities, educational experience, and so on.

alternative interpretive scheme until he succeeds in the difficult task of comprehending it on its own terms. Second, to share a conceptual system is to increase the tendency for our interpretations of society to converge also. For the shared conceptual scheme is likely to reflect fundamental common assumptions; and that conceptual scheme also exposes those who employ it to similar aspects of the environment, diverting their attention from features that might threaten shared assumptions.

Thus, for instance, the limitation of "power" to the production of intended results diverts the consensus theorist from exploring possible ways in which some members of society unintentionally produce massive and onerous consequences for other members. This conceptual focus also encourages him to translate ruling elite theories into conspiracy theories, because he will not acknowledge that such a group has power unless it collectively *intends* the results flowing from its actions.[32] He thus converts the opposing theory into a caricature and finds, not too surprisingly, abundant evidence to refute that caricature.

Second, there is not a simple or a universal connection between sharing a perspective and sharing any *particular* concept. Not all conflict theorists, for instance, will employ the concepts "power," "interest," and "class" in exactly the ways we have summarized here. We can speak of dominant tendencies, though, such as the strong propensity for conflict theorists to hold that if "we take the simple democratic view that *what men are interested in* is all that concerns us then we are accepting the values that have been inculcated, often accidentally and often deliberately by vested interests. These values are often

[32] This partly explains, I think, why theorists such as Daniel Bell *insisted* on translating the theory of the power elite into a conspiracy theory even after repeated denials by its author. See Bell, "The Power Elite Reconsidered," in his *The End of Ideology* (Glencoe, Ill.: Free Press, 1960), pp. 47–75.

the only ones men have had a chance to develop. They are unconsciously acquired habits rather than choices." [33]

If a scholar emphasizes the difference between acquired habit and conscious choice in this way, he is also quite likely to carve out conceptual distinctions between what one is interested in and what is in his interest.

Third, in posing the relationship between perspective and conceptual systems, we have considered only some dimensions of some concepts. The rules governing the use of concepts in social inquiry are much more complex than we have so far intimated, and the relationship between conceptual system and perspective shares in that complexity. For example, regarding the concept of power, the tacit decision to include unintended consequences in its definition is only one of many such decisions pertinent to that concept. Thus there are many ways to exert an effect on the conduct of others. One might employ manipulation, coercion, persuasion, authority, conditioning; one might unconsciously provide a model others identify with, and so on. Some researchers tacitly group all these forms of influence indiscriminately under "power"; others discriminate carefully among them and rule certain forms, such as persuasion, outside the rubric of "power"; still others make such subtle distinctions and yet include all types as variants of "power." The stance one adopts on these issues will reflect to some degree the perspective brought to inquiry and affect the substance of one's explanatory theory.[34]

Fourth, in isolating two opposing perspectives for the purpose of exemplifying these themes, we have given short shrift to other possible alternatives. Most notably, we have ignored an orientation also sometimes called the conflict theory to differentiate it from consensus theory. Thomas Hobbes, Vilfredo Pareto, and Roberto Michels in classical theory, and Ralf Dahrendorf and Gerhard Lenski in contemporary social science, have posed this more conservative version of conflict theory.[35] That orientation also makes fundamental presumptions about the sources of order in society, the forms and likely directions of social change, the nature and consequences of stratification.[36]

[33] C. Wright Mills, *The Sociological Imagination* (New York: Oxford University Press, 1959), p. 194. Mills goes on to warn against the temptation to *impose* what is to men's interest on them when they do not see it that way. "If we take the dogmatic view *that what is to men's interests* whether they are interested in it or not is all that need concern us, then we run the risk of violating democratic values. We may become manipulators or coercers or both, rather than persuaders" (p. 194).

[34] The specific dimensions noted here are explored by Partridge in "Some Notes on the Concept of Power" in this volume, pp. 212–227.

[35] See Thomas Hobbes, "The State of Nature," and Gerhard Lenski, "The Nature of Distributive Systems," both in this volume, pp. 68–74 and pp. 124–145.

[36] Fred Dallmayr examines the view of human nature assumed in this theory under the rubric of Homo Politicus, comparing it to Homo Sociologicus, represented in consensus theory, and Homo Economicus—a model of man and society also not covered by the two perspectives presented here. "Empirical Political Theory and the Image of Man" in this volume, pp. 168–191.

It also generates a characteristic conceptual system comprehensible within the framework of its basic presumptions.

When these caveats are noted, the fundamental themes we have advanced remain intact: A perspective is a set of presumptions about social and political life derived from selective social experience; the conceptual system it sustains focuses on those aspects of the environment most congruent with those presumptions and tends to divert attention away from other possible dimensions. Since the investigator is seldom sharply aware of his own perspective and its role in inquiry, he is likely to ignore or underplay its tendency to push his interpretations in a particular direction. He may fail to ask whether the angle of vision available to him screens out possible evidence that could challenge his most fundamental presumptions; he may forget to ask carefully whether opposing perspectives sustain conceptual systems significantly different from his own.

Unaware of the structure of his own perception, he is thus unlikely to probe opposing theories deeply. Translating opposing claims into themes more comprehensible within his own perspective, he refutes a caricature of that theory; and he thereby encourages in himself an easy confidence in the superiority of his own position. Lacking critical awareness of the structure and import of his own perspective, he lacks an essential prerequisite to objectivity in the enterprise of social science.

TOWARD THEORETICAL SELF-CONSCIOUSNESS

The responsible person seeks awareness of the wider implications of his thought and action and then strives to adjust his future activities to promote more desirable consequences. It is not easy to decide what one's responsibilities are; neither is it easy to ascertain how effectively one is meeting them. Nevertheless, the difficulty of the effort does not justify its dismissal. Assuming, then, that a social scientist seeks to advance his interpretations in a responsible way, how should he proceed? How should he proceed, particularly, when he realizes that the explanatory theory he adopts sustains moral conclusions of some import and that the explanatory theory in turn reflects the perspective brought to inquiry as well as the constraints of evidence?

We can state the objective with some clarity. *For a theory is responsibly formulated and advanced when its proponents seriously try to elaborate and defend publicly all its sustaining factors.* Such an enterprise involves, first, an effort to clarify for self and others the basic presumptions and conceptual organization of the perspective brought to inquiry; second, an assessment of the extent to which the available evidence supports or contravenes the perspective; third, a full statement of the normative import of the theory; and finally, an assessment of the extent to which available evidence and other explicit considerations justify acting in support of those normative conclusions. We shall deal with each of these in turn.

Self-Clarification of the Perspective

When I suppose I merely see what is "out there," I am oblivious to the particular spectacles I wear—oblivious, that is, to the presumptions underlying my inquiries and to the contours of the concepts organizing my perception. The result is unjustified confidence in the conclusions I reach and an inability to approach the environment from alternative angles of vision. I foreclose, in effect, avenues to the critical reappraisal of my favored interpretation.

But how should one undertake such a reappraisal? The difficulty of the enterprise becomes more apparent when I realize that my perspective itself has emerged out of my personal history of social transactions. I share it with selected others with whom I interact, and its structure helps to constitute the fabric of our relationships. I habitually turn to these others to check the adequacy of my concepts, the plausibility of my beliefs, the propriety of my values. And yet, since our shared perspective has developed out of shared social experiences, my habitual procedure hardly encourages the self-consciousness I need to develop.

The very limitation inherent in my habitual approach suggests a more promising route. For I become self-conscious of the perspective that orients my study of the political world *by exploring sympathetically alternative ways to comprehend that world.* By confronting unfamiliar presumptions in opposing theories, I render my own tacit views more explicit. By striving to perceive the world from other angles of vision, I begin to grasp more explicitly my own habits of classification. I begin to see that my disagreements with others do not only or always constitute simple disagreements of fact; they also reflect a variable weighting of the "same facts" and subtle differences in the way we slice and organize experience. The suggested approach and promised results of this enterprise are lucidly summarized by Stuart Hampshire: "The habits of self-conscious criticism may modify the habits of behavior. But the habits of criticism are themselves only revised by further criticism and comparison, and *by communication with minds that are outside the circle of convention and custom within which he is confined.*" [37]

To put the point a bit more concretely, a conflict theorist of the sort considered earlier becomes more self-conscious by immersing himself in the theoretical frame of, say, Emile Durkheim or Kingsley Davis and Wilbert Moore.

[37] Stuart Hampshire, *Thought and Action* (New York: Viking Press, 1959), pp. 208, 214. See also Stanley Benn, "The Nature of Political Philosophy," *Encyclopedia of Philosophy,* Vol. 6 (New York: Macmillan, 1967), pp. 387–392.

He must suspend the natural inclination to look at the evidence they present only through his eyes—though that too becomes appropriate at some point. But initially he must strive to comprehend their presumptions and to master the categories through which they experience political life. The task, of course, is not easy. And even when the investigator attains some success, signals do not automatically emerge telling him just which presumptions and which spectacles constitute the most adequate perspective.

Several benefits do emerge, though. Aware now more fully of my habits of classification and interpretation, I open myself to new possibilities. I convert, to some degree, unconsciously acquired predispositions that have conditioned my thought into more fully conscious constructs. What was a force acting upon me becomes more nearly one among alternative orientations that I can *choose* to develop, or to alter, or to reject. And in making conscious a tacit dimension of thought, I increase the extent to which my future choices can be influenced by rational argument.

Exposure of the perspective guiding inquiry also affects the *way* in which I hold my current views, even when the content of those views is not changed substantially. For I realize more clearly that there are other possible ways of construing and explaining the environment studied. Open to those alternatives, I am also more alert to the vulnerability and possible limitations of my favored scheme. I tend, therefore, to acknowledge the uncertain foundations of the theories I adopt and to advance my conclusions with a fuller public statement of the extent to which they rest upon a delicate blend of conjecture and evidence.

But, it is sometimes argued, the approach suggested here threatens to expand self-consciousness at the expense of immobilizing inquiry itself. As one's appreciation of the uncertainties and perplexities in his own theory increases, the natural response is to defer indefinitely the job of reaching firm conclusions. Since several alternatives are possible, commitment to a single position seems unwarranted or even arrogant. While perhaps comforting to the humble scholar, this stance is surely inadequate.

Political decisions must continually be made by private citizens and public officials, and even those of us not directly implicated must justify, repudiate, or merely acquiesce in those decisions. But such judgments on our part reflect normative orientations, and those normative orientations in turn presume explanatory theories. We thus cannot do without an explanatory theory: We can either seek to make it more susceptible to rational considerations or allow it to respond to the political world as an unreflective set of predispositions. But respond we must. When the issue is joined in these terms, the need to marry theoretical self-consciousness to theoretical commitment becomes clear. And it also becomes apparent that, though self-consciousness contributes to the rationality of theoretical commitment, more is required before these commitments meet adequate standards of rational choice.

The Relationship Between Theory and Evidence

The question now becomes, How do we best confront our preferred interpretation with evidence and other considerations that can help to warrant or defeat it? Thomas Kuhn and P. K. Feyerabend offered competing responses to a similar question in the natural sciences. In that context Kuhn emphasized the value of working consistently within one paradigm, while Feyerabend argued that the tenuous connection between any given theory and the evidence supporting it justifies persistent efforts to articulate and explore competing theoretical perspectives. I want now to suggest that Feyerabend's argument is particularly applicable to the social sciences.

The relationship between evidence and theory is even more complicated in the social sciences than in the natural sciences. Consider, as just one example of this connection, the complex role of evidence in adjudicating the debate between C. Wright Mills and Kingsley Davis–Wilbert Moore over the extent to which cumulative inequalities in wealth, income, education, and so on work to the advantage of all. A portion of the pertinent evidence concerns how people in the relevant situations think and feel about these inequalities. In the "normal" situation of stratified inequality, Mills will expect discontent among those at the bottom, and Davis–Moore will anticipate something closer to contented adjustment. But the feelings people have about existing inequalities flow in part from their *beliefs* about the comparative effects of a more egalitarian system. And those beliefs in turn flow from the *theories* these people hold about human nature, the effects of variable social arrangements on human development, and so on. And finally, those theories depend to some extent on the *theoretical alternatives* to which the people have been exposed. If they have been exposed mainly to something like the Davis–Moore theory, their attitudes toward inequality are somewhat more likely to be exactly those Davis and Moore expect. And so we have an instance where the evidence brought to adjudicate between competing theories about the effects of social inequality itself reflects the imprint of the theories of inequality held by the participants.

The situation we have described is only partially captured by noting that Mills will assume apparently contented citizens in the lower classes to suffer from "false consciousness," while Davis and Moore will tend to attribute a similar status to discontented citizens in a stable, stratified system. The more fundamental implication bears on the ability in principle to assess those competing claims about the very status of group consciousness in particular settings. When is that consciousness adequate or "true," and when "false"? What role should evidence drawn from survey analysis of the participants play in supporting or contravening such judgments?

To fix the point more firmly, consider a somewhat less complex case. Suppose, as a participant in a social setting, I hold the Hobbesian theory that human beings are essentially egoistic. Influenced by this belief, I will be tempted secretly to break community rules based on mutual trust. If I don't, my reasoning goes, others will, and I will then be placed at a comparative disadvantage. As others realize that I respond in this way to them, they will conclude that it would be dangerous for them to abide by the common rules; for such conformity threatens to put them at a disadvantage against people like me. As each suspects that the others will not do their part, the arrangements of mutual trust become unstable. My theory about human nature thereby contributes both to the instability and to the production of evidence in support of my initial theory. The evidential support in turn encourages others to conclude that the theory is correct and thus to reinforce even further defensive responses to the expected selfishness of others. The theory itself thus again encourages the behavior it expects and the behavior provides more evidence to sustain the theory. This circular relationship does not have to be completely closed to seriously complicate efforts to develop observational tests untainted by theoretical perspective.

The general point is this: *People and societies are constituted to some degree by the beliefs and concepts they have about themselves. And that means that the evidence we draw upon to test our theories does not simply stand "out there" independently of us, but is constituted in some problematic degree by the theories we, and those we study, adopt.* However, there are limits to these connections. I could not completely transform my nature by transforming my thoughts about myself. For the thoughts and beliefs that help to constitute us are to some degree collective products; others see me in certain ways and those orientations react back upon me as facts about myself. Neither do the connections just intimated mean that a society could completely transform itself by transforming its beliefs and concepts about itself (unlikely as *that* would be). For there are biological limits—themselves subject to theoretical debate—to the scope and variability of social organization. Indeed one of the theoretical issues arises from the fact that Hobbes and Lenski, by comparison to Durkheim, Marx, Mills, and Davis–Moore, construe the constraints of biology quite narrowly.[38]

[38] Lenski proposes initially the view that most people act more often in their own self-interest—where "interest" is understood quite narrowly. But when he has to *explain* what his theoretical postulates do not *expect*—the fact that industrial society, with greater surplus than agricultural society, is nevertheless less unequal—he appeals tacitly to an extended version of the view that people are constituted to some important degree by the concepts and beliefs they jointly hold. Thus "more important" than other causes of this reduction "has been the rise and spread of the new democratic ideology. . . . In fact, there appears to be as much justification for the thesis that this new ideology contributed to the emergence of industrial societies as for the converse." "The Nature of Distributive Systems," in this volume, p. 144. Thus all major theories of social structure and politics acknowledge *tacitly* the relationship between theory and evidence posed here, though few theorists have explored the methodological import of this relationship carefully.

The reciprocal connection between theory and evidence makes it prudent to do more than simply compare a single theory with "the facts." We must try to understand how those "facts" appear when assimilated to alternative theoretical frameworks. Such theoretical pluralism "allows for a much sharper criticism of accepted ideas than does the comparison with a domain of 'facts' which are supposed to sit there independently of theoretical considerations." [39]

Normative Import and Deliberative Judgment

Strive to clarify the perspective brought to inquiry and to identify the linkages between theory and evidence by viewing the several dimensions of one theory from the vantage point of another. That is the thesis so far. But as we have also seen, one of the reasons the effort to attain self-consciousness in inquiry is important is that our explanatory theories generate normative conclusions. I now want to argue that this connection itself suggests new considerations that can help to inform theoretical judgment.

I advance the following idea tentatively and cautiously, tentatively because I myself am wary of the extent to which it applies, cautiously because the idea is easily misinterpreted. Nevertheless, as we have seen, situations persist where evidence and the rationale for conceptual clarity are together insufficient to control the choice between competing theories. Perhaps pertinent evidence is inaccessible because it refers to what would happen if existing arrangements were changed. Perhaps the question turns to some degree on what would happen if the beliefs and attitudes of participants were to change in certain ways. In such recurring situations, I suggest, attention to the divergent normative implications of opposing theories can legitimately influence the choice between these theories.

Consider, first, a simple illustration of the kind of situation I have in mind. In a controversial study of the source of differences in scores on intelligence tests between whites and blacks, Arthur Jensen concludes that a significant part of the variation is explained by genetic factors. His opponents contend that the variation is explicable in terms of cultural biases in intelligence tests,

[39] P. K. Feyerabend, "How to Be a Good Empiricist," in *Criticism and the Growth of Knowledge,* ed. Lakatos and Musgrave, pp. 14–15. I would not argue, certainly, that every social scientist must be a full-fledged social theorist. A degree of specialization is surely desirable within social science. But for theoretical self-consciousness to affect inquiry as *a social enterprise,* specialists must begin to view their responsibilities differently. At least some social scientists must focus upon the task of theoretical self-clarification, and all social scientists must acknowledge a responsibility to be aware of these efforts, to explore the import for work in their specialities, to ask how research schemes and schedules of evidence adopted would look from the vantage point of alternative orientations. The specialist should devote as much time to these tasks as he now does to the perfection of techniques for processing data.

environmental obstacles to development peculiar to blacks, or some mix of these factors. Clearly if Jensen's explanation were accepted, a corollary shift would occur in normative and policy priorities. For example, special programs to close the gap in scores and new efforts to gear intelligence tests more closely to the social experiences of those tested would now seem less urgent and less justifiable expenditures of scarce resources. My point is this: concluding that the available evidence is insufficient to settle this issue, many scientists have *privileged* those interpretations that do not explain the variation genetically. And, I want to argue, tacit awareness of the divergent normative implications of each interpretation has *properly* influenced the persons involved to adopt the more optimistic interpretation in these circumstances. Underlying their judgment is a rule about "the burden of proof" in social inquiry, roughly analagous to a familiar principle of jurisprudence: a person (or class or race) is considered innocent until he is proven guilty.

Two considerations seem to me to apply generally to situations of this sort. First, when available evidence seems to support an interpretation with pessimistic implications for our conclusions about human rights and development, we should explore carefully the extent to which that evidence is compatible with a more optimistic theory. And, second, in such situations a certain presumption should operate in favor of the more optimistic view.

We have already considered arguments for the first proposal; consider now rationale for the second. It becomes pertinent, I think, under two preliminary conditions: (1) Among advocates of opposing theories it is agreed that one of two competing assumptions is more optimistic about human nature (given a broad sense of "human nature"). (2) In the considered judgment of at least one of the parties who has explored the available evidence bearing on these assumptions, that evidence is *compatible* with either view. Condition (1), or something close to it, is necessary to make the proposed criterion apply across theoretical systems. Without it we would be back where we started for an action that looks optimistic to a Marxist from *within* his theory might well look to a Freudian to have the most disastrous consequences. There are, though, many situations where condition (1) does obtain, situations in which one party says in effect to the other, "I wish your optimism about human nature were well grounded, but it is not." Debates between psychoanalytic theorists and cognitive development theorists indebted to Jean Piaget, about the extent to which social reform could increase the ability and inclination of people to act on moral principle, often have this character.[40] Disputes between theorists of alienation and anomie, and between Hobbesians and Rousseauians, often have this character as well.

[40] I have reviewed such a debate and considered its implications for political theory in "Moral Development and Civil Authority: Freud, Piaget, and Wollheim" (paper delivered at the National Meeting of The Conference for the Study of Political Thought, New York, March 31–April 3, 1972).

When the first condition applies, then, and available evidence seems insufficient to settle the issue, I want to argue that the more optimistic alternative should be given some superior weighting. Why? Consider the earlier example again. The assumption that genetic factors explain racial differences in intelligence promotes the very social norms and policies that generate and intensify such differences. In the event the presumption were in fact mistaken, our policies would hide that truth from us; they would expose us indeed to new evidence congenial to the pessimistic presumption. More generally, concepts and beliefs about social life help to some degree to constitute that life. Therefore, privileging the more optimistic assumption, in the conditions specified, might well help both to bring out evidence in its support previously unavailable *and* to *contribute itself* to the optimistic possibility. Thus the shared belief in a society that people *must* seek aggressively to exploit others justifies that conduct on the part of the privileged and contributes thereby to the assurance that such relationships are inevitable. Similarly, conduct based on more optimistic beliefs can sometimes contribute to their fulfillment. Arnold Kaufman, in his defense of citizen participation in group decisions processes, captures this idea nicely: "The effort to achieve a possible good (sometimes) depends on our belief in the possibility of that achievement—the very nerve of our effort to achieve a good may be cut by premature admission of its impossibility." [41]

Let me grant, indeed insist, that this maxim, like any such guideline (for example, "look for evidence that falsifies your theory"), is unavoidably vague and leads necessarily to controversy in particular settings about the range of its application, the proper weight to assign it by comparison to other considerations, and the risks involved in acting upon it. But that is not a defect in the maxim. For the very purpose of such a maxim is to elicit reflection and debate about theoretical issues when other available considerations are insufficient. If this has a slight air of paradox about it, consider again the concern that prompted the proposal.

The direction in which *presumptions* flow exerts a profound influence on the sort of conclusions reached in inquiry. To cope with this influence one must, first, seek to convert preconscious factors controlling thought into explicit ideas amenable to deliberative appraisal and, second, to formulate *reasons* or *rationale* capable of influencing judgment on these now conscious issues. The maxim proposed here is a *reason* designed to apply when available evidence is inconclusive. The fact that debates arise over the conditions and scope of its application is thus a victory of sorts for reason itself. For if no such maxim were available in these circumstances, theoretical judgment

[41] Arnold Kaufman, "Human Nature and Participatory Democracy," in *The Bias of Pluralism,* ed. William Connolly (New York: Atherton Press, 1969), p. 195. Similar ideas are advanced by Henry Kariel, "Creating Political Reality," *American Political Science Review* (December 1970), pp. 1088–1098.

itself would to that extent fall back upon the influence of unreflective habit and impulse. The search for rationale capable of influencing the intellect in such persisting conditions of uncertainty is part of the effort to render theoretical judgment more conscious and deliberative.

CONCLUSION

I approach theoretical self-consciousness as I attain awareness of previously unexamined assumptions at the center of my theory, as I attend to its conceptual contours and to the test procedures it supports, as I probe the inner connections among these three dimensions and explore the normative implications of the entire system. Such self-consciousness is best attained through a comparison of my theory, at each of these levels, with alternative systems. In this way I begin to make underlying assumptions more explicit and thus more amenable to critical scrutiny; I begin to see how my concepts may appear limited or even defective from the vantage point of other systems; I start to probe the ways in which my test procedures protect key assumptions; I begin to explore the possibility that my commitment to those assumptions is shaped in part by my desire to sustain the normative conclusions they support. In this way I probe the depth connections among the assumptions, concepts, test procedures, and normative commitments of my theory, considering as well possible linkages between my class, my social or sexual status, and my inclinations to protect certain normative commitments in these ways.

Although the process of comparison is not itself free from partisan elements, it does help to uncover tacit commitments at each of these levels and it does expose theories and theorists to forms of critical pressure previously unavailable. Considerations capable of modifying one or more of these commitments are now more likely to come to my attention. And because of the loose connections among the several dimensions of my theory, modifications at one level tend to put pressure on commitments at other levels; critical attention to these new questions in turn creates pressure at yet other points, forcing a revision here, crystallizing an argument there. Even if, an unlikely possibility, my theory emerges from this process unscathed, I will now understand its depth grammar more fully, I will have a solid grip on the range of its application and the reasons and evidence that support it, I will adhere to it less blindly and dogmatically, and I will be better equipped to communicate rationally with critics, adversaries, and potential converts.

To foster theoretical self-consciousness is to reestablish in two ways the nexus between political science and political philosophy: by breaking down the artificial separation between explanatory theory and normative judgment, and by encouraging an immersion in classical theories of politics and society as one path to the more critical understanding of contemporary styles of thought.[42] Indeed, it is partly because classical theorists carefully explored the normative import of their theories that this tradition lends itself to critical appraisal of contemporary work. Reassertion of the nexus between political science and political philosophy, or attainment of theoretical self-consciousness itself, does not provide assurance that truth will be attained. No theory, certainly, is or will be the product of reason and evidence alone. But the route to theoretical self-consciousness gives evidence its due and reason its best purchase.

[42] It is noteworthy that both Kuhn and Toulmin advise theorists in natural science to study the history of their disciplines in order to become more thoroughly alert to the structure of their own theories. As Toulmin suggests in celebrating theoretical comparison across historical periods, "if earlier men had never thought in terms other than we do, then we ourselves would simply be carrying on a traditional *habit*," *Foresight and Understanding*, p. 102 (my emphasis).

II
Political Man: Some Classical Images

3

The State of Nature

Thomas Hobbes

OF THE DIFFERENCE OF MANNERS

By manners I mean not here decency of behavior—as how one man should salute another, or how a man should wash his mouth or pick his teeth before company, and such other points of the *small morals*—but those qualities of mankind that concern their living together in peace and unity. To which end we are to consider that the felicity of this life consists not in the repose of a mind satisfied. For there is no such *finis ultimus,* utmost aim, nor *summum bonum,* greatest good, as is spoken of in the books of the old moral philosophers. Nor can a man any more live whose desires are at an end than he whose senses and imaginations are at a stand. Felicity is a continual progress of the desire from one object to another, the attaining of the former being still but the way to the latter. The cause whereof is that the object of man's desire is not to enjoy once only and for one instant of time, but to assure forever the way of his future desire. And therefore the voluntary actions and inclinations of all men tend, not only to the procuring, but also to the assuring of a contented life; and differ only in the way, which arises partly from the diversity of passions in divers men, and partly from the difference of the knowledge or opinion each one has of the causes which produce the effect desired.

So that, in the first place, I put for a general inclination of all mankind a perpetual and restless desire of power after power that ceases only in death. And the cause of this is not always that a man hopes for a more intensive delight than he has already attained to, or that he cannot be content with a moderate power, but because he cannot assure the power and means to live well which he has present without the acquisition of more. And from hence it is that

Source: Reprinted from Thomas Hobbes, *Leviathan,* ed. A. R. Waller (London: Cambridge University Press, 1904), Chapters 11 and 13. Spelling, capitalization, and punctuation have been revised to conform to modern American usage by the editors of this volume.

kings, whose power is greatest, turn their endeavors to the assuring it at home by laws or abroad by wars; and when that is done, there succeeds a new desire —in some, of fame from new conquest; in others, of ease and sensual pleasure; in others, of admiration or being flattered for excellence in some art or other ability of the mind.

Competition of riches, honor, command, or other power inclines to contention, enmity, and war, because the way of one competitor to the attaining of his desire is to kill, subdue, supplant, or repel the other. Particularly, competition of praise inclines to a reverence of antiquity. For men contend with the living, not with the dead; to these ascribing more than due, that they may obscure the glory of the other.

Desire of ease and sensual delight disposes men to obey a common power, because by such desires a man does abandon the protection that might be hoped for from his own industry and labor. Fear of death and wounds disposes to the same, and for the same reason. On the contrary, needy men and hardy, not contented with their present condition, as also all men that are ambitious of military command, are inclined to continue the causes of war, and to stir up trouble and sedition; for there is no honor military but by war, nor any such hope to mend an ill game as by causing a new shuffle.

Desire of knowledge and arts of peace inclines men to obey a common power, for such desire contains a desire of leisure, and consequently protection from some other power than their own.

Desire of praise disposes to laudable actions, such as please them whose judgment they value; for of those men whom we contemn, we contemn also the praises. Desire of fame after death does the same. And though after death there be no sense of the praise given us on earth, as being joys that are either swallowed up in the unspeakable joys of heaven or extinguished in the extreme torments of hell, yet is not such fame vain; because men have a present delight therein from the foresight of it and of the benefit that may redound thereby to their posterity, which, though they now see not, yet they imagine; and anything that is pleasure to the senses, the same also is pleasure in the imagination. . . .

Fear of oppression disposes a man to anticipate or to seek aid by society, for there is no other way by which a man can secure his life and liberty. . . .

Vainglorious men, such as without being conscious to themselves of great sufficiency, delight in supposing themselves gallant men, are inclined only to ostentation, but not to attempt, because when danger or difficulty appears, they look for nothing but to have their insufficiency discovered.

Vainglorious men such as estimate their sufficiency by the flattery of other men or the fortune of some precedent action, without assured ground of hope from the true knowledge of themselves, are inclined to rash engaging; and in the approach of danger or difficulty to retire if they can, because, not seeing the way of safety, they will rather hazard their honor, which may be salved with an excuse, than their lives, for which no salve is sufficient.

Men that have a strong opinion of their own wisdom in matter of government are disposed to ambition. Because without public employment in council or magistracy, the honor of their wisdom is lost. And therefore eloquent speakers are inclined to ambition, for eloquence seems wisdom, both to themselves and others. . . .

Ignorance of the signification of words, which is want of understanding, disposes men to take on trust, not only the truth they know not, but also the errors, and which is more, the nonsense of them they trust; for neither error nor nonsense can, without a perfect understanding of words, be detected.

From the same it proceeds that men give different names to one and the same thing from the difference of their own passions: as they that approve a private opinion call it "opinion," but they that mislike it, "heresy"; and yet heresy signifies no more than private opinion, but has only a greater tincture of choler. . . .

Ignorance of the causes and original constitution of right, equity, law, and justice disposes a man to make custom and example the rule of his actions; in such manner as to think that unjust which it has been the custom to punish, and that just of the impunity and approbation whereof they can produce an example or, as the lawyers which only use this false measure of justice barbarously call it, a precedent; like little children that have no other rule of good and evil manners but the correction they receive from their parents and masters, save that children are constant to their rule, whereas men are not so; because, grown old and stubborn, they appeal from custom to reason and from reason to custom as it serves their turn, receding from custom when their interest requires it and setting themselves against reason as often as reason is against them; which is the cause that the doctrine of right and wrong is perpetually disputed, both by the pen and the sword, whereas the doctrine of lines and figures is not so; because men care not, in that subject, what be truth, as a thing that crosses no man's ambition, profit, or lust. For I doubt not but if it had been a thing contrary to any man's right of dominion, or to the interest of men that have dominion, *that the three angles of a triangle should be equal to two angles of a square,* that doctrine should have been, if not disputed, yet, by the burning of all books of geometry, suppressed, as far as he whom it concerned was able.

Ignorance of remote causes disposes men to attribute all events to the causes immediate and instrumental, for these are all the causes they perceive. And hence it comes to pass that in all places men that are grieved with payments to the public, discharge their anger upon the publicans—that is to say, farmers, collectors, and other officers of the public revenue—and adhere to such as find fault with the public government, and thereby, when they have engaged themselves beyond hope of justification, fall also upon the supreme authority for fear of punishment or shame of receiving pardon.

Ignorance of natural causes disposes a man to credulity, so as to believe many times impossibilities; for such know nothing to the contrary but that they may be true, being unable to detect the impossibility. And credulity, because men like to be hearkened unto in company, disposes them to lying, so that ignorance itself without malice is able to make a man both to believe lies and tell them—and sometimes also to invent them.

Anxiety for the future time disposes men to inquire into the causes of things, because the knowledge of them makes men better able to order the present to their best advantage. Curiosity, or love of the knowledge of causes, draws a man from the consideration of the effect to seek the cause; and again, the cause of that cause; till of necessity he must come to this thought at last: that there is some cause whereof there is no former cause but is eternal—which is it men call God. So that it is impossible to make any profound inquiry into natural causes without being inclined thereby to believe there is one God eternal, though they cannot have any idea of him in their mind answerable to his nature. For as a man that is born blind, hearing men talk of warming themselves by the fire and being brought to warm himself by the same, may easily conceive and assure himself there is something there which men call *fire* and is the cause of the heat he feels, but cannot imagine what it is like nor have an idea of it in his mind such as they have that see it; so also by the visible things in this world, and their admirable order, a man may conceive there is a cause of them, which men call God, and yet not have an idea or image of him in his mind. . . .

OF THE NATURAL CONDITION OF MANKIND AS CONCERNING THEIR FELICITY AND MISERY

Nature has made men so equal in the faculties of the body and mind as that though there be found one man sometimes manifestly stronger in body or of quicker mind than another, yet, when all is reckoned together, the difference between man and man is not so considerable as that one man can thereupon claim to himself any benefit to which another may not pretend as well as he. For as to the strength of body, the weakest has strength enough to kill the strongest, either by secret machination or by confederacy with others that are in the same danger with himself.

And as to the faculties of the mind, setting aside the arts grounded upon words, and especially that skill of proceeding upon general and infallible rules called science—which very few have and but in few things, as being not a native faculty born with us, nor attained, as prudence, while we look after somewhat else—I find yet a greater equality among men than that of strength. For prudence is but experience, which equal time equally bestows on all men in those things they equally apply themselves unto. That which may perhaps make such equality incredible is but a vain conceit of one's own wisdom, which almost all men think they have in a greater degree than the vulgar—that is, than all men but themselves and a few others whom, by fame or for concurring with themselves, they approve. For such is the nature of men that howsoever they may acknowledge many others to be more witty or more eloquent or more learned, yet they will hardly believe there be many so wise as themselves; for they see their own wit at hand and other men's at a distance. But this proves rather that men are in that point equal than unequal. For there is not ordinarily a greater sign of the equal distribution of anything than that every man is contented with his share.

From this equality of ability arises equality of hope in the attaining of our ends. And therefore if any two men desire the same thing, which nevertheless they cannot both enjoy, they become enemies; and in the way to their end, which is principally their own conservation, and sometimes their delectation only, endeavor to destroy or subdue one another. And from hence it comes to pass that where an invader has no more to fear than another man's single power, if one plant, sow, build, or possess a convenient seat, others may probably be expected to come prepared with forces united to dispossess and deprive him, not only of the fruit of his labor, but also of his life or liberty. And the invader again is in the like danger of another.

And from this diffidence of one another there is no way for any man to secure himself so reasonable as anticipation—that is, by force or wiles to master the persons of all men he can, so long till he sees no other power great enough to endanger him; and this is no more than his own conservation requires, and is generally allowed. Also, because there be some that take pleasure in contemplating their own power in the acts of conquest, which they pursue farther than their security requires, if others that otherwise would be glad to be at ease within modest bounds should not by invasion increase their power, they would not be able, long time, by standing only on their defense, to subsist. And by consequence, such augmentation of dominion over men being necessary to a man's conservation, it ought to be allowed him.

Again, men have no pleasure, but on the contrary a great deal of grief, in keeping company where there is no power able to overawe them all. For every man looks that his companion should value him at the same rate he sets upon himself; and upon all signs of contempt or undervaluing naturally endeavors, as far as he dares (which among them that have no common power to keep them in quiet is far enough to make them destroy each other), to extort a greater value from his contemners by damage and from others by the example.

So that in the nature of man we find three principal causes of quarrel: first, competition; secondly, diffidence; thirdly, glory.

The first makes men invade for gain, the second for safety, and the third for reputation. The first use violence to make themselves masters of other men's persons, wives, children, and cattle; the second, to defend them; the third, for trifles, as a word, a smile, a different opinion, and any other sign of undervalue, either direct in their persons or by reflection in their kindred, their friends, their nation, their profession, or their name.

Hereby it is manifest that, during the time men live without a common power to keep them all in awe, they are in that condition which is called war, and such a war as is of every man against every man. For *war* consists not in battle only, or the act of fighting, but in a tract of time wherein the will to contend by battle is sufficiently known; and therefore the notion of *time* is to be considered in the nature of war as it is in the nature of weather. For as the nature of foul weather lies not in a shower or two of rain but in an inclination thereto of many days together, so the nature of war consists not in actual fighting but in the known disposition thereto during all the time there is no assurance to the contrary. All other time is *peace*.

Whatsoever, therefore, is consequent to a time of war where every man is enemy to every man, the same is consequent to the time wherein men live without other security than what their own strength and their own invention shall furnish them withal. In such condition there is no place for industry, because the fruit thereof is uncertain and consequently no culture of the earth; no navigation nor use of the commodities that may be imported by sea; no commodious building; no instruments of moving and removing such things as require much force; no knowledge of the face of the earth; no account of time; no arts; no letters; no society; and, which is worst of all, continual fear and danger of violent death; and the life of man solitary, poor, nasty, brutish, and short.

It may seem strange to some man that has not well weighed these things that nature should thus dissociate and render men apt to invade and destroy one another; and he may therefore, not trusting to this inference made from the passions, desire perhaps to have the same confirmed by experience. Let him therefore consider with himself—when taking a journey he arms himself and seeks to go well accompanied, when going to sleep he locks his doors, when even in his house he locks his chests, and this when he knows there be laws and public officers, armed, to revenge all injuries shall be done him—what opinion he has of his fellow subjects when he rides armed, of his fellow citizens when he locks his doors, and of his children and servants when he locks his chests. Does he not there as much accuse mankind by his actions as I do by my words? But neither of us accuse man's nature in it. The desires and other passions of man are in themselves no sin. No more are the actions that proceed from those passions till they know a law that forbids them, which, till laws be made, they cannot know, nor can any law be made till they have agreed upon the person that shall make it.

It may peradventure be thought there was never such a time nor condition of war as this, and I believe it was never generally so over all the world; but there are many places where they live so now. For the savage people in many places of America, except the government of small families, the concord whereof depends on natural lust, have no government at all and live at this day in that brutish manner as I said before. Howsoever, it may be perceived what manner of life there would be where there were no common power to fear by the manner of life which men that have formerly lived under a peaceful government use to degenerate into a civil war.

But though there had never been any time wherein particular men were in a condition of war one against another, yet in all times kings and persons of sovereign authority, because of their independency, are in continual jealousies and in the state and posture of gladiators, having their weapons pointing and their eyes fixed on one another—that is, their forts, garrisons, and guns upon the frontiers of their kingdoms, and continual spies upon their neighbors—which is a posture of war. But because they uphold thereby the industry of their subjects, there does not follow from it that misery which accompanies the liberty of particular men.

To this war of every man against every man, this also is consequent: that nothing can be unjust. The notions of right and wrong, justice and injustice, have there no place. Where there is no common power, there is no law; where no law, no injustice. Force and fraud are in war the two cardinal virtues. Justice and injustice are none of the faculties neither of the body nor mind. If they were, they might be in a man that were alone in the world, as well as his senses and passions. They are qualities that relate to men in society, not in solitude. It is consequent also to the same condition that there be no propriety, no dominion, no *mine* and *thine* distinct; but only that to be every man's that he can get, and for so long as he can keep it. And thus much for the ill condition which man by mere nature is actually placed in, though with a possibility to come out of it consisting partly in the passions, partly in his reason.

The passions that incline men to peace are fear of death, desire of such things as are necessary to commodious living, and a hope by their industry to obtain them. And reason suggests convenient articles of peace, upon which men may be drawn to agreement.

4

On Anomie

Emile Durkheim

SOCIAL ORDER AND ANOMIE

No living being can be happy or even exist unless his needs are sufficiently proportioned to his means. In other words, if his needs require more than can be granted, or even merely something of a different sort, they will be under continual friction and can only function painfully. Movements incapable of production without pain tend not to be reproduced. Unsatisfied tendencies atrophy, and as the impulse to live is merely the result of all the rest, it is bound to weaken as the others relax.[1]

In the animal, at least in a normal condition, this equilibrium is established with automatic spontaneity because the animal depends on purely material conditions. All the organism needs is that the supplies of substance and energy constantly employed in the vital process should be periodically renewed by equivalent quantities; that replacement be equivalent to use. When the void created by existence in its own resources is filled, the animal, satisfied, asks nothing further. Its power of reflection is not sufficiently developed to imagine other ends than those implicit in its physical nature. On the other hand, as the work demanded of each organ itself depends on the general state of vital energy and the needs of organic equilibrium, use is regulated in turn by replacement and the balance is automatic. The limits of one are those of

Source: "Social Order and Anomie" and "Anomie in the Economic Sphere" reprinted with permission of The Macmillan Company and Routledge and Kegan Paul Ltd. from Emile Durkheim, *Suicide,* trans. John A. Spaulding and George Simpson.

[1] To prove that an increase in prosperity diminishes suicides, the attempt has been made to show that they become less when emigration, the escape valve of poverty, is widely practiced (See Legoyt, pp. 257–259). But cases are numerous where parallelism instead of inverse proportions exist between the two. In Italy from 1876 to 1890 the number of emigrants rose from 76 per 100,000 inhabitants to 335, a figure itself exceeded between 1887 and 1889. At the same time suicides did not cease to grow in numbers.

the other; both are fundamental to the constitution of the existence in question, which cannot exceed them.

This is not the case with man, because most of his needs are not dependent on his body or not to the same degree. Strictly speaking, we may consider that the quantity of material supplies necessary to the physical maintenance of a human life is subject to computation, though this be less exact than in the preceding case and a wider margin left for the free combinations of the will; for beyond the indispensable minimum which satisfies nature when instinctive, a more awakened reflection suggests better conditions, seemingly desirable ends craving fulfillment. Such appetites, however, admittedly sooner or later reach a limit which they cannot pass. But how determine the quantity of well-being, comfort or luxury legitimately to be craved by a human being? Nothing appears in man's organic nor in his psychological constitution which sets a limit to such tendencies. The functioning of individual life does not require them to cease at one point rather than at another; the proof being that they have constantly increased since the beginnings of history, receiving more and more complete satisfaction, yet with no weakening of average health. Above all, how establish their proper variation with different conditions of life, occupations, relative importance of services, etc.? In no society are they equally satisfied in the different stages of the social hierarchy. Yet human nature is substantially the same among all men, in its essential qualities. It is not human nature which can assign the variable limits necessary to our needs. They are thus unlimited so far as they depend on the individual alone. Irrespective of any external regulatory force, our capacity for feeling is in itself an insatiable and bottomless abyss.

But if nothing external can restrain this capacity, it can only be a source of torment to itself. Unlimited desires are insatiable by definition and insatiability is rightly considered a sign of morbidity. Being unlimited, they constantly and infinitely surpass the means at their command; they cannot be quenched. Inextinguishable thirst is constantly renewed torture. It has been claimed, indeed, that human activity naturally aspires beyond assignable limits and sets itself unattainable goals. But how can such an undetermined state be any more reconciled with the conditions of mental life than with the demands of physical life? All man's pleasure in acting, moving and exerting himself implies the sense that his efforts are not in vain and that by walking he has advanced. However, one does not advance when one walks toward no goal, or—which is the same thing—when his goal is infinity. Since the distance between us and it is always the same, whatever road we take, we might as well have made the motions without progress from the spot. Even our glances behind and our feeling of pride at the distance covered can cause only deceptive satisfaction, since the remaining distance is not proportionately reduced. To pursue a goal which is by definition unattainable is to condemn oneself to a state of perpetual unhappiness. Of course, man may hope contrary to all reason, and hope has its pleasures even when unreasonable. It may sustain him for a time, but it cannot survive the repeated disappointments of experience indefinitely. What more can the future offer him than the past, since he can never reach a tenable condition nor even approach the glimpsed ideal? Thus, the more one has, the more one wants, since satisfactions received only stimulate instead of filling needs. Shall action as such be considered agreeable? First, only on condition of blindness to its uselessness. Secondly, for this pleasure to be felt and to temper and half veil the accompanying painful unrest, such unending motion must at least always be easy and unhampered. If it is interfered with only restlessness is left, with the lack of ease which it, itself, entails. But it would be a miracle if no insurmountable obstacle were never encountered. Our thread of life on these conditions is pretty thin, breakable at any instant.

To achieve any other result, the passions first must be limited. Only then can they be harmonized with the faculties and satisfied. But since the individual has no way of limiting them, this must be done by some force exterior to him. A regulative force must play the same role for moral needs which the organism plays for physical needs. This means that the force can only be moral. The awakening of conscience interrupted the state of equilibrium of the animal's dormant existence; only conscience, therefore, can furnish the means to re-establish it. Physical restraint would be ineffective; hearts cannot be touched by physio-chemical forces. So far as the appetites are not automatically restrained by physiological mechanisms, they can be halted only by a limit that they recognize as just. Men would never consent to restrict their desires if they felt justified in passing the assigned limit. But, for reasons given above, they cannot assign themselves this law of justice. So they must receive it from an authority which they respect, to which they yield spontaneously. Either directly and as a whole, or through the agency of one of its organs, society alone can play this moderating role; for it is the only moral power superior to the individual, the authority of which he accepts. It alone has the power necessary to stipulate law and to set the point beyond which the passions must not go. Finally, it alone can estimate the reward to be prospectively offered to every class of human functionary, in the name of the common interest.

As a matter of fact, at every moment of history there is a dim perception, in the moral consciousness of societies, of the respective value of different social services, the relative reward due to each, and the consequent degree of comfort appropriate on the average to workers in each occupation. The different functions are graded in public opinion and a certain coefficient of well-being assigned to each, according to its place in the hierarchy. According to accepted ideas, for example, a certain way of living is considered the upper limit to which a workman may aspire in his efforts to improve his existence, and there is another limit below which he is not willingly permitted to fall unless he has seriously bemeaned himself. Both differ for city and country workers, for the domestic servant and the day laborer, for the business clerk and the official, etc. Likewise the man of wealth is reproved if he lives the life of a poor man, but also if he seeks the refinements of luxury overmuch. Economists may protest in vain; public feeling will always be scandalized if an individual spends too much wealth for wholly superfluous use, and it even seems that this severity relaxes only in times of moral disturbances.[2] A genuine regimen exists, therefore, although not always legally formulated, which fixes with relative precision the maximum degree of ease of living to which each social class may legitimately aspire. However, there is nothing immutable about such a scale. It changes with the increase or decrease of collective revenue and the changes occurring in the moral ideas of society. Thus what appears luxury to one period no longer does so to another; and the well-being which for long periods was granted to a class only by exception and supererogation, finally appears strictly necessary and equitable.

Under this pressure, each in his sphere vaguely realizes the extreme limit set to his ambitions and aspires to nothing beyond. At least if he respects regulations and is docile to collective authority, that is, has a wholesome moral constitution, he feels that it is not well to ask more. Thus, an end and goal are set to the passions. Truly, there is nothing rigid nor absolute about such determination. The economic ideal assigned each class of citizens is itself confined to certain limits, within which the desires have free range. But it is not infinite. This relative limitation and the moderation it involves, make men contented with their lot while stimulating them moderately to improve it; and this average contentment causes the feeling of calm, active happiness, the pleasure in existing and living which characterizes health for societies as well as for individuals. Each person is then at least, generally speaking, in harmony with his condition, and desires only what he may legitimately hope for as the normal reward of his activity. Besides, this does not condemn man to a sort of immobility. He may seek to give beauty to his life; but his attempts in this direction may fail without causing him to despair. For, loving what he has and not fixing his desire solely on what he lacks, his wishes and hopes may fail of what he has happened to aspire to, without his being wholly destitute. He has the essentials. The equilibrium of his happiness is secure because it is defined, and a few mishaps cannot disconcert him.

But it would be of little use for everyone to recognize the justice of the hierarchy of functions established by public opinion, if he did not also consider the distribution of these functions just. The workman is not in harmony with his social position if he is not convinced that he has his desserts. If he feels justified in occupying another, what he has would not satisfy him. So it is not enough for the average level of needs for each social condition to be regulated by public opinion, but another, more precise rule, must fix the way in which these conditions are open to individuals. There is no society in which such

[2] Actually, this is a purely moral reprobation and can hardly be judicially implemented. We do not consider any reestablishment of sumptuary laws desirable or even possible.

regulation does not exist. It varies with times and places. Once it regarded birth as the almost exclusive principle of social classification; today it recognizes no other inherent inequality than hereditary fortune and merit. But in all these various forms its object is unchanged. It is also only possible, everywhere, as a restriction upon individuals imposed by superior authority, that is, by collective authority. For it can be established only by requiring of one or another group of men, usually of all, sacrifices and concessions in the name of the public interest.

Some, to be sure, have thought that this moral pressure would become unnecessary if men's economic circumstances were only no longer determined by heredity. If inheritance were abolished, the argument runs, if everyone began life with equal resources and if the competitive struggle were fought out on a basis of perfect equality, no one could think its results unjust. Each would instinctively feel that things are as they should be.

Truly, the nearer this ideal equality were approached, the less social restraint will be necessary. But it is only a matter of degree. One sort of heredity will always exist, that of natural talent. Intelligence, taste, scientific, artistic, literary or industrial ability, courage and manual dexterity are gifts received by each of us at birth, as the heir to wealth receives his capital or as the nobleman formerly received his title and function. A moral discipline will therefore still be required to make those less favored by nature accept the lesser advantages which they owe to the chance of birth. Shall it be demanded that all have an equal share and that no advantage be given those more useful and deserving? But then there would have to be a discipline far stronger to make these accept a treatment merely equal to that of the mediocre and incapable.

But like the one first mentioned, this discipline can be useful only if considered just by the peoples subject to it. When it is maintained only by custom and force, peace and harmony are illusory; the spirit of unrest and discontent are latent; appetites superficially restrained are ready to revolt. This happened in Rome and Greece when the faiths underlying the old organization of the patricians and plebeians were shaken, and in our modern societies when aristocratic prejudices began to lose their old ascendancy. But this state of upheaval is exceptional; it occurs only when society is passing through some abnormal crisis. In normal conditions the collective order is regarded as just by the great majority of persons. Therefore, when we say that an authority is necessary to impose this order on individuals, we certainly do not mean that violence is the only means of establishing it. Since this regulation is meant to restrain individual passions, it must come from a power which dominates individuals; but this power must also be obeyed through respect, not fear.

It is not true, then, that human activity can be released from all restraint. Nothing in the world can enjoy such a privilege. All existence being a part of the universe is relative to the remainder; its nature and method of manifestation accordingly depend not only on itself but on other beings, who consequently restrain and regulate it. Here there are only differences of degree and form between the mineral realm and the thinking person. Man's characteristic privilege is that the bond he accepts is not physical but moral; that is, social. He is governed not by a material environment brutally imposed on him, but by a conscience superior to his own, the superiority of which he feels. Because the greater, better part of his existence transcends the body, he escapes the body's yoke, but is subject to that of society.

But when society is disturbed by some painful crisis or by beneficent but abrupt transitions, it is momentarily incapable of exercising this influence; thence come the sudden rises in the curve of suicides which we have pointed out above.

In the case of economic disasters, indeed, something like a declassification occurs which suddenly casts certain individuals into a lower state than their previous one. Then they must reduce their requirements, restrain their needs, learn greater self-control. All the advantages of social influence are lost so far as they are concerned; their moral education has to be recommenced. But society cannot adjust them instantaneously to this new life and teach them to practice the increased self-repression to which they are unaccustomed. So they are not adjusted to the condition forced on them, and its very prospect is intolerable; hence the suffering which detaches them from a reduced existence even before they have made trial of it.

It is the same if the source of the crisis is an abrupt growth of power and wealth. Then, truly, as the conditions of life are changed, the standard according to which needs were regulated can no longer remain the same; for it varies with social resources, since it largely determines the share of each class of producers. The scale is upset; but a new scale cannot be immediately improvised. Time is required for the public conscience to reclassify men and things. So long as the social forces thus freed have not regained equilibrium, their respective values are unknown and so all regulation is lacking for a time. The limits are unknown between the possible and the impossible, what is just and what is unjust, legitimate claims and hopes and those which are immoderate. Consequently, there is no restraint upon aspirations. If the disturbance is profound, it affects even the principles controlling the distribution of men among various occupations. Since the relations between various parts of society are necessarily modified, the ideas expressing these relations must change. Some particular class especially favored by the crisis is no longer resigned to its former lot, and, on the other hand, the example of its greater good fortune arouses all sorts of jealousy below and about it. Appetites, not being controlled by a public opinion, become disoriented, no longer recognize the limits proper to them. Besides, they are at the same time seized by a sort of natural erethism simply by the greater intensity of public life. With increased prosperity desires increase. At the very moment when traditional rules have lost their authority, the richer prize offered these appetites stimulates them and makes them more exigent and impatient of control. The state of de-regulation or anomie is thus further heightened by passions being less disciplined, precisely when they need more disciplining.

But then their very demands make fulfillment impossible. Overweening ambition always exceeds the results obtained, great as they may be, since there is no warning to pause here. Nothing gives satisfaction and all this agitation is uninterruptedly maintained without appeasement. Above all, since this race for an unattainable goal can give no other pleasure but that of the race itself, if it is one, once it is interrupted the participants are left empty handed. At the same time the struggle grows more violent and painful, both from being less controlled and because competition is greater. All classes contend among themselves because no established classification any longer exists. Effort grows, just when it becomes less productive. How could the desire to live not be weakened under such conditions?

This explanation is confirmed by the remarkable immunity of poor countries. Poverty protects against suicide because it is a restraint in itself. No matter how one acts, desires have to depend upon resources to some extent; actual possessions are partly the criterion of those aspired to. So the less one has the less he is tempted to extend the range of his needs indefinitely. Lack of power, compelling moderation, accustoms men to it, while nothing excites envy if no one has superfluity. Wealth, on the other hand, by the power it bestows, deceives us into believing that we depend on ourselves only. Reducing the resistance we encounter from objects, it suggests the possibility of unlimited success against them. The less limited one feels, the more intolerable all limitation appears. Not without reason, therefore, have so many religions dwelt on the advantages and moral value of poverty. It is actually the best school for teaching self-restraint. Forcing us to constant self-discipline, it prepares us to accept collective discipline with equanimity, while wealth, exalting the individual, may always arouse the spirit of rebellion which is the very source of immorality. This, of course, is no reason why humanity should not improve its material condition. But though the moral danger involved in every growth of prosperity is not irremediable, it should not be forgotten.

ANOMIE IN THE ECONOMIC SPHERE

If anomie never appeared except, as in the above instances, in intermittent spurts and acute crisis, it might cause the social suicide rate to vary from time to time, but it would not be a regular, constant factor. In one sphere of social life, however—the sphere of trade and industry—it is actually in a chronic state.

For a whole century, economic progress has mainly consisted in freeing industrial relations from all regulation. Until very recently, it was the function of a whole system of moral forces to exert this discipline. First, the influence of religion was felt alike by workers and masters, the poor and the rich. It consoled the former and taught them contentment with their lot by informing them of the providential nature of the social order, that the share of each class was assigned by God himself, and by holding out the hope for just compensation in a world to come in return for the inequalities of this world. It governed the latter, recalling that worldly interests are not man's entire lot, that they must be subordinate to other and higher interests, and that they should therefore not be pursued without rule or measure. Temporal power, in turn, restrained the scope of economic functions by its supremacy over them and by the relatively subordinate role it assigned them. Finally, within the business world proper, the occupational groups by regulating salaries, the price of products and production itself, indirectly fixed the average level of income on which needs are partially based by the very force of circumstances. However, we do not mean to propose this organization as a model. Clearly it would be inadequate to existing societies without great changes. What we stress is its existence, the fact of its useful influence, and that nothing today has come to take its place.

Actually, religion has lost most of its power. And government, instead of regulating economic life, has become its tool and servant. The most opposite schools, orthodox economists and extreme socialists, unite to reduce government to the role of a more or less passive intermediary among the various social functions. The former wish to make it simply the guardian of individual contracts; the latter leave it the task of doing the collective bookkeeping, that is, of recording the demands of consumers, transmitting them to producers, inventorying the total revenue and distributing it according to a fixed formula. But both refuse it any power to subordinate other social organs to itself and to make them converge toward one dominant aim. On both sides nations are declared to have the single or chief purpose of achieving industrial prosperity; such is the implication of the dogma of economic materialism, the basis of both apparently opposed systems. And as these theories merely express the state of opinion, industry, instead of being still regarded as a means to an end transcending itself, has become the supreme end of individuals and societies alike. Thereupon the appetites thus excited have become freed of any limiting authority. By sanctifying them, so to speak, this apotheosis of well-being has placed them above all human law. Their restraint seems like a sort of sacrilege. For this reason, even the purely utilitarian regulation of them exercised by the industrial world itself through the medium of occupational groups has been unable to persist. Ultimately, this liberation of desires has been made worse by the very development of industry and the almost infinite extension of the market. So long as the producer could gain his profits only in his immediate neighborhood, the restricted amount of possible gain could not much overexcite ambition. Now that he may assume to have almost the entire world as his customer, how could passions accept their former confinement in the face of such limitless prospects?

Such is the source of the excitement predominating in this part of society, and which has thence extended to the other parts. There, the state of crisis and anomie is constant and, so to speak, normal. From top to bottom of the ladder, greed is aroused without knowing where to find the ultimate foothold. Nothing can calm it, since its goal is far beyond all it can attain. Reality seems valueless by comparison with the dreams of fevered imaginations; reality is therefore abandoned, but so too is possibility abandoned when it in turn becomes reality. A thirst arises for novelties, unfamiliar pleasures, nameless sensations, all of which lose their savor once known. Henceforth one has no strength to endure the least reverse. The whole fever subsides and the sterility of all the tumult is apparent, and it is seen that all these new sensations in their infinite quantity cannot form a solid foundation of happiness to support one during days of trial. The wise man, knowing how to enjoy achieved results without having constantly to replace them with others, finds in them an attachment to life in the hour of difficulty. But the man who has always pinned all his hopes on the future and lived with his eyes fixed upon it, has nothing in the past as a comfort against the present's afflictions, for the past was nothing to him but a series of hastily experienced stages. What blinded him to himself was his expectation always to find further on the happiness he had so far missed. Now he is stopped in his tracks; from now on nothing remains behind or ahead of him to fix his gaze upon. Weariness alone, moreover, is enough to bring disillusionment, for he cannot in the end escape the futility of an endless pursuit.

We may even wonder if this moral state is not principally what makes economic catastrophes of our day so fertile in suicides. In societies where a man is subjected to a healthy discipline, he submits more readily to the blows of chance. The necessary effort for sustaining a little more discomfort costs him relatively little, since he is used to discomfort and constraint. But when every constraint is hateful in itself, how can closer constraint not seem intolerable? There is no tendency to resignation in the feverish impatience of men's lives. When there is no other aim but to outstrip constantly the point arrived at, how painful to be thrown back! Now this very lack of organization characterizing our economic condition throws the door wide to every sort of adventure. Since imagination is hungry for novelty, and ungoverned, it gropes at random. Setbacks necessarily increase with risks and thus crises multiply, just when they are becoming more destructive.

Yet these dispositions are so inbred that society has grown to accept them and is accustomed to think them normal. It is everlastingly repeated that it is man's nature to be eternally dissatisfied, constantly to advance, without relief or rest, toward an indefinite goal. The longing for infinity is daily represented as a mark of moral distinction, whereas it can only appear within unregulated consciences which elevate to a rule the lack of rule from which they suffer. The doctrine of the most ruthless and swift progress has become an article of faith. But other theories appear parallel with those praising the advantages of instability, which, generalizing the situation that gives them birth, declare life evil, claim that it is richer in grief than in pleasure and that it attracts men only by false claims. Since this disorder is greatest in the economic world, it has most victims there.

Industrial and commercial functions are really among the occupations which furnish the greatest number of suicides. Almost on a level with the liberal professions, they sometimes surpass them; they are especially more afflicted than agriculture, where the old regulative forces still make their appearance felt most and where the fever of business has least penetrated. Here is best recalled what was once the general constitution of the economic order. And the divergence would be yet greater if, among the suicides of industry, employers were distinguished from workmen, for the former are probably most stricken by the state of anomie. The enormous rate of those with independent means (720 per million) sufficiently shows that the possessors of most comfort suffer most. Everything that enforces subordination attenuates the effects of this state. At least the horizon of the lower classes is limited by those above them, and for this same reason their desires are more modest. Those who have only empty space above them are almost inevitably lost in it, if no force restrains them. . . .

THE ANOMIC DIVISION OF LABOR

Up to now, we have studied the division of labor only as a normal phenomenon, but, like all social facts, and, more generally, all biological facts, it presents pathological forms which must be analyzed. Though normally the division of labor produces social solidarity, it sometimes happens that it has different, and even contrary results. Now, it is important to find out what makes it deviate from its natural course, for if we do not prove that these cases are exceptional, the division of labor might be accused of logically implying them. Moreover, the study of these devious forms will permit us to determine the conditions of existence of the normal state better. When we know the circumstances in which the division of labor ceases to bring forth solidarity, we shall better understand what is necessary for it to have that effect. Pathology, here as elsewhere, is a valuable aid of physiology.

One might be tempted to reckon as irregular forms of the division of labor criminal occupations and other harmful activities. They are the very negation of solidarity, and yet they take the form of special activities. But to speak

Source: "The Anomic Division of Labor" and "Conclusions" reprinted with permission of The Macmillan Company from *The Division of Labor in Society,* by Emile Durkheim, trans. George Simpson. Copyright 1947 by The Free Press.

with exactitude, there is no division of labor here, but differentiation pure and simple. The two terms must not be confused. Thus, cancer and tuberculosis increase the diversity of organic tissues without bringing forth a new specialization of biologic functions.[3] In all these cases, there is no partition of a common function, but, in the midst of the organism, whether individual or social, another is formed which seeks to live at the expense of the first. In reality, there is not even a function, for a way of acting merits this name only if it joins with others in maintaining general life. This question, then, does not enter into the body of our investigation.

We shall reduce to three types the exceptional forms of the phenomenon that we are studying. This is not because there can be no others, but rather because those of which we are going to speak are the most general and the most serious.

The first case of this kind is furnished us by industrial or commercial crises, by failures, which are so many partial breaks in organic solidarity. They evince, in effect, that at certain points in the organism certain social functions are not adjusted to one another. But, insofar as labor is divided more, these phenomena seem to become more frequent, at least in certain cases. From 1845 to 1869, failures increased 70%.[4] We cannot, however, attribute this fact to the growth in economic life, since enterprises have become a great deal more concentrated than numerous.

The conflict between capital and labor is another example, more striking, of the same phenomenon. Insofar as industrial functions become more specialized, the conflict becomes more lively, instead of solidarity increasing. In the Middle Ages, the worker everywhere lived at the side of his master, pursuing his tasks "in the same shop, in the same establishment." [5] Both were part of the same corporation and led the same existence. "They were on an almost equal footing; whoever had served his apprenticeship could, at least in many of the occupations, set himself up independently if he had the means." [6] Hence, conflicts were wholly unusual. Beginning with the fifteenth century things began to change. "The occupational circle is no longer a common organization; it is an exclusive possession of the masters, who alone decided all matters. . . . From that time, a sharp line is drawn between masters and workers. The latter formed, so to speak, an order apart; they had their customs, their rules, their independent associations." [7] Once this separation was effected, quarrels became numerous. "When the workers thought they

[3] This is a distinction that Spencer does not make. It seems that, for him, the two terms are synonymous. The differentiation, however, which disintegrates (cancerous, microbic, criminal) is very different from that which brings vital forces together (division of labor).

[4] Block, *Statistique de la France.*

[5] Levasseur, *Les Classes Ouvrières en France jusqu'à la Révolution,* II, p. 315.

[6] Ibid., I, p. 496.

[7] Ibid.

had a just complaint, they struck or boycotted a village, an employer, and all of them were compelled to obey the letter of the order. . . . The power of association gave the workers the means of combating their employers with equal force."[8] But things were then far from reaching "the point at which we now see them. Workers rebelled in order to secure higher wages or some other change in the condition of labor, but they did not consider the employer as a permanent enemy whom one obeyed because of his force. They wished to make him concede a point, and they worked energetically towards that end, but the conflict was not everlasting. The workshops did not contain two opposing classes. Our socialist doctrines were unknown."[9] Finally, in the seventeenth century, the third phase of this history of the working classes begins: the birth of large-scale industry. The worker is more completely separated from the employer. "He becomes somewhat regimented. Each has his function, and the system of the division of labor makes some progress. In the factory of Van-Robais, which employed 1692 workers, there were particular shops for wheelwrighting, for cutlery, for washing, for dyeing, for warping, and the shops for weaving themselves contained several types of workers whose labor was entirely distinct."[10] At the same time that specialization becomes greater, revolts become more frequent. "The smallest cause for discontent was enough to upset an establishment, and cause a worker unhappiness who did not respect the decision of the community."[11] We well know that, since then, the warfare has become ever more violent. . . .

To be sure, we shall see in the following chapter that this tension in social relations is due, in part, to the fact that the working classes are not really satisfied with the conditions under which they live, but very often accept them only as constrained and forced, since they have not the means to change them. This constraint alone, however, would not account for the phenomenon. In effect, it does not weigh less heavily upon all those generally bereft of fortune, and yet this state of permanent hostility is wholly special to the industrial world. Then, in the interior of this world, it is the same for all workers indiscriminately. But, small-scale industry, where work is less divided, displays a relative harmony between worker and employer.[12] It is only in large-scale industry that these relations are in a sickly state. That is because they depend in part upon a different cause. . . .

What makes these facts serious is that they have sometimes been considered a necessary effect of the division of labor after it has passed beyond a certain stage of development. In this case, it is said, the individual, hemmed in by his task, becomes isolated in a special activity. He no longer feels the idea of

[8] Ibid., I, p. 504.

[9] Hubert Valleroux, *Les Corporations d'arts et de métiers,* p. 49.

[10] Levasseur, II, p. 315.

[11] Ibid., p. 319.

[12] See Cauwes, *Précis d'économie politique,* II, p. 39.

a common work being done by those who work side by side with him. Thus, the division of labor could not be pushed farther without becoming a source of disintegration. "Since all such decomposition," says Auguste Comte, "necessarily has the tendency to determine a corresponding dispersion, the fundamental partition of human labors cannot avoid evoking, in a proportionate degree, individual divergences, both intellectual and moral, whose combined influence must, in the same measure, demand a permanent discipline able to prevent or unceasingly contain their discordant flight. If, on the one hand, indeed, the separation of social functions permits a felicitous development of the spirit of detail otherwise impossible, it spontaneously tends, on the other hand, to snuff out the spirit of togetherness or, at least, to undermine it profoundly. Likewise, from the moral point of view, at the same time that each is thus placed in strict dependence upon the mass, he is naturally deterred by the peculiar scope of his special activity which constantly links him to his own private interest whose true relation with the public interest he perceives but very vaguely. . . . Thus it is that the same principle which has alone permitted the development and the extension of general society threatens, in a different aspect, to decompose it into a multitude of incoherent corporations which almost seem not to be of the same species." [13] Espinas has expressed himself almost in the same terms: "Division," he says, "is dispersion." [14]

The division of labor would thus exercise, because of its very nature, a dissolving influence which would be particularly obvious where functions are very specialized. Comte, however, does not conclude from his principle that societies must be led to what he himself calls the age of generality, that is, to that state of indistinctness and homogeneity which was their point of departure. The diversity of functions is useful and necessary, but as unity, which is no less indispensable, does not spontaneously spring up, the care of realizing it and of maintaining it would constitute a special function in the social organism, represented by an independent organ. This organ is the state or government. "The social destiny of government," says Comte, "appears to me to consist particularly in sufficiently containing, and preventing, as far as possible, this fatal disposition towards a fundamental dispersion of ideas, sentiments, and interests, the inevitable result of the very principle of human development, and which, if it could follow its natural course without interruption, would inevitably end by arresting social progress in all important respects. This conception, in my eyes, constitutes the first positive and rational basis of an elementary and abstract theory of government properly so called, seen in its noblest and greatest scientific extension, as characterized in general by a universal and necessary reaction, at first spontaneous and then regulated, of the totality of the parts that go to make it up. It is clear, in effect, that the only real means of preventing such a dispersion consists in this indispensable

[13] Auguste Comte, *Cours de philosophie positive,* IV, p. 429.

[14] Alfred V. Espinas, *Sociétés Animales,* conclusion, IV.

reaction in a new and special function, susceptible of fittingly intervening in the habitual accomplishment of all the diverse functions of social economy, so as to recall to them unceasingly the feeling of unity and the sentiment of common solidarity. . . ."[15]

Of course, we have ourselves shown that the governmental organ develops with the division of labor, not as a repercussion of it, but because of mechanical necessity. As organs are rigorously solidary where functions are very divided, what affects one affects the others, and social events take on a more general interest. At the same time, with the effacement of the segmental type, they penetrate more easily throughout the extent of the same tissue or the same system. For these two reasons, there are more of them which are retained in the directive organ whose functional activity, more often exercised, grows with the volume. But its sphere of action does not extend further.

But beneath this general, superficial life there is an intestine, a world of organs which, without being completely independent of the first, nevertheless function without its intervention, without its even being conscious of them, at least normally. They are freed from its action because it is too remote for them. The government cannot, at every instant, regulate the conditions of the different economic markets, fixing the prices of their commodities and services, or keeping production within the bounds of consumptionary needs, etc. All these practical problems arise from a multitude of detail, coming from thousands of particular circumstances which only those very close to the problems know about. Thus, we cannot adjust these functions to one another and make them concur harmoniously if they do not concur of themselves. If, then, the division of labor has the dispersive effects that are attributed to it, they ought to develop without resistance in this region of society, since there is nothing to hold them together. What gives unity to organized societies, however, as to all organisms, is the spontaneous consensus of parts. Such is the internal solidarity which not only is as indispensable as the regulative action of higher centres, but which also is their necessary condition, for they do no more than translate it into another language and, so to speak, consecrate it. Thus, the brain does not make the unity of the organism, but expresses and completes it. Some speak of the necessity of a reaction of the totality of parts, but it still is necessary for this totality to exist; that is to say, the parts must be already solidary with one another for the whole to take conscience of itself and react in this way. Else, as work is divided, one would see a sort of progressive decomposition produced, not only at certain points, but throughout society, instead of the ever stronger concentration that we really observe.

But, it is said, there is no need for going into detail. It is sufficient to call to mind whenever necessary "the spirit of the whole and the sentiment of common solidarity," and this action the government alone can execute. This is true, but it is much too general to assure the concourse of social functions,

[15] Auguste Comte, *Cours de philosophie positive,* IV, pp. 430–431.

if that has not been realized by itself. In effect, what is the point at issue? Is it to make each individual feel that he is not self-sufficient, but is a part of a whole on which he depends? But such an abstract, vague, and, withal, intermittent representation, just as all complex representations, can avail nothing against lively, concrete impressions which occupational activity at every instant evokes in each one of us. If, then, occupational activity has the effects that are adduced, if the occupations which fill our daily life tend to detach us from the social group to which we belong, such a conception, which is quite dormant and never occupies more than a small part of the field of conscience, will not be sufficient to hold us to it. In order that the sentiment of our state of dependence be effective, it would be necessary for it also to be continuous, and it can be that only if it is linked to the very practice of each special function. But then specialization would no longer have the consequences which it is said to produce. Or else governmental action would have as its object the maintenance of a certain moral uniformity among occupations, the preventing of "social affections gradually concentrated in individuals of the same occupation from becoming more and more foreign to other classes, for want of sufficient likeness in customs and thoughts." [16] But this uniformity cannot be maintained by force and against the nature of things. Functional diversity induces a moral diversity that nothing can prevent, and it is inevitable that one should grow as the other does. We know, moreover, why these two phenomena develop in parallel fashion. Collective sentiments become more and more impotent in holding together the centrifugal tendencies that the division of labor is said to engender, for these tendencies increase as labor is more divided, and, at the same time, collective sentiments are weakened. . . .

As the market extends, great industry appears. But it results in changing the relations of employers and employees. The great strain upon the nervous system and the contagious influence of great agglomerations increase the needs of the latter. Machines replace men; manufacturing replaces hand-work. The worker is regimented, separated from his family throughout the day. He always lives apart from his employer, etc. These new conditions of industrial life naturally demand a new organization, but as these changes have been accomplished with extreme rapidity, the interests in conflict have not yet had the time to be equilibrated. . . .[17]

The preceding has removed one of the most serious charges brought against the division of labor.

It has often been accused of degrading the individual by making him a machine. And truly, if he does not know whither the operations he performs are tending, if he relates them to no end, he can only continue to work through

[16] Auguste Comte, *Cours de philosophie positive,* IV, p. 42.

[17] Let us remember, however, that, as we shall see in the following chapter, this antagonism is not entirely due to the rapidity of these changes, but, in good part, to the still very great inequality of the external conditions of the struggle. On this factor, time has no influence.

routine. Every day he repeats the same movements with monotonous regularity, but without being interested in them, and without understanding them. He is no longer a living cell of a living organism which unceasingly vibrates with neighboring cells, which acts upon them, and to whose action it responds and with whose needs and circumstances it changes. He is no longer anything but an inert piece of machinery, only an external force set going which always moves in the same direction and in the same way. Surely, no matter how one may represent the moral ideal, one cannot remain indifferent to such debasement of human nature. If morality has individual perfection as its goal, it cannot thus permit the ruin of the individual, and if it has society as its goal, it cannot let the very source of social life be drained, for the peril does not threaten only economic functions, but all social functions, as elevated as they may be. "If," says Comte, "we have often justly deplored, in the material world, the workman being exclusively occupied during his whole life with the manufacture of knife-handles or pin-heads, healthy philosophy ought not less bemoan, in the intellectual order, the exclusive and continuous employment of the human brain in the resolution of some equations or in the classification of some insects. The moral effect, in one case, as in the other, is unfortunately very much the same." [18]

As a remedy, it has sometimes been proposed that, in addition to their technical and special instruction, workers be given a general education. But, suppose that we can thus relieve some of the bad effects attributed to the division of labor; that is not a means of preventing them. The division does not change its nature because it has been preceded by general culture. No doubt, it is good for the worker to be interested in art, literature, etc., but it is none the less bad that he should be treated as a machine all day long. Who cannot see, moreover, that two such existences are too opposed to be reconciled and cannot be led by the same man! If a person has grown accustomed to vast horizons, total views, broad generalities, he cannot be confined, without impatience, within the strict limits of a special task. Such a remedy would make specialization inoffensive by making it intolerable, and, consequently, more or less impossible.

What solves the contradiction is that, contrary to what has been said, the division of labor does not produce these consequences because of a necessity of its own nature, but only in exceptional and abnormal circumstances. In order for it to develop without having such a disastrous influence on the human conscience, it is not necessary to temper it with its opposite. It is necessary and it is sufficient for it to be itself, for nothing to come from without to denature it. For, normally, the role of each special function does not require that the individual close himself in, but that he keep himself in constant relations with neighboring functions, take conscience of their needs, of the changes which they undergo, etc. The division of labor presumes that the worker,

[18] Auguste Comte, *Cours,* IV, p. 430.

far from being hemmed in by his task, does not lose sight of his collaborators, that he acts upon them, and reacts to them. He is, then, not a machine who repeats his movements without knowing their meaning, but he knows that they tend, in some way, towards an end that he conceives more or less distinctly. He feels that he is serving something. For that, he need not embrace vast portions of the social horizon; it is sufficient that he perceive enough of it to understand that his actions have an aim beyond themselves. From that time, as special and uniform as his activity may be, it is that of an intelligent being, for it has direction, and he knows it. The economists would not have left this essential character of the division of labor in the shade and, accordingly, would not have exposed it to this unmerited reproach, if they had not reduced it to being merely a means of increasing the produce of social forces, if they had seen that it is above all a source of solidarity. . . .

CONCLUSIONS

But does not the division of labor by making each of us an incomplete being bring on a diminution of individual personality? That is a reproach which has often been levelled at it.

Let us first of all remark that it is difficult to see why it would be more in keeping with the logic of human nature to develop superficially rather than profoundly. Why would a more extensive activity, but more dispersed, be superior to a more concentrated, but circumscribed, activity? Why would there be more dignity in being complete and mediocre, rather than in living a more specialized, but more intense life, particularly if it is thus possible for us to find what we have lost in this specialization, through our association with other beings who have what we lack and who complete us? We take off from the principle that man ought to realize his nature as man, to accomplish his όικεῖον ἔργον [proper work], as Aristotle said. But this nature does not remain constant throughout history; it is modified with societies. Among lower peoples, the proper duty of man is to resemble his companions, to realize in himself all the traits of the collective type which are then confounded, much more than today, with the human type. But, in more advanced societies, his nature is, in large part, to be an organ of society, and his proper duty, consequently, is to play his role as an organ.

Moreover, far more from being tramelled by the progress of specialization, individual personality develops wth the division of labor.

To be a person is to be an autonomous source of action. Man acquires this quality only insofar as there is something in him which is his alone and which individualizes him, as he is something more than a simple incarnation of the generic type of his race and his group. It will be said that he is endowed with free will and that is enough to establish his personality. But although there may be some of this liberty in him, an object of so many discussions, it is not this metaphysical, impersonal, invariable attribute which can serve as the unique basis for concrete personality, which is empirical and variable with individuals. That could not be constituted by the wholly abstract power of choice between two opposites, but it is still necessary for this faculty to be exercised towards ends and aims which are proper to the agent. In other words, the very materials of conscience must have a personal character. But we have seen in the second book of this work that this result is progressively produced as the division of labor progresses. The effacement of the segmental type, at the same time that it necessitates a very great specialization, partially lifts the individual conscience from the organic environment which supports it, as from the social environment which envelops it, and, accordingly, because of this double emancipation, the individual becomes more of an independent factor in his own conduct. The division of labor itself contributes to this enfranchisement, for individual natures, while specializing, become more complex, and by that are in part freed from collective action and hereditary influences which can only enforce themselves upon simple, general things.

It is, accordingly, a real illusion which makes us believe that personality was so much more complete when the division of labor had penetrated less. No doubt, in looking from without at the diversity of occupations which the individual then embraces, it may seem that he is developing in a very free and complete manner. But, in reality, this activity which he manifests is not really his. It is society, it is the race acting in and through him; he is only the intermediary through which they realize themselves. His liberty is only apparent and his personality borrowed. Because the life of these societies is, in certain respects, less regular, we imagine that original talents have more opportunity for free play, that it is easier for each one to pursue his own tastes, that a very large place is left to free fantasy. But this is to forget that personal sentiments are then very rare. If the motives which govern conduct do not appear as periodically as they do today, they do not leave off being collective, and, consequently, impersonal, and it is the same with the actions that they inspire. Moreover, we have shown above how activity becomes richer and more intense as it becomes more specialized.

Thus, the progress of individual personality and that of the division of labor depend upon one and the same cause. It is thus impossible to desire one without desiring the other. But no one today contests the obligatory character of the rule which orders us to be more and more of a person.

One last consideration will make us see to what extent the division of labor is linked with our whole moral life.

Men have long dreamt of finally realizing in fact the ideal of human fraternity. People pray for a state where war will no longer be the law of international relations, where relations between societies will be pacifically regulated, as those between individuals already are, where all men will collaborate in the same work and live the same life. Although these aspirations are in part neutralized by those which have as their object the particular society of which we are a part, they have not left off being active and are even gaining in force. But they can be satisfied only if all men form one society, subject to the same laws. For, just as private conflicts can be regulated only by the action of the society in which the individuals live, so intersocial conflicts can be regulated only by a society which comprises in its scope all others. The only power which can serve to moderate individual egotism is the power of the group; the only power which can serve to moderate the egotism of groups is that of some other group which embraces them.

Truly, when the problem has been posed in these terms, we must recognize that this ideal is not on the verge of being integrally realized, for there are too many intellectual and moral diversities between different social types existing together on the earth to admit of fraternalization in the same society. But what is possible is that societies of the same type may come together, and it is, indeed, in this direction that evolution appears to move. We have already seen that among European peoples there is a tendency to form, by spontaneous movement, a European society which has, at present, some idea of itself and the beginning of organization. If the formation of a single human society is forever impossible, a fact which has not been proved,[19] at least the formation of continually larger societies brings us vaguely near the goal. These facts, moreover, in no wise contradict the definition of morality that we have given, for if we cling to humanity and if we ought to cling to it, it is because it is a society which is in process of realizing itself in this way, and with which we are solidary.[20]

But we know that greater societies cannot be formed except through the development of the division of labor, for not only could they not maintain themselves in equilibrium without a greater specialization of functions, but even the increase in the number of those competing would suffice to produce this result mechanically; and that, so much the more, since the growth of volume is generally accompanied by a growth in density. We can then formulate the following proposition: the ideal of human fraternity can be realized only in proportion to the progress of the division of labor. We must choose: either to renounce our dream, if we refuse further to circumscribe our activity, or else to push forward its accomplishment under the condition we have just set forth.

But if the division of labor produces solidarity, it is not only because it

[19] There is nothing that forces the intellectual and moral diversity of societies to be maintained. The ever greater expansion of higher societies, from which there results the absorption or elimination of less advanced societies, tends, in any case, to diminish such diversity.

[20] Thus, the duties that we have toward it do not oppress those which link us to our country. For the latter is the only actually realized society of which we are members; the other is only a desideratum whose realization is not even assured.

makes each individual an *exchangist,* as the economists say;[21] it is because it creates among men an entire system of rights and duties which link them together in a durable way. Just as social similitudes give rise to a law and a morality which protect them, so the division of labor gives rise to rules which assure pacific and regular concourse of divided functions. If economists have believed that it would bring forth an abiding solidarity, in some manner of its own making, and if, accordingly, they have held that human societies could and would resolve themselves into purely economic associations, that is because they believed that it affected only individual, temporary interests. Consequently, to estimate the interests in conflict and the way in which they ought to equilibrate, that is to say, to determine the conditions under which exchange ought to take place, is solely a matter of individual competence; and, since these interests are in a perpetual state of becoming, there is no place for any permanent regulation. But such a conception is, in all ways, inadequate for the facts. The division of labor does not present individuals to one another, but social functions. And society is interested in the play of the latter; in so far as they regularly concur, or do not concur, it will be healthy or ill. Its existence thus depends upon them, and the more they are divided the greater its dependence. That is why it cannot leave them in a state of indetermination. In addition to this, they are determined by themselves. Thus are formed those rules whose number grows as labor is divided, and whose absence makes organic solidarity either impossible or imperfect.

But it is not enough that there be rules; they must be just, and for that it is necessary for the external conditions of competition to be equal. If, moreover, we remember that the collective conscience is becoming more and more a cult of the individual, we shall see that what characterizes the morality of organized societies, compared to that of segmental societies, is that there is something more human, therefore more rational, about them. It does not direct our activities to ends which do not immediately concern us; it does not make us servants of ideal powers of a nature other than our own, which follow their directions without occupying themselves with the interests of men. It only asks that we be thoughtful of our fellows and that we be just, that we fulfill our duty, that we work at the function we can best execute, and receive the just reward for our services. The rules which constitute it do not have a constraining force which snuffs out free thought; but, because they are rather made for us and, in a certain sense, by us, we are free. We wish to understand them; we do not fear to change them. We must, however, guard against finding such an ideal inadequate on the pretext that it is too earthly and too much to our liking. An ideal is not more elevated because more transcendent, but because it leads us to vaster perspectives. What is im-

[21] The word is de Molinari's, *La Morale Économique,* p. 248.

portant is not that it tower high above us, until it becomes a stranger to our lives, but that it open to our activity a large enough field. This is far from being on the verge of realization. We know only too well what a laborious work it is to erect this society where each individual will have the place he merits, will be rewarded as he deserves, where everybody, accordingly, will spontaneously work for the good of all and of each. Indeed, a moral code is not above another because it commands in a drier and more authoritarian manner, or because it is more sheltered from reflection. Of course, it must attach us to something besides ourselves but it is not necessary for it to chain us to it with impregnable bonds.

It has been said [22] with justice that morality—and by that must be understood, not only moral doctrines, but customs—is going through a real crisis. What precedes can help us to understand the nature and causes of this sick condition. Profound changes have been produced in the structure of our societies in a very short time; they have been freed from the segmental type with a rapidity and in proportions such as have never before been seen in history. Accordingly, the morality which corresponds to this social type has regressed, but without another developing quickly enough to fill the ground that the first left vacant in our consciences. Our faith has been troubled; tradition has lost its sway; individual judgment has been freed from collective judgment. But, on the other hand, the functions which have been disrupted in the course of the upheaval have not had the time to adjust themselves to one another; the new life which has emerged so suddenly has not been able to be completely organized, and above all, it has not been organized in a way to satisfy the need for justice which has grown more ardent in our hearts. If this be so, the remedy for the evil is not to seek to resuscitate traditions and practices which, no longer responding to present conditions of society, can only live an artificial, false existence. What we must do to relieve this anomie is to discover the means for making the organs which are still wasting themselves in discordant movements harmoniously concur by introducing into their relations more justice by more and more extenuating the external inequalities which are the source of the evil. Our illness is not, then, as has often been believed, of an intellectual sort; it has more profound causes. We shall not suffer because we no longer know on what theoretical notion to base the morality we have been practicing, but because, in certain of its parts, this morality is irremediably shattered, and that which is necessary to us is only in process of formation. Our anxiety does not arise because the criticism of scholars has broken down the traditional explanation we use to give to our duties; consequently, it is not a new philosophical system which will relieve the situation. Because certain of our duties are no longer founded in the reality of things, a breakdown has resulted which will be re-

[22] Beaussire, *Les Principes de la morale*, Introduction.

paired only in so far as a new discipline is established and consolidated. In short, our first duty is to make a moral code for ourselves. Such a work cannot be improvised in the silence of the study; it can arise only through itself, little by little, under the pressure of internal causes which make it necessary. But the service that thought can and must render is in fixing the goal that we must attain. That is what we have tried to do.

5

On Alienation

Karl Marx

THE DIVISION OF LABOR

Language is as old as consciousness, language is practical consciousness, as it exists for other men, and for that reason is really beginning to exist for me personally as well; for language, like consciousness, only arises from the need, the necessity, of intercourse with other men. Where there exists a relationship, it exists for me: the animal has no "relations" with anything, cannot have any. For the animal, its relation to others does not exist as a relation. Consciousness is therefore from the very beginning a social product, and remains so as long as men exist at all. Consciousness is at first, of course, merely consciousness concerning the immediate sensuous environment and consciousness of the limited connection with other persons and things outside the individual who is growing self-conscious . . . at this point man is only distinguished from sheep by the fact that with him consciousness takes the place of instinct or that his instinct is a conscious one.

This sheep-like or tribal consciousness receives its further development and extension through increased productivity, the increase of needs, and, what is fundamental to both of these, the increase of population. With these there develops the division of labor, which was originally nothing but the division of labor in the sexual act, then that division of labor which develops spontaneously or "naturally" by virtue of natural predisposition (e.g., physical strength), needs, accidents, etc., etc. Division of labor only becomes truly such from the moment when a division of material and mental labor appears . . . the division of labor implies the possibility, nay the fact that intellectual and material activity—enjoyment and labor, production and consumption—devolve on different individuals, and that the only possibility of

Source: "The Division of Labor" is taken from Karl Marx and Frederick Engels, *The German Ideology,* ed. R. Pascal (New York: International Publishers Company, Inc., New World Paperback Edition, 1947), and is reprinted by permission of International Publishers Company, Inc.

their not coming into contradiction lies in the negation in its turn of the division of labor. . . .

With the division of labor, in which all these contradictions are implicit, and which in its turn is based on the natural division of labor in the family and the separation of society into individual families opposed to one another, is given simultaneously the distribution, and indeed the unequal distribution (both quantitative and qualitative), of labor and its products, hence property: the nucleus, the first form, of which lies in the family, where wife and children are the slaves of the husband. This latent slavery in the family, though still very crude, is the first property, but even at this early stage it corresponds perfectly to the definition of modern economists who call it the power of disposing of the labor power of others. Division of labor and private property are, moreover, identical expressions: in the one the same thing is affirmed with reference to activity as is affirmed in the other with reference to the product of the activity.

Further, the division of labor implies the contradiction between the interest of the separate individual or the individual family and the communal interest of all individuals who have intercourse with one another. And indeed, this communal interest does not exist merely in the imagination, as "the general good," but first of all in reality, as the mutual interdependence of the individuals among whom the labor is divided. And finally, the division of labor offers us the first example of how, as long as man remains in natural society, that is as long as a cleavage exists between the particular and the common interest, as long therefore as activity is not voluntarily, but naturally, divided, man's own deed becomes an alien power opposed to him, which enslaves him instead of being controlled by him. For as soon as labor is distributed, each man has a particular, exclusive sphere of activity, which is forced upon him and from which he cannot escape. He is a hunter, a fisherman, a shepherd, or a critical critic, and must remain so if he does not want to lose his means of livelihood; while in communist society, where nobody has one exclusive sphere of activity but each can become accomplished in any branch he wishes, society regulates the general production and thus makes it possible for me to do one thing today and another tomorrow, to hunt in the morning, fish in the afternoon, rear cattle in the evening, criticize after dinner, just as I have a mind, without ever becoming hunter, fisherman, shepherd, or critic.

ALIENATED LABOR

Let us not begin our explanation, as does the economist, from a legendary primordial condition. Such a primordial condition does not explain any-

Source: "Alienated Labor," "The Alienation of Species Life," "Capitalist Political Economy," and "Communism and the Abolition of Private Property" taken from *Karl* thing; it merely removes the question into a grey and nebulous distance. It asserts as a fact or event what it should deduce, namely, the necessary relation between two things; for example, between the division of labor and exchange. In the same way theology explains the origin of evil by the fall of man; that is, it asserts as a historical fact what it should explain.

We shall begin from a contemporary economic fact. The worker becomes poorer the more wealth he produces and the more his production increases in power and extent. The worker becomes an ever cheaper commodity the more goods he creates. The devaluation of the human world increases in direct relation with the increase in value of the world of things. Labor does not only create goods; it also produces itself and the worker as a commodity, and indeed in the same proportion as it produces goods.

This fact simply implies that the object produced by labor, its product, now stands opposed to it as an alien being, as a power independent of the producer. The product of labor is labor which has been embodied in an object and turned into a physical thing; this product is an objectification of labor. The performance of work is at the same time its objectification. The performance of work appears in the sphere of political economy as a vitiation of the worker, objectification as a loss and as servitude to the object, and appropriation as alienation.

So much does the performance of work appear as vitiation that the worker is vitiated to the point of starvation. So much does objectification appear as loss of the object that the worker is deprived of the most essential things not only of life but also of work. Labor itself becomes an object which he can acquire only by the greatest effort and with unpredictable interruptions. So much does the appropriation of the object appear as alienation that the more objects the worker produces the fewer he can possess and the more he falls under the domination of his product, of capital.

All these consequences follow from the fact that the worker is related to the product of his labor as to an alien object. For it is clear on this presupposition that the more the worker expends himself in work the more powerful becomes the world of objects which he creates in face of himself, the poorer he becomes in his inner life, and the less he belongs to himself. It is just the same as in religion. The more of himself man attributes to God the less he has left in himself. The worker puts his life into the object, and his life then belongs no longer to himself but to the object. The greater his activity, therefore, the less he possesses. What is embodied in the product of his labor is no longer his own. The greater this product is, therefore, the more he is diminished. The alienation of the worker in his product means not only that his labor becomes an object, assumes an external existence, but that it exists independently, outside himself, and alien to him, and that it stands opposed to him as an autonomous power. The life which he has given to the object sets itself against him as an alien and hostile force. . . .

(The alienation of the worker in his object is expressed as follows in the laws of political economy: the more the worker produces the less he has to consume; the more value he creates the more worthless he becomes; the more refined his product the more crude and misshapen the worker; the more civilized the product the more barbarous the worker; the more powerful the work the more feeble the worker; the more the work manifests intelligence the more the worker declines in intelligence and becomes a slave of nature.)

Political economy conceals the alienation in the nature of labor in so far as it does not examine the direct relationship between the worker (work) and production. Labor certainly produces marvels for the rich but it produces privation for the worker. It produces palaces, but hovels for the worker. It produces beauty, but deformity for the worker. It replaces labor by machinery, but it casts some of the workers back into a barbarous kind of work and turns the others into machines. It produces intelligence, but also stupidity and cretinism for the workers.

The direct relationship of labor to its products is the relationship of the worker to the objects of his production. The relationship of property owners to the objects of production and to production itself is merely a consequence of this first relationship and confirms it. We shall consider this second aspect later.

Thus, when we ask what is the important relationship of labor, we are concerned with the relationship of the *worker* to production.

So far we have considered the alienation of the worker only from one aspect; namely, his relationship with the products of his labor. However, alienation appears not merely in the result but also in the process of production, within productive activity itself. How could the worker stand in an alien relationship to the product of his activity if he did not alienate himself in the act of production itself? The product is indeed only the résumé of activity, of production. Consequently, if the product of labor is alienation, production itself must be active alienation—the alienation of activity and the activity of alienation. The alienation of the object of labor merely summarizes the alienation in the work activity itself.

What constitutes the alienation of labor? First, that the work is *external* to the worker, that it is not part of his nature; and that, consequently, he does not fulfil himself in his work but denies himself, has a feeling of misery rather than well-being, does not develop freely his mental and physical energies but is physically exhausted and mentally debased. The worker, therefore, feels himself at home only during his leisure time, whereas at work he feels homeless. His work is not voluntary but imposed, forced labor. It is not the satisfaction of a need, but only a means for satisfying other needs. Its alien character is clearly shown by the fact that as soon as there is no physical or other compulsion it is avoided like the plague. External labor, labor in which man alienates himself, is a labor of self-sacrifice, of mortification. Finally, the external character of work for the worker is shown by the fact that it is not his own work but work for someone else, that in work he does not belong to himself but to another person.

Just as in religion the spontaneous activity of human fantasy, of the human brain and heart, reacts independently as an alien activity of gods or devils upon the individual, so the activity of the worker is not his own spontaneous activity. It is another's activity and a loss of his own spontaneity.

We arrive at the result that man (the worker) feels himself to be freely active only in his animal functions—eating, drinking, and procreating, or at most also in his dwelling and in personal adornment—while in his human functions he is reduced to an animal. The animal becomes human and the human becomes animal.

Eating, drinking, and procreating are of course also genuine human functions. But abstractly considered, apart from the environment of human activities, and turned into final and sole ends, they are animal functions.

We have now considered the act of alienation of practical human activity, labor, from two aspects: (1) the relationship of the worker to the product of labor as an alien object which dominates him. This relationship is at the same time the relationship to the sensuous external world, to natural objects, as an alien and hostile world; (2) the relationship of labor to the act of production within labor. This is the relationship of the worker to his own activity as something alien and not belonging to him, activity as suffering (passivity), strength as powerlessness, creation as emasculation, the personal physical and mental energy of the worker, his personal life (for what is life but activity?), as an activity which is directed against himself, independent of him and not belonging to him. This is self-alienation as against the above-mentioned alienation of the thing.

THE ALIENATION OF SPECIES LIFE

We have now to infer a third characteristic of alienated labor from the two we have considered.

Man is a species being not only in the sense that he makes the community (his own as well as those of other things) his object both practically and theoretically, but also (and this is simply another expression for the same thing) in the sense that he treats himself as the present, living species, as a universal and consequently free being.

Species life, for man as for animals, has its physical basis in the fact that man (like animals) lives from inorganic nature, and since man is more universal than an animal so the range of inorganic nature from which he lives is more universal. Plants, animals, minerals, air, light, etc., constitute, from the theoretical aspect, a part of human consciousness as objects of natural science and art; they are man's spiritual inorganic nature, his intellectual means of life, which he must first prepare for enjoyment and perpetuation. So also, from the practical aspect, they form a part of human life and activity. In practice man lives only from these natural products, whether in the form of food, heating, clothing, housing, etc. The universality of man appears in practice in the universality which makes the whole of nature into his inorganic body: (1) as a direct means of life; and equally (2) as the material object and instrument of his life activity. Nature is the inorganic body of man; that is to say nature, excluding the human body itself. To say that man *lives* from nature means that nature is his *body* with which he must remain in a continuous interchange in order not to die. The statement that the physical and mental life of man, and nature, are interdependent means simply that nature is interdependent with itself, for man is a part of nature.

Since alienated labor: (1) alienates nature from man; and (2) alienates man from himself, from his own active function, his life activity; so it alienates him from the species. It makes *species life* into a means of individual life. In the first place it alienates species life and individual life, and secondly, it turns the latter, as an abstraction, into the purpose of the former, also in its abstract and alienated form.

For labor, life activity, productive life, now appears to man only as means for the satisfaction of a need, the need to maintain his physical existence. Productive life is, however, species life. It is life creating life. In the type of life activity resides the whole character of a species, its species character; and free, conscious activity is the species character of human beings. Life itself appears only as a *means of life*.

The animal is one with its life activity. It does not distinguish the activity from itself. It is its activity. But man makes his life activity itself an object of his will and consciousness. He has a conscious life activity. It is not a determination with which he is completely identified. Conscious life activity distinguishes man from the life activity of animals. Only for this reason is he a species being. Or rather, he is only a self-conscious being, i.e., his own life is an object for him, because he is a species being. Only for this reason is his activity free activity. Alienated labor reverses the relationship, in that man because he is a self-conscious being makes his life activity, his being, only a means for his existence.

The practical construction of an objective world, the manipulation of inorganic nature, is the confirmation of man as a conscious species being, i.e., a being who treats the species as his own being or himself as a species being. Of course, animals also produce. They construct nests, dwellings, as in the case of bees, beavers, ants, etc. But they only produce what is strictly necessary for themselves or their young. They produce only in a single direction, while man produces universally. They produce only under the compulsion of direct physical needs, while man produces when he is free from physical need and only truly produces in freedom from such need. Animals produce only themselves, while man reproduces the whole of nature. The products of animal production belong directly to their physical bodies, while man is free in face of his product. Animals construct only in accordance with the standards and needs of the species to which they belong, while man knows how to produce in accordance with the standards of every species and knows how to apply the appropriate standard to the object. Thus man constructs also in accordance with the laws of beauty.

It is just in his work upon the objective world that man really proves himself as a species being. This production is his active species life. By means of it nature appears as his work and his reality. The object of labor is, therefore, the objectification of man's species life; for he no longer reproduces himself merely intellectually, as in consciousness, but actively and in a real sense, and he sees his own reflection in a world which he has constructed. While, therefore, alienated labor takes away the object of production from man, it also takes away his species life, his real objectivity as a species being, and changes his advantage over animals into a disadvantage in so far as his inorganic body, nature, is taken from him.

Just as alienated labor transforms free and self-directed activity into a means, so it transforms the species life of man into a means of physical existence.

Consciousness, which man has from his species, is transformed through alienation so that species life becomes only a means for him. (3) Thus alienated labor turns the species life of man, and also nature as his mental species property, into an alien being and into a means for his individual existence. It alienates from man his own body, external nature, his mental life and his human life. (4) A direct consequence of the alienation of man from the product of his labor, from his life activity and from his species life, is that man is alienated from other men. When man confronts himself he also confronts other men. What is true of man's relationship to his work, to the product of his work and to himself, is also true of his relationship to other men, to their labor, and to the objects of their labor.

In general, the statement that man is alienated from his species life means that each man is alienated from others, and that each of the others is likewise alienated from human life.

Human alienation, and above all the relation of man to himself, is first realized and expressed in the relationship between each man and other men. Thus in the relationship of alienated labor every man regards other men according to the standards and relationships in which he finds himself placed as a worker. . . .

CAPITALIST POLITICAL ECONOMY

Political economy, the science of wealth, is, therefore, at the same time, the science of renunciation, of privation and of saving, which actually succeeds in depriving man of fresh air and of physical activity. This science of a marvelous industry is at the same time the science of asceticism. Its true ideal is the ascetic but usurious miser and the ascetic but productive slave. Its moral ideal is the worker who takes a part of his wages to the savings bank. It has even found a servile art to embody this favorite idea, which has been produced in a sentimental manner on the stage. Thus, despite its worldly and pleasure-seeking appearance, it is a truly moral science, and the most moral of all sciences. Its principal thesis is the renunciation of life and of human needs. The less you eat, drink, buy books, go to the theater or to balls, or to the public house, and the less you think, love, theorize, sing, paint, fence, etc., the more you will be able to save and the greater will become your treasure which neither moth nor rust will corrupt—your capital. The less you are, the less you express your life, the more you have, the greater is your alienated life and the greater is the saving of your alienated being. Everything which the economist takes from you in the way of life and humanity, he restores to you in the form of money and wealth. And everything which you are unable to do, your money can do for you; it can eat, drink, go to the ball and to the theater. It can acquire art, learning, historical treasures, political power; and it can travel. It can appropriate all these things for you, can purchase everything; it is the true opulence. But although it can do all this, it only desires to create itself, and to buy itself, for everything else is subservient to it. When one owns the master, one also owns the servant, and one has no need of the master's servant. Thus all passions and activities must be submerged in avarice. The worker must have just what is necessary for him to want to live, and he must want to live only in order to have this. . . .

Society, as it appears to the economist, is *civil* society, in which each individual is a totality of needs and only exists for another person, as the other exists for him, in so far as each becomes a means for the other. The economist (like politics in its *rights of man*) reduces everything to man, i.e., to the individual, whom he deprives of all characteristics in order to classify him as a capitalist or a worker.

The division of labor is the economic expression of the social character of labor within alienation. Or, since labor is only an expression of human activity within alienation, of life activity as alienation of life, the division of labor is nothing but the alienated establishment of human activity as a real species activity or the activity of man as a species being.

The economists are very confused and self-contradictory about the nature of the division of labor (which of course has to be regarded as a principal motive force in the production of wealth once labor is recognized as the essence of private property), i.e., about the alienated form of human activity as species activity.

Adam Smith:

> The division of labor . . . is not originally the effect of any human wisdom. . . . It is the necessary, though very slow and gradual consequence of the propensity to truck, barter, and exchange one thing for another. [Whether this propensity be one of those original principles of human nature . . .] or whether, as seems more probable, it be the necessary consequence of the faculties of reason and of speech [it belongs not to our present subject to inquire]. It is common to all men, and to be found in no other race of animals . . . [In almost every other race of animals the individual] when it is grown up to maturity is entirely independent. . . . But man has almost constant occasion for the help of his brethren, and it is in vain for him to expect it from their benevolence only. He will be more likely to prevail if he can interest their self-love in his favor, and show them that it is for their own advantage to do for him what he requires of them. . . . We address ourselves not to their humanity but to their self-love, and never talk to them of our own necessities but of their advantages.[1]
>
> As it is by treaty, by barter, and by purchase that we obtain from one another the greater part of those mutual good offices that we stand in need of, so it is this same trucking disposition which originally gives occasion to the division of labor. In a tribe of hunters or shepherds a particular person makes bows and arrows, for example, with more readiness and dexterity than any other. He frequently exchanges them for cattle or for venison with his companions; and he finds at last that he can in this manner get more cattle and venison than if he himself went to the field to catch them. From a regard to his own interest, therefore, the making of bows and arrows grows to be his chief business. . . .[2]

The whole of modern political economy is agreed, however, upon the fact that division of labor and abundance of production, division of labor and accumulation of capital, are mutually determining; and also that liberated and autonomous private property alone can produce the most effective and extensive division of labor.

Adam Smith's argument may be summarized as follows: The division of labor confers upon labor an unlimited capacity to produce. It arises from the propensity to exchange and barter, a specifically human propensity which is probably not fortuitous but determined by the use of reason and speech. The motive of those who engage in exchange is not humanity but *egoism*. The diversity of human talents is more the effect than the cause of the division of labor, i.e., of exchange. Furthermore, it is only the latter which makes this diversity useful. The particular qualities of the different tribes within

[1] Adam Smith, *The Wealth of Nations,* I (Everyman Edition), pp. 12–13. I have indicated the parts of this quotation which Marx paraphrased by square brackets. [*Bottomore's note.*]

[2] Ibid., pp. 13–14.

an animal species are by nature more pronounced than the differences between the aptitudes and activities of human beings. But since animals are not able to exchange, the diversity of qualities in animals of the same species but of different tribes is of no benefit to any individual animal. Animals are unable to combine the various qualities of their species, or to contribute to the common advantage and comfort of the species. It is otherwise with men, whose most diverse talents and forms of activity are useful to each other, because they can bring their different products together in a common stock, from which each man can buy. As the division of labor arises from the propensity to exchange, so it develops and is limited by the extent of exchange, by the extent of the market. In developed conditions every man is a merchant and society is a commercial association. Say regards exchange as fortuitous and not fundamental. Society could exist without it. It becomes indispensable in an advanced state of society. Yet production cannot take place without it. The division of labor is a convenient and useful means, a skilful deployment of human powers for social wealth, but it diminishes the capacity of each person taken individually. . . .

That which exists for me through the medium of money, that which I can pay for (i.e., which money can buy), that I *am,* the possessor of the money. My own power is as great as the power of money. The properties of money are my own (the possessor's) properties and faculties. What I am and can do is, therefore, not at all determined by my individuality. I am ugly, but I can buy the most beautiful woman for myself. Consequently, I am not ugly, for the effect of ugliness, its power to repel, is annulled by money. As an individual I am lame, but money provides me with twenty-four legs. Therefore, I am not lame. I am a detestable, dishonorable, unscrupulous, and stupid man, but money is honored and so also is its possessor. Money is the highest good, and so its possessor is good. Besides, money saves me the trouble of being dishonest; therefore, I am presumed honest. I am stupid, but since money is the real mind of all things, how should its possessor be stupid? Moreover, he can buy talented people for himself, and is not he who has power over the talented more talented than they? I who can have, through the power of money, everything for which the human heart longs, do I not possess all human abilities? Does not my money, therefore, transform all my incapacities into their opposites?

If money is the bond which binds me to human life, and society to me, and which links me with nature and man, is it not the bond of all bonds? Is it not, therefore, also the universal agent of separation? It is the real means of both *separation* and *union,* the galvano-chemical power of society. . . .

Money, then, appears as a disruptive power for the individual and for the social bonds, which claim to be self-subsistent entities. It changes fidelity into infidelity, love into hate, hate into love, virtue into vice, vice into virtue, servant into master, stupidity into intelligence and intelligence into stupidity. . . .

He who can purchase bravery is brave, though a coward. Money is not exchanged for a particular quality, a particular thing, or a specific human faculty, but for the whole objective world of man and nature. Thus, from the standpoint of its possessor, it exchanges every quality and object for every other, even though they are contradictory. It is the fraternization of incompatibles; it forces contraries to embrace.

Let us assume *man* to be *man,* and his relation to the world to be a human one. Then love can only be exchanged for love, trust for trust, etc. If you wish to enjoy art you must be an artistically cultivated person; if you wish to influence other people you must be a person who really has a stimulating and encouraging effect upon others. Every one of your relations to man and to nature must be a specific expression, corresponding to the object of your will, of your real individual life. If you love without evoking love in return, i.e., if you are not able, by the manifestation of yourself as a loving person, to make yourself a *beloved person,* then your love is impotent and a misfortune.

COMMUNISM AND THE ABOLITION OF PRIVATE PROPERTY

But the antithesis between propertylessness and property is still an indeterminate antithesis, which is not conceived in its active reference to its intrinsic relations, not yet conceived as a contradiction, so long as it is not understood as an antithesis between labor and capital. . . .

Finally, communism is the positive expression of the abolition of private property, and in the first place of universal private property. In taking this relation in its universal aspect communism is, in its first form, only the generalization and fulfilment of the relation. As such it appears in a double form; the domination of material property looms so large that it aims to destroy everything which is incapable of being possessed by everyone as private property. It wishes to eliminate talent, etc., by force. Immediate physical possession seems to it the unique goal of life and existence. The role of worker is not abolished, but is extended to all men. The relation of private property remains the relation of the community to the world of things. Finally, this tendency to oppose general private property to private property is expressed in an animal form; marriage (which is incontestably a form of exclusive private property) is contrasted with the community of women, in which women become communal and common property. One may say that this idea of the community of women is the open secret of this entirely crude and unreflective communism. Just as women are to pass from marriage to universal prostitution, so the whole world of wealth (i.e., the objective being of man) is to pass from the relation of exclusive marriage with the private owner to the relation of universal prostitution with the community. This communism, which negates the personality of man in every sphere, is only the logical expression of private property, which is this negation. Universal envy setting itself up as a power is only a camouflaged form of cupidity which reestablishes itself and satisfies itself in a different way. The thoughts of every individual private property are at least directed against any wealthier private property, in the form of envy and the desire to reduce everything to a common level; so that this envy and levelling in fact constitute the essence of competition. Crude communism is only the culmination of such envy and levelling down on the basis of a preconceived minimum. How little this abolition of private property represents a genuine appropriation is shown by the abstract negation of the whole world of culture and civilization and the regression to the unnatural simplicity of the poor and wantless individual who has not only not surpassed private property but has not yet even attained to it.

The community is only a community of work and of equality of wages paid out by the communal capital, by the community as universal capitalist. The two sides of the relation are raised to a supposed universality; labor as a condition in which everyone is placed, and capital as the acknowledged universality and power of the community.

In the relationship with woman, as the prey and the handmaid of communal lust, is expressed the infinite degradation in which man exists for himself; for the secret of this relationship finds its unequivocal, incontestable, open, and revealed expression in the relation of man to woman and in the way in which the direct and natural species relationship is conceived. The immediate, natural and necessary relation of human being to human being is also the relation of man to woman. In this natural species relationship man's relation to nature is directly his relation to man, and his relation to man is directly his relation to nature, to his own natural function. Thus, in this relation is sensuously revealed, reduced to an observable fact, the extent to which human nature has become nature for man and to which nature has become human nature for him. From this relationship man's whole level of development can be assessed. It follows from the character of this relationship how far man has become, and has understood himself as, a species being, a human being. The relation of man to woman is the most natural relation of human being to human being. It indicates, therefore, how far man's *natural* behavior has become *human,* and how far his *human* essence has become a *natural* essence for him, how far his *human nature* has become *nature* for him. It also shows how far man's needs have become *human* needs, and consequently how far the other person, as a person, has become one of his needs, and to what extent he is in his individual existence at the same time a social being. The first positive annulment of private property, crude communism, is, therefore, only a phenomenal form of the infamy of private property representing itself as positive community.

Communism (*a*) still political in nature, democratic or despotic; (*b*) with the abolition of the state, yet still incomplete and influenced by private property, that is, by the alienation of man. In both forms communism is already aware of being the reintegration of man, his return to himself, the supersession of man's self-alienation. But since it has not yet grasped the positive nature of private property, or the human nature of needs, it is still captured and contaminated by private property. It has well understood the concept, but not the essence.

Communism is the positive abolition of private property, of human self-alienation, and thus the real appropriation of human nature through and for man. It is, therefore, the return of man himself as a *social,* i.e., really human, being, a complete and conscious return which assimilates all the wealth of previous development. Communism as a fully developed naturalism is humanism and as a fully developed humanism is naturalism. It is the definitive resolution of the antagonism between man and nature, and between man and man. It is the true solution of the conflict between existence and essence, between objectification and self-affirmation, between freedom and necessity, between individual and species. It is the solution of the riddle of history and knows itself to be this solution. . . .

We have seen how, on the assumption that private property has been positively superseded, man produces man, himself and then other men; how the object which is the direct activity of his personality is at the same time his existence for other men and their existence for him. Similarly, the material of labor and man himself as a subject are the starting point as well as the result of this movement (and because there must be this starting point private property is a historical necessity). Therefore, the social character is the universal character of the whole movement; as society itself produces man as man, so it is produced by him. Activity and mind are social in their content as well as in their origin; they are social activity and social mind. The human significance of nature only exists for social man, because only in this case is nature a bond with other men, the basis of his existence for others and of their existence for him. Only then is nature the basis of his own human experience and a vital element of human reality. The natural existence of man has here become his *human* existence and nature itself has become human for him. Thus *society* is the accomplished union of man with nature, the veritable resurrection of nature, the realized naturalism of man and the realized humanism of nature.

III
Contemporary Models of Society and Politics

6

Some Principles of Stratification

Kingsley Davis and Wilbert E. Moore

In a previous paper some concepts for handling the phenomena of social inequality were presented.[1] In the present paper a further step in stratification theory is undertaken—an attempt to show the relationship between stratification and the rest of the social order.[2] Starting from the proposition that no society is "classless," or unstratified, an effort is made to explain, in functional terms, the universal necessity which calls forth stratification in any social system. Next, an attempt is made to explain the roughly uniform distribution of prestige as between the major types of positions in every society. Since, however, there occur between one society and another great differences in the degree and kind of stratification, some attention is also given to the varieties of social inequality and the variable factors that give rise to them.

Clearly, the present task requires two different lines of analysis—one to understand the universal, the other to understand the variable features of stratification. Naturally each line of inquiry aids the other and is indispensable, and in the treatment that follows the two will be interwoven, although, because of space limitations, the emphasis will be on the universals.

Throughout, it will be necessary to keep in mind one thing—namely, that the discussion relates to the system of positions, not to the individuals occupying those positions. It is one thing to ask why different positions carry different degrees of prestige, and quite another to ask how certain individuals get into those positions. Although, as the argument will try to show, both ques-

Source: *American Sociological Review* 10 (April 1945), pp. 242–249. Reprinted by permission of the authors and the American Sociological Association.

[1] Kingsley Davis, "A Conceptual Analysis of Stratification," *American Sociological Review* 7 (June 1942), pp. 309–321.

[2] The writers regret (and beg indulgence) that the present essay, a condensation of a longer study, covers so much in such short space that adequate evidence and qualification cannot be given and that as a result what is actually very tentative is presented in an unfortunately dogmatic manner.

tions are related, it is essential to keep them separate in our thinking. Most of the literature on stratification has tried to answer the second question (particularly with regard to the ease or difficulty of mobility between strata) without tackling the first. The first question, however, is logically prior and, in the case of any particular individual or group, factually prior.

THE FUNCTIONAL NECESSITY OF STRATIFICATION

Curiously, however, the main functional necessity explaining the universal presence of stratification is precisely the requirement faced by any society of placing and motivating individuals in the social structure. As a functioning mechanism a society must somehow distribute its members in social positions and induce them to perform the duties of these positions. It must thus concern itself with motivation at two different levels: to instill in the proper individuals the desire to fill certain positions, and, once in these positions, the desire to perform the duties attached to them. Even though the social order may be relatively static in form, there is a continuous process of metabolism as new individuals are born into it, shift with age, and die off. Their absorption into the positional system must somehow be arranged and motivated. This is true whether the system is competitive or noncompetitive. A competitive system gives greater importance to the motivation to achieve positions, whereas a noncompetitive system gives perhaps greater importance to the motivation to perform the duties of the positions; but in any system both types of motivation are required.

If the duties associated with the various positions were all equally pleasant to the human organism, all equally important to societal survival, and all equally in need of the same ability or talent, it would make no difference who got into which positions, and the problem of social placement would be greatly reduced. But actually it does make a great deal of difference who gets into which positions, not only because some positions are inherently more agreeable than others, but also because some require special talents or training and some are functionally more important than others. Also, it is essential that the duties of the positions be performed with the diligence that their importance requires. Inevitably, then, a society must have, first, some kind of rewards that it can use as inducements, and, second, some way of distributing these rewards differentially according to positions. The rewards and their distribution become a part of the social order, and thus give rise to stratification.

One may ask what kind of rewards a society has at its disposal in distributing its personnel and securing essential services. It has, first of all, the things that contribute to sustenance and comfort. It has, second, the things that contribute to humor and diversion. And it has, finally, the things that contribute to self-respect and ego expansion. The last, because of the peculiarly social character of the self, is largely a function of the opinion of others, but it nonetheless ranks in importance with the first two. In any social system all three kinds of rewards must be dispensed differentially according to positions.

In a sense the rewards are "built into" the position. They consist in the "rights" associated with the position, plus what may be called its accompaniments or perquisites. Often the rights, and sometimes the accompaniments, are functionally related to the duties of the position. (Rights as viewed by the incumbent are usually duties as viewed by other members of the community.) However, there may be a host of subsidiary rights and perquisites that are not essential to the function of the position and have only an indirect and symbolic connection with its duties, but which still may be of considerable importance in inducing people to seek the positions and fulfil the essential duties.

If the rights and prerequisites of different positions in a society must be unequal, then the society must be stratified, because that is precisely what stratification means. Social inequality is thus an unconsciously evolved device by which societies insure that the most important positions are conscientiously filled by the most qualified persons. Hence every society, no matter how simple or complex, must differentiate persons in terms of both prestige and esteem, and must therefore possess a certain amount of institutionalized inequality.

It does not follow that the amount or type of inequality need be the same in all societies. This is largely a function of factors that will be discussed presently.

THE TWO DETERMINANTS OF POSITIONAL RANK

Granting the general function that inequality subserves, one can specify the two factors that determine the relative rank of different positions. In general those positions convey the best reward, and hence have the highest rank, which (a) have the greatest importance for the society and (b) require the greatest training or talent. The first factor concerns function and is a matter of relative significance; the second concerns means and is a matter of scarcity.

Differential Functional Importance

Actually a society does not need to reward positions in proportion to their functional importance. It merely needs to give sufficient reward to them to insure that they will be filled competently. In other words, it must see that less essential positions do not compete successfully with more essential ones. If a position is easily filled, it need not be heavily rewarded, even though important. On the other hand, if it is important but hard to fill, the reward must be high enough to get it filled anyway. Functional importance is therefore a necessary but not a sufficient cause of high rank being assigned to a position.[3]

Differential Scarcity of Personnel

Practically all positions, no matter how acquired, require some form of skill or capacity for performance. This is implicit in the very notion of position, which implies that the incumbent must, by virtue of his incumbency, accomplish certain things.

There are, ultimately, only two ways in which a person's qualifications come about: through inherent capacity or through training. Obviously, in concrete activities both are always necessary, but from a practical standpoint the scarcity may lie primarily in one or the other, as well as in both. Some positions require innate talents of such high degree that the persons who fill them are bound to be rare. In many cases, however, talent is fairly abundant in the population but the training process is so long, costly, and elaborate that relatively few can qualify. Modern medicine, for example, is within the mental capacity of most individuals, but a medical education is so burdensome and expensive that virtually none would undertake it if the position of the M.D. did not carry a reward commensurate with the sacrifice.

If the talents required for a position are abundant and the training easy, the method of acquiring the position may have little to do with its duties. There may be, in fact, a virtually accidental relationship. But if the skills required are scarce by reason of the rarity of talent or the costliness of training, the position, if functionally important, must have an attractive power that will draw the necessary skills in competition with other positions. This means, in effect, that the position must be high in the social scale—must command great prestige, high salary, ample leisure, and the like.

How Variations Are to Be Understood

Insofar as there is a difference between one system of stratification and another, it is attributable to whatever factors affect the two determinants of

3 Unfortunately, functional importance is difficult to establish. To use the position's prestige to establish it, as is often unconsciously done, constitutes circular reasoning from our point of view. There are, however, two independent clues: (a) the degree to which a position is functionally unique, there being no other positions that can perform the same function satisfactorily; (b) the degree to which other positions are dependent on the one in question. Both clues are best exemplified in organized systems of positions built around one major function. Thus, in most complex societies the religious, political, economic, and educational functions are handled by distinct structures not easily interchangeable. In addition, each structure possesses many different positions, some clearly dependent on, if not subordinate to, others. In sum, when an institutional nucleus becomes differentiated around one main function, and at the same time organizes a large portion of the population into its relationships, the *key* positions in it are of the highest functional importance. The absence of such specialization does not prove functional unimportance, for the whole society may be relatively unspecialized; but it is safe to assume that the more important functions receive the first and clearest structural differentiation.

differential reward—namely, functional importance and scarcity of personnel. Positions important in one society may not be important in another, because the conditions faced by the societies, or their degree of internal development, may be different. The same conditions, in turn, may affect the question of scarcity; for in some societies the stage of development, or the external situation, may wholly obviate the necessity of certain kinds of skill or talent. Any particular system of stratification, then, can be understood as a product of the special conditions affecting the two aforementioned grounds of differential reward.

MAJOR SOCIETAL FUNCTIONS AND STRATIFICATION

Religion

The reason why religion is necessary is apparently to be found in the fact that human society achieves its unity primarily through the possession by its members of certain ultimate values and ends in common. Although these values and ends are subjective, they influence behavior, and their integration enables the society to operate as a system. Derived neither from inherited nor from external nature, they have evolved as a part of culture by communication and moral pressure. They must, however, appear to the members of the society to have some reality, and it is the role of religious belief and ritual to supply and reinforce this appearance of reality. Through belief and ritual the common ends and values are connected with an imaginary world symbolized by concrete sacred objects, which world in turn is related in a meaningful way to the facts and trials of the individual's life. Through the worship of the sacred objects and the beings they symbolize, and the acceptance of supernatural prescriptions that are at the same time codes of behavior, a powerful control over human conduct is exercised, guiding it along lines sustaining the institutional structure and conforming to the ultimate ends and values.

If this conception of the role of religion is true, one can understand why in every known society the religious activities tend to be under the charge of particular persons, who tend thereby to enjoy greater rewards than the ordinary societal member. Certain of the rewards and special privileges may attach to only the highest religious functionaries, but others usually apply, if such exists, to the entire sacerdotal class.

Moreover, there is a peculiar relation between the duties of the religious official and the special privileges he enjoys. If the supernatural world governs the destinies of men more ultimately than does the real world, its earthly representative, the person through whom one may communicate with the supernatural, must be a powerful individual. He is a keeper of sacred tradition, a skilled performer of the ritual, and an interpreter of lore and myth. He is in such close contact with the gods that he is viewed as possessing some of their characteristics. He is, in short, a bit sacred, and hence free from some of the more vulgar necessities and controls.

It is no accident, therefore, that religious functionaries have been associated with the very highest positions of power, as in theocratic regimes. Indeed, looking at it from this point of view, one may wonder why it is that they do not get *entire* control over their societies. The factors that prevent this are worthy of note.

In the first place, the amount of technical competence necessary for the performance of religious duties is small. Scientific or artistic capacity is not required. Anyone can set himself up as enjoying an intimate relation with deities, and nobody can successfully dispute him. Therefore, the factor of scarcity of personnel does not operate in the technical sense.

One may assert, on the other hand, that religious ritual is often elaborate and religious lore abstruse, and that priestly ministrations require tact, if not intelligence. This is true, but the technical requirements of the profession are for the most part adventitious, not related to the end in the same way that science is related to air travel. The priest can never be free from competition, since the criteria of whether or not one has genuine contact with the supernatural are never strictly clear. It is this competition that debases the priestly position below what might be expected at first glance. That is why priestly prestige is highest in those societies where membership in the profession is rigidly controlled by the priestly guild itself. That is why, in part at least, elaborate devices are utilized to stress the identification of the person with his office—spectacular costume, abnormal conduct, special diet, segregated residence, celibacy, conspicuous leisure, and the like. In fact, the priest is always in danger of becoming somewhat discredited—as happens in a secularized society—because in a world of stubborn fact, ritual and sacred knowledge alone will not grow crops or build houses. Furthermore, unless he is protected by a professional guild, the priest's identification with the supernatural tends to preclude his acquisition of abundant wordly goods.

As between one society and another it seems that the highest general position awarded the priest occurs in the medieval type of social order. Here there is enough economic production to afford a surplus, which can be used to support a numerous and highly organized priesthood; and yet the populace is unlettered and therefore credulous to a high degree. Perhaps the most extreme example is to be found in the Buddhism of Tibet, but others are encountered in the Catholicism of feudal Europe, the Inca regime of Peru, the Brahminism of India, and the Mayan priesthood of Yucatan. On the other hand, if the society is so crude as to have no surplus and little differentiation, so that every priest must be also a cultivator or hunter, the separation of the priestly status from the others has hardly gone far enough for priestly prestige to mean much. When the priest actually has high prestige under these circumstances, it is because he also performs other important functions (usually political and medical).

In an extremely advanced society built on scientific technology, the priesthood tends to lose status, because sacred tradition and supernaturalism drop into the background. The ultimate values and common ends of the society tend to be expressed in less anthropomorphic ways, by officials who occupy fundamentally political, economic, or educational rather than religious positions. Nevertheless, it is easily possible for intellectuals to exaggerate the degree to which the priesthood in a presumably secular milieu has lost prestige. When the matter is closely examined the urban proletariat, as well as the rural citizenry, proves to be surprisingly god-fearing and priest-ridden. No society has become so completely secularized as to liquidate entirely the belief in transcendental ends and supernatural entities. Even in a secularized society some system must exist for the integration of ultimate values, for their ritualistic expression, and for the emotional adjustments required by disappointment, death, and disaster.

Government

Like religion, government plays a unique and indispensable part in society. But in contrast to religion, which provides integration in terms of sentiments, beliefs, and rituals, it organizes the society in terms of law and authority. Furthermore, it orients the society to the actual rather than the unseen world.

The main functions of government are, internally, the ultimate enforcement of norms, the final arbitration of conflicting interests, and the overall planning and direction of society; and externally, the handling of war and diplomacy. To carry out these functions it acts as the agent of the entire people, enjoys a monopoly of force, and controls all individuals within its territory.

Political action, by definition, implies authority. An official can command because he has authority, and the citizen must obey because he is subject to that authority. For this reason stratification is inherent in the nature of political relationships.

So clear is the power embodied in political position that political inequality is sometimes thought to comprise all inequality. But it can be shown that there are other bases of stratification, that the following controls operate in practice to keep political power from becoming complete: (a) The fact that the actual holders of political office, and especially those determining top policy, must necessarily be few in number compared to the total population. (b) The fact that the rulers represent the interest of the group rather than of themselves, and are therefore restricted in their behavior by rules and mores designed to enforce this limitation of interest. (c) The fact that the holder of political office has his authority by virtue of his office and nothing else, and therefore any special knowledge, talent, or capacity he may claim is purely incidental, so that he often has to depend upon others for technical assistance.

In view of these limiting factors, it is not strange that the rulers often have less power and prestige than a literal enumeration of their formal rights would lead one to expect.

Wealth, Property, and Labor

Every position that secures for its incumbent a livelihood is, by definition, economically rewarded. For this reason there is an economic aspect to those positions (e.g., political and religious) the main function of which is not economic. It therefore becomes convenient for the society to use unequal economic returns as a principal means of controlling the entrance of persons into positions and stimulating the performance of their duties. The amount of the economic return therefore becomes one of the main indices of social status.

It should be stressed, however, that a position does not bring power and prestige *because* it draws a high income. Rather, it draws a high income because it is functionally important and the available personnel is for one reason or another scarce. It is therefore superficial and erroneous to regard high income as the cause of a man's power and prestige, just as it is erroneous to think that a man's fever is the cause of his disease.[4]

The economic source of power and prestige is not income primarily, but the ownership of capital goods (including patents, good will, and professional reputation). Such ownership should be distinguished from the possession of consumers' goods, which is an index rather than a cause of social standing. In other words, the ownership of producers' goods is, properly speaking, a source of income like other positions, the income itself remaining an index. Even in situations where social values are widely commercialized and earnings are the readiest method of judging social position, income does not confer prestige on a position so much as it induces people to compete for the position. It is true that a man who has a high income as a result of one position may find this money helpful in climbing into another position as well, but this again reflects the effect of his initial, economically advantageous status, which exercises its influence through the medium of money.

In a system of private property in productive enterprise, an income above what an individual spends can give rise to possession of capital wealth. Presumably such possession is a reward for the proper management of one's finances originally and of the productive enterprise later. But as social differentiation becomes highly advanced and yet the institution of inheritance persists, the phenomenon of pure ownership, and reward for pure ownership, emerges. In such a case it is difficult to prove that the position is functionally important or that the scarcity involved is anything other than extrinsic and

4 The symbolic rather than intrinsic role of income in social stratification has been succinctly summarized by Talcott Parsons, "An Analytical Approach to the Theory of Social Stratification," *American Journal of Sociology* 45 (May 1940), pp. 841–862.

accidental. It is for this reason, doubtless, that the institution of private property in productive goods becomes more subject to criticism as social development proceeds toward industrialization. It is only this pure, that is, strictly legal and functionless ownership, however, that is open to attack; for some form of active ownership, whether private or public, is indispensable.

One kind of ownership of production goods consists in rights over the labor of others. The most extremely concentrated and exclusive of such rights are found in slavery, but the essential principle remains in serfdom, peonage, encomienda, and indenture. Naturally this kind of ownership has the greatest significance for stratification, because it necessarily entails an unequal relationship.

But property in capital goods inevitably introduces a compulsive element even into the nominally free contractual relationship. Indeed, in some respects the authority of the contractual employer is greater than that of the feudal landlord, inasmuch as the latter is more limited by traditional reciprocities. Even the classical economics recognized that competitors would fare unequally, but it did not pursue this fact to its necessary conclusion that, however it might be acquired, unequal control of goods and services must give unequal advantage to the parties to a contract.

Technical Knowledge

The function of finding means to single goals, without any concern with the choice between goals, is the exclusively technical sphere. The explanation of why positions requiring great technical skill receive fairly high rewards is easy to see, for it is the simplest case of the rewards being so distributed as to draw talent and motivate training. Why they seldom if ever receive the highest rewards is also clear: the importance of technical knowledge from a societal point of view is never so great as the integration of goals, which takes place on the religious, political, and economic levels. Since the technological level is concerned solely with means, a purely technical position must ultimately be subordinate to other positions that are religious, political, or economic in character.

Nevertheless, the distinction between expert and layman in any social order is fundamental, and cannot be entirely reduced to other terms. Methods of recruitment, as well as of reward, sometimes lead to the erroneous interpretation that technical positions are economically determined. Actually, however, the acquisition of knowledge and skill cannot be accomplished by purchase, although the opportunity to learn may be. The control of the avenues of training may inhere as a sort of property right in certain families or classes, giving them power and prestige in consequence. Such a situation adds an artificial scarcity to the natural scarcity of skills and talents. On the other hand, it is possible for an opposite situation to arise. The rewards of technical position may be so great that a condition of excess supply is created, leading to at least temporary devaluation of the rewards. Thus "unemployment in the learned professions" may result in a debasement of the prestige of those positions. Such adjustments and readjustments are constantly occurring in changing societies; and it is always well to bear in mind that the efficiency of a stratified structure may be affected by the modes of recruitment for positions. The social order itself, however, sets limits to the inflation or deflation of the prestige of experts: an oversupply tends to debase the rewards and discourage recruitment or produce revolution, whereas an undersupply tends to increase the rewards or weaken the society in competition with other societies.

Particular systems of stratification show a wide range with respect to the exact position of technically competent persons. This range is perhaps most evident in the degree of specialization. Extreme division of labor tends to create many specialists without high prestige since the training is short and the required native capacity relatively small. On the other hand it also tends to accentuate the high position of the true experts—scientists, engineers, and administrators—by increasing their authority relative to other functionally important positions. But the idea of a technocratic social order or a government or priesthood of engineers or social scientists neglects the limitations of knowledge and skills as a basis for performing social functions. To the extent that the social structure is truly specialized the prestige of the technical person must also be circumscribed.

VARIATION IN STRATIFIED SYSTEMS

The generalized principles of stratification here suggested form a necessary preliminary to a consideration of types of stratified systems, because it is in terms of these principles that the types must be described. This can be seen by trying to delineate types according to certain modes of variation. For instance, some of the most important modes (together with the polar types in terms of them) seem to be as follows:

(a) *The Degree of Specialization.* The degree of specialization affects the fineness and multiplicity of the gradations in power and prestige. It also influences the extent to which particular functions may be emphasized in the invidious system, since a given function cannot receive much emphasis in the hierarchy until it has achieved structural separation from the other functions. Finally, the amount of specialization influences the bases of selection. Polar types: *Specialized, Unspecialized.*

(b) *The Nature of the Functional Emphasis.* In general when emphasis is put on sacred matters, a rigidity is introduced that tends to limit specialization and hence the development of technology. In addition, a brake is placed on social mobility, and on the development of bureaucracy. When the preoccupation with the sacred is withdrawn, leaving greater scope for purely secular preoccupations, a great development, and rise in status, of economic and technological positions seemingly takes place. Curiously, a concomitant rise in political position is not likely, because it has usually been allied with the religious and stands to gain little by the decline of the latter. It is also possible for a society to emphasize family functions—as in relatively undifferentiated societies where high mortality requires high fertility and kinship forms the main basis of social organization. Main types: *Familistic, Authoritarian* (*Theocratic* or sacred, and *Totalitarian* or secular), *Capitalistic.*

(c) *The Magnitude of Invidious Differences.* What may be called the amount of social distance between positions, taking into account the entire scale, is something that should lend itself to quantitative measurement. Considerable differences apparently exist between different societies in this regard, and also between parts of the same society. Polar types: *Equalitarian, Inequalitarian.*

(d) *The Degree of Opportunity.* The familiar question of the amount of mobility is different from the question of the comparative equality or inequality of rewards posed above, because the two criteria may vary independently up to a point. For instance, the tremendous divergences in monetary income in the United States are far greater than those found in primitive societies, yet the equality of opportunity to move from one rung to the other in the social scale may also be greater in the United States than in a hereditary tribal kingdom. Polar types: *Mobile* (open), *Immobile* (closed).

(e) *The Degree of Stratum Solidarity.* Again, the degree of "class solidarity" (or the presence of specific organizations to promote class interests) may vary to some extent independently of the other criteria, and hence is an important principle in classifying systems of stratification. Polar types: *Class organized, Class unorganized.*

EXTERNAL CONDITIONS

What state any particular system of stratification is in with reference to each of these modes of variation depends on two things: (1) its state with reference to the other ranges of variation, and (2) the conditions outside the system of stratification which nevertheless influence that system. Among the latter are the following:

(a) *The Stage of Cultural Development.* As the cultural heritage grows, increased specialization becomes necessary, which in turn contributes to the enhancement of mobility, a decline of stratum solidarity, and a change of functional emphasis.

(b) *Situation with Respect to Other Societies.* The presence or absence of open conflict with other societies, of free trade relations or cultural diffusion, all influence the class structure to some extent. A chronic state of warfare tends to place emphasis upon the military functions, especially when the opponents are more or less equal. Free trade, on the other hand, strengthens the hand of the trader at the expense of the warrior and priest. Free movement of ideas generally has an equalitarian effect. Migration and conquest create special circumstances.

(c) *Size of the Society*. A small society limits the degree to which functional specialization can go, the degree of segregation of different strata, and the magnitude of inequality.

COMPOSITE TYPES

Much of the literature on stratification has attempted to classify concrete systems into a certain number of types. This task is deceptively simple, however, and should come at the end of an analysis of elements and principles, rather than at the beginning. If the preceding discussion has any validity, it indicates that there are a number of modes of variation between different systems, and that any one system is a composite of the society's status with reference to all these modes of variation. The danger of trying to classify whole societies under such rubrics as *caste, feudal,* or *open class* is that one or two criteria are selected and others ignored, the result being an unsatisfactory solution to the problem posed. The present discussion has been offered as a possible approach to the more systematic classification of composite types.

7

The Nature of Distributive Systems

Gerhard E. Lenski

FUNCTIONALISTS AND CONFLICT THEORISTS

Most modern theories of inequality fall into one or the other of two major categories. Those which stem from the conservative tradition are usually referred to as "functionalist" theories. Those which have their roots in the radical tradition are commonly labeled "conflict" theories.

Among the leading functionalist theorists of the present day, at least two have spelled out their views on inequality and stratification in some detail. These are Talcott Parsons and his former student, Kingsley Davis. Both approach the problem of inequality from the perspective of society at large, seeing it as a necessary feature of any properly functioning human society. Davis summed up the functionalist approach in a single sentence when he wrote: "Social inequality is thus an unconsciously evolved device by which societies insure that the most important positions are conscientiously filled by the most qualified persons." [1] This is the essence of the functionalist position: stratification arises basically out of the needs of societies, not out of the needs or desires of individuals.

Neither Parsons nor Davis says that all of the characteristics of any given system of stratification arise in response to societal needs. Both concede that other factors operate in the real world to modify systems of inequality to some degree. However, judging from their failure to pursue this aspect of the problem, neither considers such factors to be of major importance.

Davis argues that systems of stratification arise in response to two specific needs common to every human society. First, there is the need to instill in the abler members the motivation to occupy important and difficult positions

[1] Kingsley Davis, *Human Society* (New York: Macmillan, 1949), p. 367.

which require greater than average ability. Second, society must motivate such men, once they are in these positions, to perform the duties attached to them. Hence, it must provide them with greater rewards.

Davis cites two factors as the major determinants of the magnitude of the rewards attached to positions: (1) their functional importance for the society and (2) the relative scarcity of qualified personnel. Positions which are extremely important and which suffer from a shortage of qualified personnel receive the highest rewards. Those which are unimportant and for which there is an abundance of qualified personnel receive minimal rewards. Since all positions can never be of equal importance, nor all men equally qualified for the more responsible positions, inequality is inevitable. Not only is it inevitable, it is necessarily beneficial to everyone, since the survival and well-being of every individual is contingent on the survival and well-being of society.

Parsons' approach to the subject differs more in form than in substance. He starts from the assumption that in every human society there are certain shared values. Since values arise out of the needs of society and since the basic needs of all societies are more or less similar, these values tend to be similar the world over. What differs from one society to the next is the relative ranking of these values. One society may value efficiency more highly than stability, while another may reverse the order, but every society is obliged to value both efficiency and stability to some degree.

The system of stratification in any society is essentially an expression of the value system of that society. The rewards which men and positions enjoy are a function of the degree to which their qualities, performances, and possessions measure up to the standards set by their society. Since men necessarily differ in these respects, inequality is inevitable.[2]

By contrast with the functionalists, conflict theorists approach the problem of social inequality from the standpoint of the various individuals and subgroups within society.[3] *Their* needs and desires, rather than the needs of society as a whole, provide the basic postulates for this school of theorists. The difference between the two schools can be seen most clearly in their members' approach to the phenomenon of power. In reviewing C. Wright Mills's book, *The Power Elite,* Parsons charged: "The essential point is that, to Mills, power is not a facility for the performance of function in and on behalf of the

[2] For the chief statement of Parsons' views on stratification, see "A Revised Analytical Approach to the Theory of Social Stratification," in *Class, Status and Power: A Reader in Social Stratification,* eds. Reinhard Bendix and S. M. Lipset (New York: Free Press, 1953), pp. 92–128.

[3] Labels can sometimes be misleading when applied to groups of scholars, and this one is no exception. I do not include under the heading of conflict theorists writers such as Lewis Coser, author of *The Functions of Social Conflict* (New York: Free Press, 1956). Though this volume is focused on conflict, its basic purpose is to show how conflict serves society as a whole. In short, the underlying theoretical orientation is functionalist.

society as a system, but is interpreted exclusively as a facility for getting what one group, the holders of power, wants by preventing another group, the 'outs,' from getting what it wants." [4]

Conflict theorists, as their name suggests, see social inequality as arising out of the struggle for valued goods and services in short supply. Where the functionalists emphasize the common interests shared by the members of a society, conflict theorists emphasize the interests which divide. Where functionalists stress the common advantages which accrue from social relationships, conflict theorists emphasize the element of domination and exploitation. Where functionalists emphasize consensus as the basis of social unity, conflict theorists emphasize coercion. Where functionalists see human societies as social systems, conflict theorists see them as stages on which struggles for power and privilege take place. . . .

THE EMERGING SYNTHESIS

A third approach to the subject of social inequality is already becoming evident, an approach which slowly but surely is laying the foundation of what in Hegelian terms would be called the "synthesis." Like the Hegelian synthesis it integrates the valid insights of thesis and antithesis by approaching the problem on a different level. Whereas both thesis and antithesis are essentially *normative* theories of inequality, i.e., primarily concerned with moral evaluation and the question of justice, the synthesis is essentially *analytical,* i.e., concerned with empirical relationships and their causes. Whereas both thesis and antithesis rely on logic and isolated illustrations as methods of validating propositions, the synthesis relies on the systematic mobilization of empirical data. In short, *the synthesis is largely the result of the modern application of the scientific method to the study of the age-old problem of human inequality. . . .*

The chief objective of this chapter is to set forth certain postulates about the nature of man and society which form the foundation for the emerging synthesis. Some are drawn from the conservative tradition, some from the radical, and some from neither. No attempt will be made to give a total view of either man or society. Rather, attention will be concentrated on those aspects of both which are most relevant to the theory of distribution.

THE NATURE OF MAN

The starting point in every sociological discussion of the nature of man is the deceptively simple assertion that *man is a social being obliged by nature*

[4] Talcott Parsons, "The Distribution of Power in American Society," *World Politics* 10 (October 1957), p. 139.

to live with others as a member of society. On this proposition at least, radicals and conservatives agree, and this serves as the *first postulate* in our general theory.

To say that man is a social being is not to deny that a few individuals withdraw from society and live as hermits. The human race could not survive on this basis, however, since its chief weapon in the struggle for existence has always been culture, and culture is uniquely a social product. Social life is essential not only for the survival of the species but also for the maximum satisfaction of human needs and desires. Through cooperative activity men can satisfy many needs and desires which could never be met otherwise and can satisfy most other needs much more efficiently, i.e., with greater return for less effort or other investment.

To say that man is a social being is also to say that the society into which he is born shapes his character and personality in ways over which he has no control and of which he is often unaware. . . .

If our first postulate is relatively noncontroversial, the same cannot be said of the second. It takes us directly into the realm of one of the bitterest disputes between radicals and conservatives—the dispute concerning the origin of evil. As noted in the last chapter, the radical view of man and society steadily gained in popularity and intellectual respectability after the English revolution of the seventeenth century. In an era of European growth and expansion, this optimistic view, which postulated society as the source of evil, found increasing acceptance, especially among intellectuals. Since the rise of Nazism and the outbreak of World War II, however, the trend has been halted and, for the first time in roughly three centuries, the pendulum seems to be moving in the opposite direction. On every hand the evidence mounts that the evil in men's actions is rooted more deeply than radical theorists had supposed. Neither the French Revolution nor the Russian produced the utopias that were promised despite revolutionary institutional change.[5] Though the patterns of men's lives have been changed greatly by the social and technological revolutions of modern times, egoism, selfishness, and cruelty continue to loom large.

Paralleling the argument from modern history is that from contemporary psychology, where current theory and research undermine our faith in the natural goodness of man no less than do political events. Recent research reveals the human infant as an extremely self-centered creature, motivated solely by his own needs and desires. If we rid ourselves of the romantic aura which surrounds babies in our society, we discover that they are totally

[5] For example, Marxist theory is a radical theory critical of social institutions only so long as Marxists are out of power. Once they gain power, as in Russia and China, the profoundly conservative elements in this theory come to the fore. The drastic shift in ideological orientation required of Communists in the era following the 1917 Revolution was undoubtedly one reason for the frequent purges of Old Bolsheviks.

involved in reducing the various tensions created by their biological nature and the environment. Their early actions are simply trial-and-error probings to discover methods of reducing or relieving these tensions.

In time, of course, the normal child learns to take the wishes of others into account. But this does not mean that he is any less motivated to maximize his own satisfactions. Rather, it means that he has learned that the attainment of his own goals is inextricably linked with the interests of others. . . .

Children's games afford far more insights into the nature of social organization than is usually recognized. In particular, they demonstrate the process by which institutions with their elements of cooperation and morality and their concepts of right and justice can emerge from the actions of an originally unorganized aggregation of individuals each selfishly seeking to maximize his own personal satisfactions. To achieve the maximization individuals are forced to work (and play) together, but they find that this can be rewarding only if the activity takes place within the framework of a system of rules which, above all else, protects the cooperative activity itself. This can only be done if certain basic rights are guaranteed to all of the essential participants; e.g., each boy is guaranteed his turn at bat. This may seem to entail some sacrifice on the part of the stronger or abler participants, but really it does not, since the only alternative is the cessation of the cooperative activity and all its benefits. Thus, for them, as for the other participants, adherence to the rules can be accounted for merely as a form of *enlightened self-interest*. . . .

Lest it seem that all human action is motivated solely by self-interest, it must be affirmed that some is clearly motivated by a genuine concern for others, with no overtones of self-interest. Clearly there are forces in human experience which are capable of evoking the response of *unselfish or altruistic love*.[6] However, since in most persons this pattern of response has only a limited development, altruistic action is most likely to occur in the minor events of daily life where little is at stake. Apparently many men develop a genuine desire to be generous and kind in their dealings with others but find it "impossible" to act in this way when much is at stake. Thus altruistic action is concentrated on the level of lesser events and decisions, and is infrequent on the level of major social decisions. In fact, it appears that one can state as a generalization that *the frequency of altruistic action varies inversely with the magnitude of the values involved.*

This is not to say that men are immoral when major values are at stake. Rather, it points to the need to differentiate between two kinds of morality, *pragmatic morality* and *ideal morality*. Pragmatic morality is the basis of all popular moral codes, and is based on the recognition that men need one another, and therefore condemns many kinds of harmful actions, especially those which threaten to undermine the social order. Ideal morality, by contrast, has

[6] Certain religious ideologies, in combination with the personal experience and recognition of undeserved love, seem to be the chief sources of this.

never been accepted as the basis of any popular moral code, since it not only condemns harmful actions but requires that men love others as they love themselves and without regard to possible rewards.

This does not mean that altruism, or unselfish love, is of little or no importance. It is extremely important from both the psychological and moral standpoints, and human existence would be much poorer and harsher if it were absent. It is not, however, a major determinant of the distribution of power and privilege.

Thus, when one surveys the human scene, one is forced to conclude that *when men are confronted with important decisions where they are obliged to choose between their own, or their group's, interests and the interests of others, they nearly always choose the former*—though often seeking to hide this fact from themselves and others. This is the *second postulate* in our theory. As is evident, it leans far in the direction of the conservative position with its skeptical view of the innate goodness of man. . . .

The *third postulate* in our theory pertains to the objects of men's strivings. Some, such as the air we breathe, are readily available to all, but most are not. *Most are in short supply*—that is, the demand for them exceeds the available supply.

This is a normal feature of the world of nature. Though we often speak of nature's bounty, the fact remains that all living things have a reproductive capacity which, in view of the limited supply of food and other resources, makes it inevitable that large numbers will die well before the end of their normal life span and most of the others live close to the margin of subsistence.

To some extent man has been able to free himself from these difficulties. Thousands of years ago he learned to increase his food supply and, more recently, he has learned to control reproduction. Yet while man enjoys certain advantages when compared with other living things, he also suffers from certain disadvantages. Unlike the various plants and animals, *man has an insatiable appetite for goods and services.* No matter how much he produces and consumes, he always desires more. This is true chiefly because the goods and services he consumes have a *status value* as well as a utilitarian value. If automobiles were simply a means of transportation, a society able to control its reproduction could eventually satisfy this demand. However, automobiles are also status symbols; hence there is no limit to the demand for their improvement and for the goods and services utilized in their production. The very nature of status striving makes it inevitable that the demand will exceed the supply: those of lower status constantly strive to equal those of higher status and those of higher status always seek to preserve the difference. Given these conditions, satiation is impossible no matter how much man increases production or restricts population increase.

If our first three postulates are correct, that is, if man is a social being, and if most of his important actions are motivated by self-interest or partisan group interest, and if many or most of the objects of his striving are in short supply, then it follows logically that *a struggle for rewards will be present in every human society.* This struggle need not always assume violent forms. On the contrary, it can be carried on within the framework of some system of rules. However, the absence of violence does not mean that the struggle is any less real or serious for the parties involved.

Before concluding this portion of our discussion, two further postulates should be entered into the record. The first of these, and fourth in our series, is that *men are unequally endowed by nature with the attributes necessary to carry on these struggles.* Some are born with serious physical handicaps which severely limit their chances. Others are handicapped in less obvious ways, such as by poor physical coordination, mild brain damage, lack of stamina, or even ugliness.

These inequalities in natural endowment are not the primary source of social inequality. But they are important enough to provide some foundation for the ancient conservative thesis that nature is the source of social inequality.

Fifth, and finally, for the present, we postulate that *man tends to be a creature of habit and powerfully influenced by the social counterpart of habit, namely, custom.* William James once called habit "the enormous flywheel of society" and this still seems a fair characterization since habit, like the flywheel, brings the powerful factor of inertia into play in human affairs. The same is true of custom. From the standpoint of the distributive process both habit and custom are tremendously important since they tend to stabilize existing systems of distribution by causing men to accept and take for granted even those distributive arrangements which work to their disadvantage and are not essential. Thus such arrangements prove far more durable and stable than one would expect and persist far longer than a careful analysis of the pattern itself would otherwise indicate.

THE NATURE OF SOCIETY

Building on this view of man, it is now possible to turn to the more difficult problem of the nature of human societies. . . . In the first place, if there is no such thing as a perfect social system, we should stop spinning theories which postulate their existence and direct our energies toward the building of theories which explicitly assume that all human organizations are *imperfect systems.*[7] Second, social theorists (and researchers too) should stop trying to find *social* utility in all the varied behavior patterns of men; they should recognize that many established patterns of action are thoroughly antisocial and contribute

[7] Hobbes saw this clearly as his comparison of man with the bees and ants indicates. Of the latter he wrote, "among these creatures the common good differs not from the private; and being by nature inclined to the private, they procure thereby the common benefit. But man, whose joy consists in comparing himself with other men, can relish nothing but what is eminent." Thomas Hobbes, *Leviathan* (New York: Liberal Arts, 1958), Chap. 17.

nothing to the general good. Third, we should expect to find *both* cooperation and conflict as continuous and normal features of human life and should stop viewing conflict as a pathological or abnormal condition, as is often done in contemporary functionalist theory. Fourth, we should devote more attention to the causes and consequences of variations in the degree of group integration. Finally, we must learn to think of distributive systems as reflecting *simultaneously* system needs and unit needs, with each often subverting the other. . . .

Logically, it is not possible for the interests of society to be compatible with the interests of all its members if the interests of these members are themselves incompatible to any appreciable degree. Yet, as we have seen, this is precisely the case. Under such conditions, the most that is possible is that the interests of society are consistent with the interests of *some* of its members. As we shall see later, there is good reason to believe that in many societies throughout history the interests of only a small minority of the members were significantly identified with the interests of the total society.

The conflict between societal interests and individual interests can be shown in yet another way. From the standpoint of society as a whole, it is desirable that the key positions be filled by the best qualified men. From the standpoint of the individual motivated by self-interest, it is usually desirable that he fill one of these positions himself. In most instances, the interests of the individual will be subversive of the interests of the society and vice versa.

Conservative theorists have often argued that occupancy of the key positions in a society is evidence of superior ability and therefore that the actions of the occupants benefit all. However, critics reply, "Superior ability at what? Picking one's parents? Force? Deceit?" Unhappily, these have often been major factors in the acquisition of key positions. The circularity in the logic of the conservative defense is of such a nature as to render it meaningless.

INDIVIDUAL INTERESTS: THEIR NATURE

Up to this point we have frequently referred to societal interests and individual interests, but without ever stating precisely what either is. On first consideration, it may seem that the nature of these interests is so obvious that no discussion is needed. When one reflects on these matters, however, certain difficulties are encountered, especially with respect to the concept of societal interests.

One of the great temptations in this area is to play God and identify these interests with what one feels they ought to be, or what they "really" are. This is, in effect, the practice of the Marxists and other ideologues who know what is good for an individual or a society even better than the persons involved. Such an approach may be fruitful politically, but not scientifically.

If we reject this deductive approach, we are forced back on induction. Two alternatives present themselves: (1) inductions based on *statements* made by the individual or group; (2) inductions based on *inferences from the actions* of the individual or group. Of these two, the latter seems wiser for two reasons. First, both individuals and groups often have reasons for misrepresenting their true interests: dissimulation is often profitable. Second, since the work of Freud, we cannot ignore the role of the subconscious in human behavior. Men's actions are often motivated by desires and goals of which they are only dimly aware. For both reasons it is wiser to base our judgments of the interests which prompt men's actions on what they do rather than on what they say. . . .

To begin with, it is clear that the great majority of men have always accorded *survival* the highest priority. Though there have been exceptions, such as religious and political martyrs and heroic warriors, most men have not shared their values. . . .

The fact that survival is usually given the highest priority has far-reaching implications for the social life of man. First of all, *it causes might or force to be the most effective deterrent and also the supreme sanction in human affairs.* It is no coincidence that violence is the last court of appeal in human conflicts. As will become evident in later chapters, this is a matter of great importance for our theory of distribution.

Because most men value survival so highly, anything which facilitates survival is also valued highly. Practically, this means that food and other goods and services which provide *sustenance* are highly valued, especially since they are normally in short supply.

After survival, it is more difficult to say which is man's most important goal. Probably the two chief contenders are *health* and *status,* or *prestige.* Little needs to be said concerning health since the value men attach to it is evident in every society. Everywhere men are prepared to pay dearly for the sake of health and freely admit it.

Status, or prestige, is a different matter. Men often deny that they are greatly concerned with it. In our own society, for example, few people will admit to others, or even to themselves, that they value status highly. When we examine their actions, however, the concern for status quickly becomes evident. It influences almost every kind of decision from the choice of a car to the choice of a spouse. Fear of the loss of status, or honor, is one of the few motives that can make men lay down their lives on the field of battle. . . .

SOCIETAL INTERESTS: THEIR NATURE

At the risk of oversimplification, one may say that the coordinated actions of societies are directed largely toward one or the other of two basic goals. First and foremost, they are directed toward *the maintenance of the political status quo within the group.* Since perfect stability or equilibrium is impossible, this goal might better be described as *the minimization of the rate of internal political change.* This manifests itself in various ways, but particularly in the development of the machinery of state and other agencies and instruments of social control, in the great concern for law and order which every society's leaders express, and in the cultivation of political ideologies which justify the *status quo.* It is also seen in the universal concern of societies and their leaders with defense against foreign aggression.

The second basic goal of societies is *the maximization of production and the resources on which production depends.* Sometimes this has been sought by efforts to promote technological advance; more often it has been through war and conquest.

Neither of these two basic goals receives priority in every society. In some, efforts to minimize political change seem to take preference over efforts to maximize production, while in others the reverse is true. In general it appears that *the goal of maximizing production has priority in relatively unstratified societies and that the goal of minimizing political change has priority in societies in which power and privilege are monopolized by a few.* In societies in which neither of these conditions exists, the two goals seem to be given roughly equal priority. . . .

TWO LAWS OF DISTRIBUTION

When one seeks to build a theory of distribution on the postulates about the nature of man and society set forth in the last chapter, one soon discovers that these lead to a curious, but important, *dualism.* If those postulates are sound, one would predict that almost all the products of men's labors will be distributed on the basis of two seemingly contradictory principles, *need* and *power.*

In our discussion of the nature of man, it was postulated that where important decisions are involved, most human action is motivated either by self-interest or by partisan group interests. This suggests that power alone governs the distribution of rewards. This cannot be the case, however, since we also postulated that most of these essentially selfish interests can be satisfied only by the establishment of cooperative relations with others. Cooperation is absolutely essential both for survival and for the efficient attainment of most other goals. In other words, men's selfish interests compel them to remain members of society and to share in the division of labor.

If these two postulates are correct, then it follows that *men will share the product of their labors to the extent required to insure the survival and continued productivity of those others whose actions are necessary or beneficial to themselves.* This might well be called the first law of distribution, since the survival of mankind as a species depends on compliance with it.

This first law, however, does not cover the entire problem. It says nothing about how any *surplus,* i.e., goods and services over and above the minimum required to keep producers alive and productive, which men may be able to produce will be distributed. This leads to what may be called the second law of distribution. If we assume that in important decisions human action is motivated almost entirely by self-interest or partisan group interests, and if we assume that many of the things men most desire are in short supply, then, as noted before, this surplus will inevitably give rise to conflicts and struggles aimed at its control. If, following Weber, we define power as the probability of persons or groups carrying out their will even when opposed by others,[8] then it follows that *power will determine the distribution of nearly all of the surplus possessed by a society.* The qualification "nearly all" takes account of the very limited influence of altruistic action which our earlier analysis of the nature of man leads us to expect.

This second law points the way to another very important relationship, that between our two chief variables, power and privilege. If privilege is defined as possession or control of a portion of the surplus produced by a society, then it follows that *privilege is largely a function of power, and to a very limited degree, a function of altruism.* This means that to explain most of the distribution of privilege in a society, we have but to determine the distribution of power.

To state the matter this way suggests that the task of explaining the distribution of privilege is simple. Unfortunately, this is not the case since there are many forms of power and they spring from many sources. Nevertheless, the establishment of this key relationship reduces the problem to more manageable proportions, since it concentrates attention on one key variable, power. Thus if we can establish the pattern of its distribution in a given society, we have largely established the pattern for the distribution of privilege, and if we can discover the causes of a given distribution of power we have also discovered the causes of the distribution of privilege linked with it.

To put the matter this way is to invite the question of how the third basic element in every distributive system, *prestige,* is related to power and privilege. It would be nice if one could say that prestige is a simple function of privilege, but unfortunately this does not seem to be the case. Without going into a complex analysis of the matter at this point, the best that can be said is that empirical evidence strongly suggests that *prestige is largely, though not solely, a function of power and privilege, at least in those societies where there is a substantial surplus.*[9] If this is true, it follows that even though the

[8] See Max Weber, *The Theory of Social and Economic Organization,* trans. A. M. Henderson and Talcott Parsons (New York: Free Press, 1947), p. 152, or Max Weber, *From Max Weber: Essays in Sociology,* trans. H. H. Gerth and C. Wright Mills (Fair Lawn, N.J.: Oxford University Press, 1946), p. 180.

[9] I have not attempted to establish this generalization by deductive logic since this would be a major undertaking requiring the introduction of new postulates and would divert the analysis from its primary task. For the same reason I have not attempted to deal with prestige in other parts of this volume except incidentally.

subject of prestige is not often mentioned in this volume, its pattern of distribution and its causes can largely be deduced from discussion of the distribution of power and privilege and their causes in those societies where there is an appreciable surplus. . . .

Power is the key variable in the triad from the causal and explanatory standpoint. Hence, it is with this variable that we shall be primarily concerned in the analysis which follows.

THE VARIABLE ASPECTS OF DISTRIBUTIVE SYSTEMS

As the statement of the two laws indicates, the second law does not have any effect on the distributive process until the conditions specified in the first have been satisfied. Until the necessities of life have been made available to enough productive, mutually interdependent members of the group, there is no surplus to be fought over and distributed on the basis of power. Thus, as a first hypothesis we would be led to predict that *in the simplest societies, or those which are technologically most primitive, the goods and services available will be distributed wholly, or largely, on the basis of need.*

As the productivity of societies increases, the possibility of producing a surplus steadily increases, though it should be noted that the existence of a surplus is not a function of technological advance alone. Even though we cannot say that the surplus available to a society increases proportionately with advances in the level of technology, such advances increase the probability that there will be a surplus and also that there will be a sizable surplus. Hence, as a second hypothesis we are led to predict that *with technological advance, an increasing proportion of the goods and services available to a society will be distributed on the basis of power.* . . . If the first two laws of distribution and the two hypotheses based on them are valid, then *the nature of distributive systems will vary greatly, depending on the degree of technological advance in the societies involved.* The variations should be every bit as great as those which differentiate markets where perfect competition prevails from those where imperfect competition holds sway. . . .

No two societies are identical from the technological standpoint, and their classification into technological types is based on similarities (or identity) with respect to certain fundamental characteristics and ignores secondary differences. If primary differences in technology cause major differences in distributive systems, *one would expect these secondary differences in technology to generate lesser differences in distributive systems.* Thus, one would expect considerable differences between a society in the first stages of industrialization and one which is highly industrialized, just as one would expect differences between a hunting and gathering society with no alternative mode of food production and one which has some rudimentary forms of horticulture to supplement its diet. . . .

FORCE AND ITS TRANSFORMATION

Of the two principles which govern the distributive process, need and power, the first is relatively simple and poses few problems of great importance or difficulty. Unhappily, the same cannot be said of the second. Of all the concepts used by sociologists, few are the source of more confusion and misunderstanding than power. Hence it is necessary to spell out in some detail the nature of this concept and how it functions in the distributive process.

As a starting point, it may be well to return briefly to one of the postulates introduced in the last chapter. There it was assumed that survival is the chief goal of the great majority of men. If this is so, then it follows that *the ability to take life is the most effective form of power.* In other words, more men will respond readily to the threat of the use of *force* than to any other. In effect, it constitutes the final court of appeals in human affairs; there is no appeal from force in a given situation except the exercise of superior force. Hence force stands in the same relationship to other forms of power as trumps to the other suits in the game of bridge, and those who can exercise the greatest force are like those who control trumps.

This fact has been recognized by countless observers of the human scene in every age. As Pascal put it, "Not being able to make that which is just strong, man has made that which is strong just." Cicero made the same point when he said, "Laws are dumb in the midst of arms," and Hobbes asserted that "Covenants without the sword are but words, and of no strength to secure a man at all. . . ."

Though force is the most effective instrument for seizing power in a society, and though it always remains the foundation of any system of inequality, it is not the most effective instrument for retaining and exploiting a position of power and deriving the maximum benefits from it. Therefore, regardless of the objectives of a new regime, once organized opposition has been destroyed it is to its advantage to make increasing use of other techniques and instruments of control, and to allow force to recede into the background to be used only when other techniques fail.

If the new elite has materialistic goals and is concerned solely with self-aggrandizement, it soon discovers that the rule of might is both inefficient and costly. So long as it relies on force, much of the profit is consumed by the costs of coercion. If the population obeys only out of fear of physical violence, a large portion of the time, energy, and wealth of the elite are invariably consumed in the effort to keep it under control and separate the producers from the product of their labors. Even worse, honor, which normally ranks high in the scale of human values, is denied to those who rule by force alone. . . .[10]

[10] For a good discussion of the limitations of rule by force, see Robert Dahl and Charles

Thus *those who seize power by force find it advantageous to legitimize their rule once effective organized opposition is eliminated.* Force can no longer continue to play the role it did. It can no longer function as the private resource of a special segment of the population. Rather it must be transformed into a public resource used in the defense of law and order. . . .

There are various means by which this transformation can be effected. To begin with, by virtue of its coercive power, a new elite is in a good position to rewrite the law of the land as it sees fit. This affords them a unique opportunity, since by its very nature law is identified with justice and the rule of right. Since legal statutes are stated in general and impersonal terms, they appear to support abstract principles of justice rather than the special interests of particular men or classes of men. The fact that laws exist prior to the events to which they are applied suggests an objective impartiality which also contributes to their acceptance. Yet laws can always be written in such a way that they favor some particular segment of society. Anatole France saw this clearly when he wrote, "The law in its majestic equality forbids the rich as well as the poor to sleep under bridges, to beg in the street, and to steal bread. . . ."

Institutions which shape public opinion serve as a second instrument for legitimizing the position of new elites. Through the use of a combination of inducements and threats, educational and religious institutions, together with the mass media and other molders of public opinion, can usually be transformed into instruments of propaganda for the new regime. A determined and intelligent elite working through them can usually surround itself with an aura of legitimacy within a few months or years.

The concept of "propaganda," or the manipulation of consensus, is an integral element in the synthetic theory of stratification. A recognition of this phenomenon and the special role it plays in the distributive process enables us to avoid the impasse which has driven Dahrendorf and others to despair of ever reconciling the conservative and radical traditions. Consensus and coercion are more closely related than those who preach the Janus-headed character of society would have us believe. *Coercive power can often be used to create a new consensus. . . .*

THE MIDDLE CLASSES AND THE INSTITUTIONALIZATION OF POWER

As historians and students of politics have long recognized, revolutions are the work of small minorities. Hence, when the revolution is over, the new elite is obliged to employ the services of others to achieve their objectives.

Lindblom, *Politics, Economics, and Welfare* (New York: Harper & Row, 1953), pp. 107–109. See also Karl A. Wittfogel, *Oriental Despotism: A Comparative Study of Total Power* (New Haven, Conn.: Yale University Press, 1957), Chap. 4.

Only in this way can they hope to bring the surplus of the society effectively under their control and effect its transformation into the kinds of goods and services they desire.

Fortunately for the new elite, their position of power provides them with the necessary resources for securing the help they need. The portion of the economic surplus they already control can be used to hire an army of technicians and specialists who can bring still more of the surplus under control. This can then be used to hire others to transform the raw materials into fine homes, beautiful clothes, works of art, public monuments, personal services, and the thousand and one things that men of power and privilege desire, or, in the case of an ideological elite, to staff the institutions which will transform society.

This process leads to the creation, extension, or perpetuation of a middle stratum of technicians and specialists working in the service of the elite. These include public officials, craftsmen, artists, servants, merchants, soldiers, priests, and scholars. The chief task of the officials is to locate the economic surplus and separate it from its producers. As Shaw's Caesar put it when challenged to explain his great interest in Egyptian taxes, "My friend, taxes are the chief business of a conqueror of the world." Craftsmen and artists are necessary to transform the surplus into the kinds of goods and services desired by the elite. Merchants facilitate the movement of goods to the places where they are wanted by those with the means to purchase them. Personal servants provide the innumerable services which men of rank cannot provide for themselves. Priests and scholars contribute to the maintenance of public order and, when they fail, the military can take over. In short, a complex apparatus is brought into being, the primary function of which is to insure the elite's continued control over the economic surplus and its transformation into the varied kinds of goods and services the elite desires.

As should be evident, those in the employ of the elite are rewarded in proportion to the value of their services to the elite, and the scarcity of the supply of replacements. Contrary to such functionalist theorists as Kingsley Davis and Wilbert Moore, these roles are not rewarded in proportion to their contribution to the common good.[11] It is the needs of the elite, not the needs of the total society, which determine the demand curve for such services. *The distribution of rewards in a society is a function of the distribution of power, not of system needs.* This is inevitable in such imperfect systems as human societies.

When a political cycle survives for an appreciable period of time, the nature of the middle classes and their relation to the political elite gradually changes. In eras of constitutional rule there is a tendency for those classes to arrogate to themselves certain of the powers and privileges of the elite. This

[11] Kingsley Davis and Wilbert Moore, "Some Principles of Stratification," *American Sociological Review* 10 (1945), pp. 242–249.

is not difficult since it is their normal function to act on behalf of the elite. Powers delegated often become powers lost; once lost they are not easily recovered. Thus it appears that *the greater the degree of constitutionalism in a society, the less the middle classes function merely as agents of the elite and the greater their personal independence, autonomy, and security.* This is an important development and we shall have frequent occasion to refer to it in later pages. However, it should not be allowed to obscure the more basic relation between the middle classes and the elite which continues even in an era of constitutionalism. . . .

REVERSAL OF A BASIC TREND

Of all the types of societies we have examined, none illustrates better than the industrial, the difficulties and limitations of a *purely* deductive and highly general approach to stratification theory. Given the vastly increased productivity of this type of society and the greatly enlarged powers of industrial states, nothing would be more logical than to predict inequalities in power and privilege even greater than those found in agrarian societies. However, even a limited survey of the contemporary scene suggests that this is not the case, and a more intensive examination confirms this impression. If anything, inequalities in power and privilege seem usually somewhat *less* pronounced in mature industrial societies than in agrarian. In short, *the appearance of mature industrial societies marks the first significant reversal in the age-old evolutionary trend toward ever increasing inequality.*

The evidence supporting these assertions takes several basic forms. To begin with, a comparison of the political systems of agrarian and industrial societies makes it clear that political power is much more concentrated in the former. In agrarian societies, the powers of government were nearly always vested in the hands of the few; the great majority were *wholly excluded* from the political process. In industrial societies this is a minority pattern, limited only to those societies in the earlier stages of industrialization and to those ruled by totalitarian parties. In the majority of industrial societies, all adult citizens not only enjoy voting privileges but, far more important, the right to organize politically to promote their own special interests or beliefs, even when these are in opposition to the interests or beliefs of those in power.[12] While this does not mean that all inequalities in political power are eliminated or the democratic millennium ushered in, it does mean a significant reduction in political inequality and a substantial diffusion of political power, both of which are readily evident when these societies are compared with agrarian. This can be seen most clearly in the case of the Scandinavian democracies,

[12] In some countries the right of opposition is limited to those who are willing to support democratic procedures, with the result that Communist and Fascist parties are excluded by law, but even this limitation is absent in the majority of democratic nations.

where Socialist Parties have been the dominant political force in recent decades, but the pattern is also evident in countries such as the United States and France, where the political influence of the lower classes has not been nearly so great. It should also be noted that even in some of those industrial societies where democracy was not permitted, as in post-Stalinist Russia or Perón's Argentina, the political elite used much of its power to promote programs designed to benefit the lower classes, a practice virtually unknown in agrarian societies.

A second indication of declining inequalities can be found in data on the distribution of income. Earlier we saw evidence which indicated that in agrarian societies the top 1 or 2 percent of the population usually received *not less than half* of the total income of the nation.[13] In the case of industrial societies the comparable figure is substantially less. According to official governmental reports, the top 2 percent of the population of democratic nations receives about 10 percent of the total personal cash income after taxes. For example, British figures for 1954 indicate that the top 2 percent received 8.5 percent of the total income after taxes; Swedish figures for 1950 show the top 1.8 percent received 9.9 percent before taxes; Danish figures for 1949 show the top 1.1 percent received 10.3 percent *before taxes;* United States figures for 1958 show the top 1.3 percent received 8.1 percent, and the top 2.3 percent received 11.6 percent, *before taxes. . . .*[14]

CAUSES OF THE REVERSAL

From the theoretical standpoint, the decline in political and economic inequality associated with the emergence of industrial societies is extremely important. This constitutes a reversal in a major historical trend, and the reasons for this reversal are by no means obvious. On the contrary, given the increased productivity of industrial societies and the growth in the powers of the state, one would normally predict even greater inequality than in agrarian societies. The fact that the opposite occurred indicates either that one or more of the basic postulates with which we began is in error, or that other factors are at work which were not taken into account (or, at least, not sufficiently) in our original, highly general formulation. The evidence, as I

[13] Gerhard E. Lenski, *Power and Privilege* (New York: McGraw-Hill, 1966), p. 228.

[14] British figures are calculated from G. D. H. Cole, *The Post-War Condition of Britain* (London: Routledge, 1956), p. 223; Swedish figures are from George R. Nelson, ed., *Freedom and Welfare: Social Patterns in the Northern Countries of Europe* (sponsored by the Ministries of Social Affairs of Denmark, Finland, Iceland, Norway, and Sweden, 1953), p. 54; Danish figures are from K. Lemberg and N. Ussing, "Redistribution of Income in Denmark," in Alan Peacock, ed., *Income Redistribution and Social Policy* (London: Cape, 1954), p. 72; United States figures are calculated from *The World Almanac, 1961* (New York: World-Telegram, 1961), p. 744. All figures are from official governmental sources.

shall show, favors the latter interpretation, indicating again the serious difficulties which attend any effort to develop a general theory by purely deductive means.

Among the factors not considered in our earlier assumptions about the nature of man and society was the relationship between technological and cultural complexity on the one hand, and administrative efficiency on the other. In modern industrial societies, technology in particular, and culture in general, are far more complex than in even the most advanced agrarian societies.[15] In fact, they are so complex that it is no longer possible for those in positions of high command to begin to understand the work of all those beneath them. In effect, there is a growing "ignorance" on the part of those in positions of command. This is not to say that those in authority in industrial societies are less intelligent or knowledgeable than their counterparts in agrarian societies, but rather that they are masters of *a smaller proportion* of what they need to know to maintain effective control over those beneath them. Thus, because of the many gaps in their knowledge, they are often compelled either to issue commands based on insufficient information, or to leave matters to the discretion of their subordinates, thus opening the door to encroachments on their prerogatives. In the former case, authority is preserved, but at the expense of efficiency and productivity, while in the latter case a measure of authority is sacrificed to increase efficiency and productivity. In short, *the relationship between productivity and authority appears to be curvilinear in industrial societies, at least up to the present time.*[16] Thus, unless political authorities are willing and able to sacrifice productivity, it is unlikely that they will be able to rely on the technique of command to the extent their agrarian counterparts did. However, to the degree that they delegate authority or rely on market mechanisms, they facilitate the diffusion of power and privilege.

[15] One of the best evidences of this is the rapid growth of vocabulary in the language of every industrial society.

[16] Recent events in the Soviet Union provide a good illustration of this. The increasing reliance on market mechanisms in economic decision making represents a deliberate effort to increase efficiency and productivity while sacrificing centralized authority. This development was forced on Soviet authorities by the physical impossibility of developing an adequate, workable, and comprehensive plan for the whole Soviet economy. According to reports, one Soviet economist predicted that unless there were drastic reforms, planning work would increase thirty-six-fold by 1980, and would require the services of the entire adult population, and this presumably would not raise the level of efficiency of the planning procedures. Another Soviet economist is reported to have argued that a sound plan must take account of all the possible interrelationships between products in the plan and the number of these interrelations is the square of the number of products. Since the Soviet machine industry alone now turns out 125,000 different products, a comprehensive plan for this one industry would require provision for more than 15 billion interrelations. See Joseph Alsop, "Matter of Fact," *The Washington Post,* Jan. 13, 1964. While the use of modern high-speed computers will undoubtedly alleviate the problems of planners to a considerable degree, it is not likely that in the foreseeable future the curvilinearity in the relationship between productivity and authority can be eliminated, especially in societies in which the diversity of goods and services produced is constantly increasing.

A second factor which seems to have contributed to the reversal in the historic trend toward greater inequality is *the rapidity and magnitude of the increases in productivity.* In societies in which the gross national product and per capita income are rapidly rising, and promise to continue rising, elites find themselves in the paradoxical situation in which they can maximize their *net* input of rewards by responding to pressures from below and making certain concessions. By granting the lower classes some share in the economic surplus, they can reduce worker hostility and the accompanying losses from strikes, slowdowns, and industrial sabotage. In an expanding economy, an elite can make economic concessions in *relative* terms without necessarily suffering any loss in *absolute* terms. In fact, if the concessions are not too large, and the rate of the economy's growth is great enough, relative losses can even be accompanied by *substantial* absolute gains. For example, an elite would enjoy a substantially greater income if it took 40 percent of the gross national product in a $100 billion economy, than if it stubbornly fought to maintain a 50 percent share and thereby held the economy at the $50 billion level. *If we assume that the majority of men would willingly make modest relative concessions for the sake of substantial absolute gains, and if we also assume that leading members of the elites in industrial societies have an awareness of the benefits they can obtain from concessions, then we can only predict they will make them.*

A willingness to make concessions may also be encouraged by the principle of marginal utility. This principle serves as a reminder that the first million dollars normally has greater value to a man than any subsequent million he may acquire. In societies with very productive economies, many members of the elite may be prepared to make some *economic* concessions in order to maximize other kinds of rewards, such as safety, respect, and leisure. In other words, after a certain level of wealth has been attained, elites may prefer to sacrifice a portion of the economic surplus in order to reduce hostility and the dangers of revolution, and to win for themselves a greater measure of respect and affection. Or, they may find it impossible to maintain tight control over political and economic organizations and at the same time enjoy the benefits of leisure, and so permit a portion of the economic surplus to pass into other hands. In short, *because elites have multiple goals, and are not concerned with maximizing material rewards alone, they may be willing to make certain economic concessions in a highly productive and expanding economy.*

Yet another factor which has played a role in reducing inequality is the development of new and highly effective methods of birth control. In the past, the natural tendency of the human race to multiply usually had the effect of offsetting whatever economic gains might otherwise have resulted from technological advance. Numbers tended to increase up to the carrying power of the economy *except as limited by the development of tyrannical political systems which diverted the "economic surplus" to the elite at the expense of further population increase.* One consequence, of course, was the large and wretched class of expendables, whose very presence served to prevent any substantial long-run improvement in the lot of the peasants and artisans with whom they constantly competed for employment.

Today the situation is rapidly changing, and promises to change even more in the future. For the first time in history, mankind has found safe, simple, and effective means of controlling population growth. In societies where these have been most widely used, the rate of population growth has been slowed to the point where real and substantial gains in per capita income have been achieved in a fairly short time, thus reducing the intensity of the competitive pressures. Now, for almost the first time in centuries, the lower classes are able to bargain for wages in markets no longer perennially glutted with labor. This development has almost certainly contributed to the decline in inequality.

Another factor that has probably contributed to the decline in inequality is the great expansion in human knowledge. In the past, the dominant class chiefly needed unskilled labor, and thanks to human fecundity, this was always plentiful. This put the vast majority of men in a poor bargaining position, and hence the price of labor was minimal. Today, in the more advanced industrial societies, the situation is radically changed. Because of the great functional utility of so much of the new knowledge, a host of occupational specialists have appeared who are not interchangeable to any great degree. This introduces into the labor market certain rigidities which favor the sellers of labor, especially in an era in which the demand for technical skills is rapidly rising. Furthermore, even if the dominant classes could obtain the necessary labor for a subsistence wage, it is doubtful that this would prove expedient. The efficiency of work requiring mental effort or alertness can be seriously reduced when those performing it are not physically fit. Two men working at 50 percent efficiency in this situation are not the equal of one man working at top efficiency, as in work requiring brute strength alone. Moreover expensive machines and tight production schedules are vulnerable to the mistakes of inattentive workers to a degree that is not characteristic of agrarian societies. These factors all prevent the dominant classes from driving the wages of this increasingly numerous segment of the population down to the subsistence level, and prevent the system from reaching the level of economic inequality that is found in agrarian societies, both past and present.

The egalitarian trend in modern industrial societies is evident in the *political* area no less than in the economic. In many respects the trend toward greater political equality is more surprising than the corresponding economic trend, because the struggle for political power is essentially a zero-sum "game," i.e., gains by one party necessarily entail corresponding losses by opponents. The struggle for privilege, on the other hand, is a positive-sum "game," thanks to the constantly rising level of productivity. Thus in the political realm the privileged classes cannot accept losses in relative terms and still realize absolute gains.

All the reasons for the spread of democratic government are still not completely understood. Obviously, it has not been dictated by economic necessity, as shown by the vigor of a number of nondemocratic, totalitarian nations. On the other hand, the relative frequency of democratic government in industrial states and its virtual absence in agrarian, strongly indicate some connection. Specifically, this suggests that industrialization creates conditions favorable to the growth of democracy, but does not make it inevitable.

One favorable condition is the spread of literacy and the extension of education. An illiterate peasantry lacking access to mass media of information is in a poor position to participate in the political process; a literate middle and working class with many media of information available is much more favorably situated. Advances in the level of living have a similar effect. Peasants and artisans living at, or near, the subsistence level cannot afford the luxury of sustained political activity; workers in an industrial society have more leisure, energy, and money to devote to this. Still another factor favoring the growth of democracy is the modern pattern of warfare which involves the entire population to an extent unknown in agrarian societies.[17] As many observers have noted, the traditional distinction between the military and civilian segments of the population has been almost obliterated, and military men have come to regard urban centers of production as prime military targets. If Andrzejewski and other writers are correct, this trend should have an egalitarian influence, since inequality tends to be most pronounced where military activities are limited to the few.

More important than any of these, however, has been the rise and spread of *the new democratic ideology* which asserts that the state belongs to the people.[18] This ideology is not simply a reflection of changing economic conditions, though, as we have seen, it has been affected by them. Rather, the historical record indicates it had its origin in religious and philosophical developments of the seventeenth century and spread rather widely in the eighteenth century in countries which were still thoroughly agrarian in character, e.g., the United States and France. In fact, there appears to be as much justification for the thesis that this new ideology contributed to the emergence of industrial societies as for the converse.

[17] See, for example, Walter Millis, *Arms and Men: A Study of American Military History* (New York: Putnam, 1956).

[18] In one sense this ideology is not at all new, as shown in Chap. 1 and also in the practices of hunting and gathering and simple horticultural peoples. In another sense, however, modern democratic beliefs can be said to derive from the work of seventeenth-century political theorists such as John Locke, who put this ancient idea in a modern form which made it a significant force first in the intellectual world and then in the political.

In any case, this new ideology became an important force in the political life of industrial societies. It captured the imagination of all kinds of men, even some of the political elite, thus making the traditional monopoly of political power increasingly untenable. As the democratic ideology spread, those who governed had to make substantial concessions in order to avoid massive challenges to their power—challenges which would have been costly to resist, and might even have led to their overthrow. The idea that the state should be the servant of all the people continues to be a major force in the modern era, mobilizing the egoistic impulses of the disadvantaged classes in an idealistic cause, thereby uniting morality and egoism in a manner reminiscent of their union under the banner of "the divine right of kings," but with the opposite effect.

Wherever democratic theory has become institutionalized, a dramatic new possibility has arisen: *now the many can combine against the few, and even though individually the many are weaker, in combination they may be as strong or stronger.* With this development, the door is opened to a host of revolutionary developments in the distributive realm. . . .

8

The Structure of Power in American Society

C. Wright Mills

THE NATURE OF POWER

Power has to do with whatever decisions men make about the arrangements under which they live, and about the events which make up the history of their times. Events that are beyond human decision do happen; social arrangements do change without benefit of explicit decision. But insofar as such decisions are made, the problem of who is involved in making them is the basic problem of power. Insofar as they could be made but are not, the problem becomes who fails to make them?

We cannot today merely assume that in the last resort men must always be governed by their own consent. For among the means of power which now prevail is the power to manage and to manipulate the consent of men. That we do not know the limits of such power, and that we hope it does have limits, does not remove the fact that much power today is successfully employed without the sanction of the reason or the conscience of the obedient.

Surely nowadays we need not argue that, in the last resort, coercion is the "final" form of power. But then, we are by no means constantly at the last resort. Authority (power that is justified by the beliefs of the voluntarily obedient) and manipulation (power that is wielded unbeknown to the powerless)—must also be considered, along with coercion. In fact, the three types must be sorted out whenever we think about power.

Source: *Power, Politics and People, The Collected Essays of C. Wright Mills,* ed. Irving Louis Horowitz, published by The Oxford University Press. The section titles have been provided by the editors of this volume.

A draft of this lecture was presented at a residential weekend at the Beatrice Webb House, Surrey, on 2 March 1957; and at the University of Frankfurt on 3 May 1957. A more detailed exposition of the general argument, as well as documentation, will be found in *The Power Elite* (New York City: Oxford University Press), 1956.

In the modern world, we must bear in mind, power is often not so authoritative as it seemed to be in the medieval epoch: ideas which justify rulers no longer seem so necessary to their exercise of power. At least for many of the great decisions of our time—especially those of an international sort—mass "persuasion" has not been "necessary"; the fact is simply accomplished. Furthermore, such ideas as are available to the powerful are often neither taken up nor used by them. Such ideologies usually arise as a response to an effective debunking of power; in the United States such opposition has not been effective enough recently to create the felt need for new ideologies of rule.

There has, in fact, come about a situation in which many who have lost faith in prevailing loyalties have not acquired new ones, and so pay no attention to politics of any kind. They are not radical, not liberal, not conservative, not reactionary. They are inactionary. They are out of it. If we accept the Greek's definition of the idiot as an altogether private man, then we must conclude that many American citizens are now idiots. And I should not be surprised, although I do not know, if there were not some such idiots even in Germany. This—and I use the word with care—this spiritual condition seems to me the key to many modern troubles of political intellectuals, as well as the key to much political bewilderment in modern society. Intellectual "conviction" and moral "belief" are not necessary, in either the rulers or the ruled, for a ruling power to persist and even to flourish. So far as the role of ideologies is concerned, their frequent absences and the prevalence of mass indifference are surely two of the major political facts about the western societies today.

How large a role any explicit decisions do play in the making of history is itself a historical problem. For how large that role may be depends very much upon the means of power that are available at any given time in any given society. In some societies, the innumerable actions of innumerable men modify their milieux, and so gradually modify the structure itself. These modifications—the course of history—go on behind the backs of men. History is drift, although in total "men make it." Thus, innumerable entrepreneurs and innumerable consumers by ten thousand decisions per minute may shape and reshape the free-market economy. Perhaps this was the chief kind of limitation Marx had in mind when he wrote, in *The 18th Brumaire:* that "Men make their own history, but they do not make it just as they please; they do not make it under circumstances chosen by themselves. . . ."

But in other societies—certainly in the United States and in the Soviet Union today—a few men may be so placed within the structure that by their decisions they modify the milieux of many other men, and in fact nowadays the structural conditions under which most men live. Such elites of power also make history under circumstances not chosen altogether by themselves, yet compared with other men, and compared with other periods of world history, these circumstances do indeed seem less limiting.

I should contend that "men are free to make history," but that some men are indeed much freer than others. For such freedom requires access to the means of decision and of power by which history can now be made. It has not always been so made; but in the later phases of the modern epoch it is. It is with reference to this epoch that I am contending that if men do not make history, they tend increasingly to become the utensils of history-makers as well as the mere objects of history.

The history of modern society may readily be understood as the story of the enlargement and the centralization of the means of power—in economic, in political, and in military institutions. The rise of industrial society has involved these developments in the means of economic production. The rise of the nation-state has involved similar developments in the means of violence and in those of political administration.

In the western societies, such transformations have generally occurred gradually, and many cultural traditions have restrained and shaped them. In most of the Soviet societies, they are happening very rapidly indeed and without the great discourse of western civilization, without the Renaissance and without the Reformation, which so greatly strengthened and gave political focus to the idea of freedom. In those societies, the enlargement and the coordination of all the means of power has occurred more brutally, and from the beginning under tightly centralized authority. But in both types, the means of power have now become international in scope and similar in form. To be sure, each of them has its own ups and downs; neither is as yet absolute; how they are run differs quite sharply.

Yet so great is the reach of the means of violence, and so great the economy required to produce and support them, that we have in the immediate past witnessed the consolidation of these two world centers, either of which dwarfs the power of ancient Rome. As we pay attention to the awesome means of power now available to quite small groups of men we come to realize that Caesar could do less with Rome than Napoleon with France; Napoleon less with France than Lenin with Russia. But what was Caesar's power at its height compared with the power of the changing inner circles of Soviet Russia and the temporary administrations of the United States? We come to realize—indeed they continually remind us—how a few men have access to the means by which in a few days continents can be turned into thermonuclear wastelands. That the facilities of power are so enormously enlarged and so decisively centralized surely means that the powers of quite small groups of men, which we may call elites, are now of literally inhuman consequence.

My concern here is not with the international scene but with the United States in the middle of the twentieth century. I must emphasize "in the middle of the twentieth century" because in our attempt to understand any society we come upon images which have been drawn from its past and which often confuse our attempt to confront its present reality. That is one minor reason why history is the shank of any social science: we must study it if only to rid ourselves of it. In the United States, there are indeed many such images and usually they have to do with the first half of the nineteenth century. At that time the economic facilities of the United States were very widely dispersed and subject to little or to no central authority.

The state watched in the night but was without decisive voice in the day.

One man meant one rifle and the militia were without centralized orders.

Any American as old-fashioned as I can only agree with R. H. Tawney that "Whatever the future may contain, the past has shown no more excellent social order than that in which the mass of the people were the masters of the holdings which they ploughed and the tools with which they worked, and could boast . . . 'It is a quietness to a man's mind to live upon his own and to know his heir certain.' "

But then we must immediately add: all that is of the past and of little relevance to our understanding of the United States today. Within this society three broad levels of power may now be distinguished. I shall begin at the top and move downward.

THE POWER ELITE

The power to make decisions of national and international consequence is now so clearly seated in political, military, and economic institutions that other areas of society seem off to the side and, on occasion, readily subordinated to these. The scattered institutions of religion, education, and family are increasingly shaped by the big three, in which history-making decisions now regularly occur. Behind this fact there is all the push and drive of a fabulous technology; for these three institutional orders have incorporated this technology and now guide it, even as it shapes and paces their development.

As each has assumed its modern shape, its effects upon the other two have become greater, and the traffic between the three has increased. There is no longer, on the one hand, an economy, and, on the other, a political order, containing a military establishment unimportant to politics and to money making. There is a political economy numerously linked with military order and decision. This triangle of power is now a structural fact, and it is the key to any understanding of the higher circles in America today. For as each of these domains has coincided with the others, as decisions in each have become broader, the leading men of each—the high military, the corporation executives, the political directorate—have tended to come together to form the power elite of America.

The political order, once composed of several dozen states with a weak federal center, has become an executive apparatus which has taken up into itself many powers previously scattered, legislative as well as administrative, and which now reaches into all parts of the social structure. The long-time tendency of business and government to become more closely connected has since World War II reached a new point of explicitness. Neither can now be seen clearly as a distinct world. The growth of executive government does not mean merely the "enlargement of government" as some kind of autonomous bureaucracy: under American conditions, it has meant the ascendency of the corporation man into political eminence. Already during the New Deal, such men had joined the political directorate; as of World War II they came to dominate it. Long involved with government, now they have moved into quite full direction of the economy of the war effort and of the post-war era.

The economy, once a great scatter of small productive units in somewhat automatic balance, has become internally dominated by a few hundred corporations, administratively and politically interrelated, which together hold the keys to economic decision. This economy is at once a permanent-war economy and a private-corporation economy. The most important relations of the corporation to the state now rest on the coincidence between military and corporate interests, as defined by the military and the corporate rich, and accepted by politicians and public. Within the elite as a whole, this coincidence of military domain and corporate realm strengthens both of them and further subordinates the merely political man. Not the party politician, but the corporation executive, is now more likely to sit with the military to answer the question: what is to be done?

The military order, once a slim establishment in a context of civilian distrust, has become the largest and most expensive feature of government; behind smiling public relations, it has all the grim and clumsy efficiency of a great and sprawling bureaucracy. The high military have gained decisive political and economic relevance. The seemingly permanent military threat places a premium upon them and virtually all political and economic actions are now judged in terms of military definitions of reality: the higher military have ascended to a firm position within the power elite of our time.

In part at least this is a result of an historical fact, pivotal for the years since 1939: the attention of the elite has shifted from domestic problems—centered in the thirties around slump—to international problems—centered in the forties and fifties around war. By long historical usage, the government of the United States has been shaped by domestic clash and balance; it does not have suitable agencies and traditions for the democratic handling of international affairs. In considerable part, it is in this vacuum that the power elite has grown.

1. To understand the unity of this power elite, we must pay attention to the psychology of its several members in their respective milieux. Insofar as the power elite is composed of men of similar origin and education, of similar career and style of life, their unity may be said to rest upon the fact that they are of similar social type, and to lead to the fact of their easy intermingling. This kind of unity reaches its frothier apex in the sharing of that prestige which is to be had in the world of the celebrity. It achieves a more solid culmination

in the fact of the interchangeability of positions between the three dominant institutional orders. It is revealed by considerable traffic of personnel within and between these three, as well as by the rise of specialized go-betweens as in the new style high-level lobbying.

2. Behind such psychological and social unity are the structure and the mechanics of those institutional hierarchies over which the political directorate, the corporate rich, and the high military now preside. How each of these hierarchies is shaped and what relations it has with the others determine in large part the relations of their rulers. Were these hierarchies scattered and disjoined, then their respective elites might tend to be scattered and disjointed; but if they have many interconnections and points of coinciding interest, then their elites tend to form a coherent kind of grouping. The unity of the elite is not a simple reflection of the unity of institutions, but men and institutions are always related; that is why we must understand the elite today in connection with such institutional trends as the development of a permanent-war establishment, alongside a privately incorporated economy, inside a virtual political vacuum. For the men at the top have been selected and formed by such institutional trends.

3. Their unity, however, does not rest solely upon psychological similarity and social intermingling, nor entirely upon the structural blending of commanding positions and common interests. At times it is the unity of a more explicit coordination.

   To say that these higher circles are increasingly coordinated, that this is *one* basis of their unity, and that at times—as during open war—such coordination is quite wilful, is not to say that the coordination is total or continuous, or even that it is very surefooted. Much less is it to say that the power elite has emerged as the realization of a plot. Its rise cannot be adequately explained in any psychological terms.

   Yet we must remember that institutional trends may be defined as opportunities by those who occupy the command posts. Once such opportunities are recognized, men may avail themselves of them. Certain types of men from each of these three areas, more far-sighted than others, have actively promoted the liaison even before it took its truly modern shape. Now more have come to see that their several interests can more easily be realized if they work together, in informal as well as in formal ways, and accordingly they have done so.

The idea of the power elite is of course an interpretation. It rests upon and it enables us to make sense of major institutional trends, the social similarities and psychological affinities of the men at the top. But the idea is also based upon what has been happening on the middle and lower levels of power, to which I now turn.

THE MIDDLE LEVELS OF POWER

There are of course other interpretations of the American system of power. The most usual is that it is a moving balance of many competing interests. The image of balance, at least in America, is derived from the idea of the economic market: in the nineteenth century, the balance was thought to occur between a great scatter of individuals and enterprises; in the twentieth century, it is thought to occur between great interest blocks. In both views, the politician is the key man of power because he is the broker of many conflicting powers.

I believe that the balance and the compromise in American society—the "countervailing powers" and the "veto groups," of parties and associations, of strata and unions—must now be seen as having mainly to do with the middle levels of power. It is these middle levels that the political journalist and the scholar of politics are most likely to understand and to write about—if only because, being mainly middle class themselves, they are closer to them. Moreover, these levels provide the noisy content of most "political" news and gossip; the images of these levels are more or less in accord with the folklore of how democracy works; and, if the master-image of balance is accepted, many intellectuals, especially in their current patrioteering, are readily able to satisfy such political optimism as they wish to feel. Accordingly, liberal interpretations of what is happening in the United States are now virtually the only interpretations that are widely distributed.

But to believe that the power system reflects a balancing society is, I think, to confuse the present era with earlier times, and to confuse its top and bottom with its middle levels.

By the top levels, as distinguished from the middle, I intend to refer, first of all, to the scope of the decisions that are made. At the top today, these decisions have to do with all the issues of war and peace. They have also to do with slump and poverty which are now so very much problems of international scope. I intend also to refer to whether or not the groups that struggle politically have a chance to gain the positions from which such top decisions are made, and indeed whether their members do usually hope for such top national command. Most of the competing interests which make up the clang and clash of American politics are strictly concerned with their slice of the existing pie. Labor unions, for example, certainly have no policies of an international sort other than those which given unions adopt for the strict economic protection of their members. Neither do farm organizations. The actions of such middle-level powers may indeed have consequence for top-level policy; certainly at times they hamper these policies. But they are not truly concerned with them, which means of course that their influence tends to be quite irresponsible.

The facts of the middle levels may in part be understood in terms of the rise of the power elite. The expanded and centralized and interlocked hierarchies over which the power elite preside have encroached upon the old balance and relegated it to the middle level. But there are also independent developments of the middle levels. These, it seems to me, are better understood as an affair of intrenched and provincial demands than as a center of national decision. As such, the middle level often seems much more of a stalemate than a moving balance.

1. The middle level of politics is not a forum in which there are debated the big decisions of national and international life. Such debate is not carried on by nationally responsible parties representing and clarifying alternative policies. There are no such parties in the United States. More and more, fundamental issues never come to any point or decision before the Congress, much less before the electorate in party campaigns. In the case of Formosa, in the spring of 1955, the Congress abdicated all debate concerning events and decisions which surely bordered on war. The same is largely true of the 1957 crisis in the Middle East. Such decisions now regularly by-pass the Congress, and are never clearly focused issues for public decision.

   The American political campaign distracts attention from national and international issues, but that is not to say that there are no issues in these campaigns. In each district and state, issues are set up and watched by organized interests of sovereign local importance. The professional politician is of course a party politician, and the two parties are semi-feudal organizations: they trade patronage and other favors for votes and for protection. The differences between them, so far as national issues are concerned, are very narrow and very mixed up. Often each seems to be forty-eight parties, one to each state; and accordingly, the politician as campaigner and as Congressman is not concerned with national party lines, if any are discernible. Often he is not subject to any effective national party discipline. He speaks for the interests of his own constituency, and he is concerned with national issues only insofar as they affect the interests effectively organized there, and hence his chances of reelection. That is why, when he does speak of national matters, the result is so often such an empty rhetoric. Seated in his sovereign locality, the politician is not at the national summit. He is on and of the middle levels of power.

2. Politics is not an arena in which free and independent organizations truly connect the lower and middle levels of society with the top

levels of decision. Such organizations are not an effective and major part of American life today. As more people are drawn into the political arena, their associations become mass in scale, and the power of the individual becomes dependent upon them; to the extent that they are effective, they have become larger, and to that extent they have become less accessible to the influence of the individual. This is a central fact about associations in any mass society: it is of most consequence for political parties and for trade unions.

In the thirties, it often seemed that labor would become an insurgent power independent of corporation and state. Organized labor was then emerging for the first time on an American scale, and the only political sense of direction it needed was the slogan, "organize the unorganized." Now without the mandate of the slump, labor remains without political direction. Instead of economic and political struggles it has become deeply entangled in administrative routines with both corporation and state. One of its major functions, as a vested interest of the new society, is the regulation of such irregular tendencies as may occur among the rank and file.

There is nothing, it seems to me, in the make-up of the current labor leadership to allow us to expect that it can or that it will lead, rather than merely react. Insofar as it fights at all it fights over a share of the goods of a single way of life and not over that way of life itself. The typical labor leader in the U.S.A. today is better understood as an adaptive creature of the main business drift than as an independent actor in a truly national context.

3. The idea that this society is a balance of powers requires us to assume that the units in balance are of more or less equal power and that they are truly independent of one another. These assumptions have rested, it seems clear, upon the historical importance of a large and independent middle class. In the latter nineteenth century and during the Progressive Era, such a class of farmers and small businessmen fought politically—and lost—their last struggle for a paramount role in national decision. Even then, their aspirations seemed bound to their own imagined past.

   This old, independent middle class has of course declined. On the most generous count, it is now 40 percent of the total middle class (at most 20 percent of the total labor force). Moreover, it has become politically as well as economically dependent upon the state, most notably in the case of the subsidized farmer.

   The *new* middle class of white-collar employees is certainly not the political pivot of any balancing society. It is in no way polit-

> ically unified. Its unions, such as they are, often serve merely to incorporate it as hanger-on of the labor interest. For a considerable period, the old middle class *was* an independent base of power; the new middle class cannot be. Political freedom and economic security *were* anchored in small and independent properties; they are not anchored in the worlds of the white-collar job. Scattered property holders were economically united by more or less free markets; the jobs of the new middle class are integrated by corporate authority. Economically, the white-collar classes are in the same condition as wage workers; politically, they are in a worse condition, for they are not organized. They are no vanguard of historic change; they are at best a rear guard of the welfare state.

The agrarian revolt of the nineties, the small-business revolt that has been more or less continuous since the eighties, the labor revolt of the thirties—each of these has failed as an independent movement which could countervail against the powers that be; they have failed as politically autonomous third parties. But they have succeeded, in varying degree, as interests vested in the expanded corporation and state; they have succeeded as parochial interests seated in particular districts, in local divisions of the two parties, and in the Congress. What they would become, in short, are well-established features of the *middle* levels of balancing power, on which we may now observe all those strata and interests which in the course of American history have been defeated in their bids for top power or which have never made such bids.

Fifty years ago many observers thought of the American state as a mask behind which an invisible government operated. But nowadays, much of what was called the old lobby, visible or invisible, is part of the quite visible government. The "governmentalization of the lobby" has proceeded in both the legislative and the executive domain, as well as between them. The executive bureaucracy becomes not only the center of decision but also the arena within which major conflicts of power are resolved or denied resolution. "Administration" replaces electoral politics; the maneuvering of cliques (which include leading senators as well as civil servants) replaces the open clash of parties.

The shift of corporation men into the political directorate has accelerated the decline of the politicians in the Congress to the middle levels of power; the formation of the power elite rests in part upon this relegation. It rests also upon the semiorganized stalemate of the interests of sovereign localities, into which the legislative function has so largely fallen; upon the virtually complete absence of a civil service that is a politically neutral but politically relevant, depository of brain power and executive skill; and it rests upon the increased official secrecy behind which great decisions are made without benefit of public or even of congressional debate.

THE MASS SOCIETY

There is one last belief upon which liberal observers everywhere base their interpretations and rest their hopes. That is the idea of the public and the associated idea of public opinion. Conservative thinkers, since the French Revolution, have of course Viewed With Alarm the rise of the public, which they have usually called the masses, or something to that effect. "The populace is sovereign," wrote Gustave Le Bon, "and the tide of barbarism mounts." But surely those who have supposed the masses to be well on their way to triumph are mistaken. In our time, the influence of publics or of masses within political life is in fact decreasing, and such influence as on occasion they do have tends, to an unknown but increasing degree, to be guided by the means of mass communication.

In a society of publics, discussion is the ascendant means of communication, and the mass media, if they exist, simply enlarge and animate this discussion, linking one face-to-face public with the discussions of another. In a mass society, the dominant type of communication is the formal media, and publics become mere markets for these media: the "public" of a radio program consists of all those exposed to it. When we try to look upon the United States today as a society of publics, we realize that it has moved a considerable distance along the road to the mass society.

In official circles, the very term, "the public," has come to have a phantom meaning, which dramatically reveals its eclipse. The deciding elite can identify some of those who clamor publicly as "Labor," others as "Business," still others as "Farmer." But these are not the public. "The public" consists of the unidentified and the nonpartisan in a world of defined and partisan interests. In this faint echo of the classic notion, the public is composed of these remnants of the old and new middle classes whose interests are not explicitly defined, organized, or clamorous. In a curious adaptation, "the public" often becomes, in administrative fact, "the disengaged expert," who, although ever so well informed, has never taken a clear-cut and public stand on controversial issues. He is the "public" member of the board, the commission, the committee. What "the public" stands for, accordingly is often a vagueness of policy (called "open-mindedness"), a lack of involvement in public affairs (known as "reasonableness"), and a professional disinterest (known as "tolerance").

All this is indeed far removed from the eighteenth-century idea of the public of public opinion. That idea parallels the economic idea of the magical market. Here is the market composed of freely competing entrepreneurs; there is the public composed of circles of people in discussion. As price is the result of anonymous, equally weighted, bargaining individuals, so public opinion is the result of each man's having thought things out for himself and then contributing his voice to the great chorus. To be sure, some may have more influence on the state of opinion than others, but no one group monopolizes the discussion, or by itself determines the opinions that prevail.

In this classic image, the people are presented with problems. They discuss them. They formulate viewpoints. These viewpoints are organized, and they compete. One viewpoint "wins out." Then the people act on this view, or their representatives are instructed to act it out, and this they promptly do.

Such are the images of democracy which are still used as working justifications of power in America. We must now recognize this description as more a fairy tale than a useful approximation. The issues that now shape man's fate are neither raised nor decided by any public at large. The idea of a society that is at bottom composed of publics is not a matter of fact; it is the proclamation of an ideal, and as well the assertion of a legitimation masquerading as fact.

I cannot here describe the several great forces within American society as well as elsewhere which have been at work in the debilitation of the public. I want only to remind you that publics, like free associations, can be deliberately and suddenly smashed, or they can more slowly wither away. But whether smashed in a week or withered in a generation, the demise of the public must be seen in connection with the rise of centralized organizations, with all their new means of power, including those of the mass media of distraction. These, we now know, often seem to expropriate the rationality and the will of the terrorized or—as the case may be—the voluntarily indifferent society of masses. In the more democratic process of indifference the remnants of such publics as remain may only occasionally be intimidated by fanatics in search of "disloyalty." But regardless of that, they lose their will for decision because they do not possess the instruments for decision; they lose their sense of political belonging because they do not belong; they lose their political will because they see no way to realize it.

The political structure of a modern democratic state requires that such a public as is projected by democratic theorists not only exist but that it be the very forum within which a politics of real issues is enacted.

It requires a civil service that is firmly linked with the world of knowledge and sensibility, and which is composed of skilled men who, in their careers and in their aspirations, are truly independent of any private, which is to say, corporation, interests.

It requires nationally responsible parties which debate openly and clearly the issues which the nation, and indeed the world, now so rigidly confronts.

It requires an intelligentsia, inside as well as outside the universities, who carry on the big discourse of the western world, and whose work is relevant to and influential among parties and movements and publics.

And it certainly requires, as a fact of power, that there be free associations standing between families and smaller communities and publics, on the one hand, and the state, the military, the corporation, on the other. For unless these do exist, there are no vehicles for reasoned opinion, no instruments for the rational exertion of public will.

Such democratic formations are not now ascendant in the power structure of the United States, and accordingly the men of decision are not men selected and formed by careers within such associations and by their performance before such publics. The top of modern American society is increasingly unified, and often seems wilfully coordinated: at the top there has emerged an elite whose power probably exceeds that of any small group of men in world history. The middle levels are often a drifting set of stalemated forces: the middle does not link the bottom with the top. The bottom of this society is politically fragmented, and even as a passive fact, increasingly powerless: at the bottom there is emerging a mass society.

These developments, I believe, can be correctly understood neither in terms of the liberal nor the Marxian interpretation of politics and history. Both these ways of thought arose as guidelines to reflection about a type of society which does not now exist in the United States. We confront there a new kind of social structure, which embodies elements and tendencies of all modern society, but in which they have assumed a more naked and flamboyant prominence.

That does not mean that we must give up the ideals of these classic political expectations. I believe that both have been concerned with the problem of rationality and of freedom: liberalism, with freedom and rationality as supreme facts about the individual; Marxism, as supreme facts about man's role in the political making of history. What I have said here, I suppose, may be taken as an attempt to make evident why the ideas of freedom and of rationality now so often seem so ambiguous in the new society of the United States of America.

9

Troubles in Mass Society

C. Wright Mills

Perhaps the most fruitful distinction with which the sociological imagination works is between "the personal troubles of milieu" and "the public issues of social structure." This distinction is an essential tool of the sociological imagination and a feature of all classic work in social science.

Troubles occur within the character of the individual and within the range of his immediate relations with others; they have to do with his self and with those limited areas of social life of which he is directly and personally aware. Accordingly, the statement and the resolution of troubles properly lie within the individual as a biographical entity and within the scope of his immediate milieu—the social setting that is directly open to his personal experience and to some extent to his willful activity. A trouble is a private matter: values cherished by an individual are felt by him to be threatened.

Issues have to do with matters that transcend these local environments of the individual and the range of his inner life. They have to do with the organization of many such milieux into the institutions of an historical society as a whole, with the ways in which various milieux overlap and interpenetrate to form the larger structure of social and historical life. An issue is a public matter: some value cherished by publics is felt to be threatened. Often there is a debate about what that value really is and about what it is that really threatens it. This debate is often without focus if only because it is the very nature of an issue, unlike even widespread trouble, that it cannot very well be defined in terms of the immediate and everyday environments of ordinary men. An issue, in fact, often involves a crisis in institutional arrangements, and often too it involves what Marxists call "contradictions" or "antagonisms."

In these terms, consider unemployment. When, in a city of 100,000, only one man is unemployed, that is his personal trouble, and for its relief we properly look to the character of the man, his skills, and his immediate opportunities. But when in a nation of 50 million employees, 15 million men are unemployed, that is an issue, and we may not hope to find its solution within the range of opportunities open to any one individual. The very structure of opportunities has collapsed. Both the correct statement of the problem and the range of possible solutions require us to consider the economic and political institutions of the society, and not merely the personal situation and character of a scatter of individuals.

Consider war. The personal problem of war, when it occurs, may be how to survive it or how to die in it with honor; how to make money out of it; how to climb into the higher safety of the military apparatus; or how to contribute to the war's termination. In short, according to one's values, to find a set of milieux and within it to survive the war or make one's death in it meaningful. But the structural issues of war have to do with its causes; with what types of men it throws up into command; with its effects upon economic and political, family and religious institutions, with the unorganized irresponsibility of a world of nation-states.

Consider marriage. Inside a marriage a man and a woman may experience personal troubles, but when the divorce rate during the first four years of marriage is 250 out of every 1,000 attempts, this is an indication of a structural issue having to do with the institutions of marriage and the family and other institutions that bear upon them.

Or consider the metropolis—the horrible, beautiful, ugly, magnificent sprawl of the great city. For many upper-class people, the personal solution to "the problem of the city" is to have an apartment with private garage under it in the heart of the city, and forty miles out, a house by Henry Hill, garden by Garrett Eckbo, on a hundred acres of private land. In these two controlled environments—with a small staff at each end and a private helicopter connection—most people could solve many of the problems of personal milieux caused by the facts of the city. But all this, however splendid, does not solve the public issues that the structural fact of the city poses. What should be done with this wonderful monstrosity? Break it all up into scattered units, combining residence and work? Refurbish it as it stands? Or, after evacuation, dynamite it and build new cities according to new plans in new places? What should those plans be? And who is to decide and to accomplish whatever choice is made? These are structural issues; to confront them and to solve them requires us to consider political and economic issues that affect innumerable milieux.

Insofar as an economy is so arranged that slumps occur, the problem of unemployment becomes incapable of personal solution. Insofar as war is inherent in the nation-state system and in the uneven industrialization of the world, the ordinary individual in his restricted milieu will be powerless—with or without psychiatric aid—to solve the troubles this system or lack of system imposes upon him. Insofar as the family as an institution turns women into darling little slaves and men into their chief providers and unweaned dependents, the problem of a satisfactory marriage remains incapable of purely private solution. Insofar as the overdeveloped megalopolis and the overdeveloped automobile are built-in features of the overdeveloped society, the issues of urban living will not be solved by personal ingenuity and private wealth.

What we experience in various and specific milieux, I have noted, is often caused by structural changes. Accordingly, to understand the changes of many personal milieux we are required to look beyond them. And the number and variety of such structural changes increase as the institutions within which we live become more embracing and more intricately connected with one another. To be aware of the idea of social structure and to use it with sensibility is to be capable of tracing such linkages among a great variety of milieux. To be able to do that is to possess the sociological imagination.

What are the major issues for publics and the key troubles of private individuals in our time? To formulate issues and troubles, we must ask what values are cherished yet threatened, and what values are cherished and supported, by the characterizing trends of our period. In the case both of threat and of support we must ask what salient contradictions of structure may be involved.

When people cherish some set of values and do not feel any threat to them, they experience *well-being.* When they cherish values but *do* feel them to be threatened, they experience a crisis—either as a personal trouble or as a public issue. And if all their values seem involved, they feel the total threat of panic.

But suppose people are neither aware of any cherished values nor experience any threat? That is the experience of *indifference,* which, if it seems to involve all their values, becomes apathy. Suppose, finally, they are unaware of any cherished values, but still are very much aware of a threat? That is the experience of *uneasiness,* of anxiety, which, if it is total enough, becomes a deadly unspecified malaise.

Ours is a time of uneasiness and indifference—not yet formulated in such ways as to permit the work of reason and the play of sensibility. Instead of troubles—defined in terms of values and threats—there is often the misery of vague uneasiness; instead of explicit issues there is often merely the beat feeling that all is somehow not right. Neither the values threatened nor whatever threatens them has been stated; in short, they have not been carried to the point of decision. Much less have they been formulated as problems of social science.

In the thirties there was little doubt—except among certain deluded business circles—that there was an economic issue which was also a pack of personal troubles. In these arguments about "the crisis of capitalism," the formulations of Marx and the many unacknowledged reformulations of his work probably set the leading terms of the issue, and some men came to understand their personal troubles in these terms. The values threatened were plain to see and cherished by all; the structural contradictions that threatened them also seemed plain. Both were widely and deeply experienced. It was a political age.

But the values threatened in the era after World War II are often neither widely acknowledged as values nor widely felt to be threatened. Much private uneasiness goes unformulated; much public malaise and many decisions of enormous structural relevance never become public issues. For those who accept such inherited values as reason and freedom, it is the uneasiness itself that is the trouble; it is the indifference itself that is the issue. And it is this condition, of uneasiness and indifference, that is the signal feature of our period.

All this is so striking that it is often interpreted by observers as a shift in the very kinds of problems that need now to be formulated. We are frequently told that the problems of our decade, or even the crises of our period, have shifted from the external realm of economics and now have to do with the quality of individual life—in fact with the question of whether there is soon going to be anything that can properly be called individual life. Not child labor but comic books, not poverty but mass leisure, are at the center of concern. Many great public issues as well as many private troubles are described in terms of "the psychiatric"—often, it seems, in a pathetic attempt to avoid the large issues and problems of modern society. Often this statement seems to rest upon a provincial narrowing of interest to the Western societies, or even to the United States—thus ignoring two thirds of mankind; often, too, it arbitrarily divorces the individual life from the larger institutions within which that life is enacted, and which on occasion bear upon it more grievously than do the intimate environments of childhood.

Problems of leisure, for example, cannot even be stated without considering problems of work. Family troubles over comic books cannot be formulated as problems without considering the plight of the contemporary family in its new relations with the newer institutions of the social structure. Neither leisure nor its debilitating uses can be understood as problems without recognition of the extent to which malaise and indifference now form the social and personal climate of contemporary American society. In this climate, no problems of "the private life" can be stated and solved without recognition of the crisis of ambition that is part of the very career of men at work in the incorporated economy.

It is true, as psychoanalysts continually point out, that people do often have "the increasing sense of being moved by obscure forces within themselves which they are unable to define." But it is *not* true, as Ernest Jones asserted, that "man's chief enemy and danger is his own unruly nature and the dark forces pent up within him." On the contrary: "Man's chief danger" today lies in the unruly forces of contemporary society itself, with its alienating methods of production, its enveloping techniques of political domination, its international anarchy—in a word, its pervasive transformations of the very "nature" of man and the conditions and aims of his life.

10

Alienation and Social Structure

C. Wright Mills

The underlying trends are well known. Great and rational organizations—in brief, bureaucracies—have indeed increased, but the substantive reason of the individual at large has not. Caught in the limited milieux of their everyday lives, ordinary men often cannot reason about the great structures—rational and irrational—of which their milieux are subordinate parts. Accordingly, they often carry out series of apparently rational actions without any ideas of the ends they serve, and there is the increasing suspicion that those at the top as well—like Tolstoy's generals—only pretend they know. The growth of such organizations, within an increasing division of labor, sets up more and more spheres of life, work, and leisure, in which reasoning is difficult or impossible. The soldier, for example, "carries out an entire series of functionally rational actions accurately without having any idea as to the ultimate end of this action" or the function of each act within the whole.* Even men of technically supreme intelligence may efficiently perform their assigned work and yet not know that it is to result in the first atom bomb.

Science, it turns out, is not a technological Second Coming. That its techniques and its rationality are given a central place in a society does not mean that men live reasonably and without myth, fraud, and superstition. Universal education may lead to technological idiocy and nationalist provinciality—rather than to the informed and independent intelligence. The mass distribution of historic culture may not lift the level of cultural sensibility, but rather, merely banalize it—and compete mightily with the chance for creative innovation. A high level of bureaucratic rationality and of technology does not mean a high level of either individual or social intelligence. From the first you cannot infer the second. For social, technological, or bureaucratic rationality is not merely a grand summation of the individual will and capacity

Source: *The Sociological Imagination* by C. Wright Mills, pp. 168–170.

* Cf. Mannheim, *Man and Society* (New York: Harcourt, Brace, 1940), p. 54.

to reason. The very chance to acquire that will and that capacity seems in fact often to be decreased by it. Rationally organized social arrangements are not necessarily a means of increased freedom—for the individual or for the society. In fact, often they are a means of tyranny and manipulation, a means of expropriating the very chance to reason, the very capacity to act as a free man.

Only from a few commanding positions or—as the case may be—merely vantage points, in the rationalized structure is it readily possible to understand the structural forces at work in the whole which thus affect each limited part of which ordinary men are aware.

The forces that shape these milieux do not originate within them, nor are they controllable by those sunk in them. Moreover, these milieux are themselves increasingly rationalized. Families as well as factories, leisure as well as work, neighborhoods as well as states—they, too, tend to become parts of a functionally rational totality—or they are subject to uncontrolled and irrational forces.

The increasing rationalization of society, the contradiction between such rationality and reason, the collapse of the assumed coincidence of reason and freedom—these developments lie back of the rise into view of the man who is "with" rationality but without reason, who is increasingly self-rationalized and also increasingly uneasy. It is in terms of this type of man that the contemporary problem of freedom is best stated. Yet such trends and suspicions are often not formulated as problems, and they are certainly not widely acknowledged as issues or felt as a set of troubles. Indeed, it is the fact of its unrecognized character, its lack of formulation, that is the most important feature of the contemporary problem of freedom and reason.

From the individual's standpoint, much that happens seems the result of manipulation, of management, of blind drift; authority is often not explicit; those with power often feel no need to make it explicit and to justify it. That is one reason why ordinary men, when they are in trouble or when they sense that they are up against issues, cannot get clear targets for thought and for action; they cannot determine what it is that imperils the values they vaguely discern as theirs.

Given these effects of the ascendant trend of rationalization, the individual "does the best he can." He gears his aspirations and his work to the situation he is in, and from which he can find no way out. In due course, he does not seek a way out: he adapts. That part of his life which is left over from work, he uses to play, to consume, "to have fun." Yet this sphere of consumption is also being rationalized. Alienated from production, from work, he is also alienated from consumption, from genuine leisure. This adaptation of the individual and its effects upon his milieux and self results not only in the loss of his chance, and in due course, of his capacity and will to reason; it also affects his chances and his capacity to act as a free man. Indeed, neither the value of freedom nor of reason, it would seem, are known to him.

Such adapted men are not necessarily unintelligent, even after they have lived and worked and played in such circumstances for quite some time. Karl Mannheim has made the point in a clear way by speaking of "self rationalization," which refers to the way in which an individual, caught in the limited segments of great, rational organizations, comes systematically to regulate his impulses and his aspirations, his manner of life and his ways of thought, in rather strict accordance with "the rules and regulations of the organization." The rational organization is thus an alienating organization: the guiding principles of conduct and reflection, and in due course of emotion as well, are not seated in the individual conscience of the Reformation man, or in the independent reason of the Cartesian man. The guiding principles, in fact, are alien to and in contradiction with all that has been historically understood as individuality. It is not too much to say that in the extreme development the chance to reason of most men is destroyed, as rationality increases and its locus, its control, is moved from the individual to the big-scale organization. There is then rationality without reason. Such rationality is not commensurate with freedom but the destroyer of it.

IV
Theoretical Conflict and Critical Choice

11

Empirical Political Theory and the Image of Man

Fred R. Dallmayr

In past centuries social science was commonly designated as the science or study of man, a usage which lingers on in contemporary literature.[1] Despite changes in terminology, it remains a fond belief of many professionals and most laymen that the basic objective of social science is the comprehension of man and of the diverse patterns of man's conduct. While other disciplines may investigate his biological and physiological dimensions, social science boldly seems to grasp man at his core, as a thinking, feeling, and acting creature. To be sure, the tools and strategies of inquiry have varied over time. It is now a commonplace to assert that the social sciences, including political science, have experienced a revolution in recent decades, a revolution bent on reshaping these disciplines in accordance with the canons of natural science. This development has resulted not only in the careful collection and rapid accumulation of empirical data, but also in efforts to absorb empirical findings into new conceptual and explanatory schemes. As in other social disciplines, one of the most intensive endeavors of recent political science has been the search for a general framework of explanation, for an "empirical" or scientific theory of politics. My purpose here is not to lament or praise these developments and innovations; for the moment I simply accept them as a consequence of man's indomitable intellectual curiosity. What I would like to explore is one aspect of the described revolution: its implication for the study and comprehension of man. Has science brought us closer to the perennial focus of social inquiry? What image of man is

Source: *Polity* 2 (Summer 1970), 443–478. Reprinted by permission of *Polity*.

[1] Compare, for example, Ralph Linton, *The Study of Man, An Introduction* (New York, 1936); Lynn T. White, ed., *Frontiers of Knowledge in the Study of Man* (New York, 1956); Michael Polanyi, *The Study of Man* (Chicago, 1963); also the chapters "The Root Is Man" and "The Goal Is Man" in Heinz Eulau, *The Behavioral Persuasion in Politics* (New York, 1963), pp. 3–11, 133–137.

reflected in the mirror of recent political science and to what extent are we able to recognize ourselves in this mirror?

Unhappily this task is encumbered at the outset by impressive obstacles. Even a cursory acquaintance with contemporary political science literature reveals not one, but a great variety of conceptual frameworks, theories, and approaches. There is considerable dispute over the requisite ingredients of a scientific or empirical "theory," and the adherents of one persuasion are by no means eager to grant the label to their opponents in other camps. Also, the "empirical" foundations of some current theories are by no means obvious or beyond question. I cannot hope to resolve these questions or controversies; nor do I wish to insist on a narrow definition. For my own purposes I would tend to assign the label of "empirical" or "analytical" theory to a coherent set of researchable propositions which, at least within a hypothetical framework, possess explanatory and predictive capacity. In the present context, however, I am quite willing to concede the label to conceptual frameworks or approaches which approximate the preceding criteria.[2] The stipulation of such broad boundaries, of course, does not significantly reduce the thicket of prevailing orientations. Fortunately, a path or clearing has been cut into the underbrush by means of a distinction recently expounded by Maurice Duverger. Political theory, Duverger pointed out, has always "oscillated between two dramatically opposed interpretations. According to one, politics is conflict, a struggle in which power allows those who possess it to ensure their hold on society and to profit by it. According to the other view, politics is an effort to bring about the rule of order and justice." In the first interpretation, he added, politics "serves to maintain the privileges of a minority against the majority"; in the second, it is a "means of realizing the integration of all citizens into the community." [3]

The dichotomy of integration and conflict, to be sure, is not Duverger's invention. Using a variety of labels and formulations, many contemporary social scientists subscribe to a similar distinction of theoretical perspectives. According to this dichotomous scheme, some social and political theories focus on the integration, consensus, and stability of a community, while

[2] On empirical theory, frameworks and approaches, see Alan C. Isaak, *Scope and Methods of Political Science* (Homewood, Ill., 1969), pp. 135–160; Oran R. Young, *Systems of Political Science* (Englewood Cliffs, 1968), pp. 8–12, 95–102; Eugene J. Meehan, *Contemporary Political Thought, A Critical Study* (Homewood, Ill., 1967), 23–26, and *The Theory and Method of Political Analysis* (Homewood, Ill., 1965), pp. 130–163; Fred M. Frohock, *The Nature of Political Inquiry* (Homewood, Ill., 1967), pp. 4–13; Gordon J. DiRenzo, ed., *Concepts, Theory and Explanation in the Behavioral Sciences* (New York, 1966), pp. 239–259; Vernon Van Dyke, *Political Science, A Philosophical Analysis* (Stanford, 1960), pp. 89–109. Some current scientific theories are actually axiomatic or "normative" (in a formal sense) rather than empirical; on this distinction compare Jügen Habermas, "Zur Logik der Sozialwissenschaften," *Philosophishche Rundschau,* Beiheft 5 (Tübingen, 1967), 49–58.

[3] Maurice Duverger, *The Idea of Politics* (Indianapolis, 1966), Chapter 12.

others are preoccupied with conflict, constraint, and dynamic change.[4] The scheme clearly has the advantage of simplicity and may be adequate for purposes of broad orientation. However, as it seems to me, the dichotomy is too blunt an instrument to capture the richness of contemporary social and political theories. Cutting across the categories of integration and conflict, another distinction can be discerned: a distinction deriving from different units of analysis. As I intend to show, some contemporary theories focus on the system or political community as the major unit of investigation, while others accord primary status to individual actors or groups and their interrelationships. A combination or pairing of the above criteria would seem to result in at least three types of theoretical orientations: an orientation which, proceeding from a system focus, is preoccupied with systemic integration and stability; a perspective which, while largely concerned with consensus, starts from the analysis of individual actors and groups; and finally an approach which, relying on individual actors and groups, explores their discord and dynamic interactions.[5] Adhering to this typology I shall try to delineate the main premises and propositions of the three perspectives, using the labels of "systemic," "exchange," and "conflict" theories; in each case I shall make an effort to trace, as far as possible, the human features implicit in the theoretical framework.

SYSTEMIC THEORIES

Among the great variety of contemporary empirical approaches, one perspective has probably exercised a dominant influence, at least in political science, during the last decade. This perspective is characterized by its focus on the social or political "system" as the unit of analysis and by its ambition to identify the determinants of system stability, equilibrium, and integration. Despite differences in usage, the term "system" in this context refers commonly to a set of elements standing in close interaction, although writers are not agreed on whether their unit of investigation is a physically concrete or a purely analytic structure. Apart from and connected with the identification of a system as an investigative unit, the perspective also attempts to explain the persistence of the unit over time and under changing environmental con-

[4] Compare Ralf Dahrendorf, *Class and Class Conflict in Industrial Society* (Stanford, 1959), p. 159 (integration theory versus coercion or conflict theory); Irving L. Horowitz, "Consensus, Conflict and Cooperation: A Sociological Inventory," *Social Forces* 41 (1962), 177–188; John Horton, "Order and Conflict Theories of Social Problems as Competing Ideologies," *American Journal of Sociology* 71 (1966), 701–713; Bert N. Adams, "Coercion and Consensus Theories: Some Unresolved Issues," ibid., 714–717; Robert Cole, "Structural-Functional Theory, the Dialectic, and Social Change," *The Sociological Quarterly* 7 (1966), 48 (dialectical versus integration models).

[5] A fourth alternative might be found in the combination of a system focus with a conflict perspective; however, except on a subsystem level, the combination is difficult to conceive and little developed in the literature.

ditions. As Morton Kaplan informs us, systems analysis refers to "the study of a set of interrelated variables, as distinguished from the environment of the set, and of the ways in which this set is maintained under the impact of environmental disturbances."[6] Explanation of system stability may rely on various interrelated factors, including functional requisites and value consensus. While conceptually distinguishable from system persistence and equilibrium, "integration" frequently serves as an overarching or unifying theme, denoting "those characteristics of a unit system's structure which explain the maintenance of the system as a stable and distinct (i.e., cohesive) entity under a range of boundary conditions."[7] The perspective delineated here is exemplified in several contemporary frameworks, including that ambitious product of scientific synthesis called general systems theory. However, due perhaps to its abstract and elusive character, general systems theory has received only scant attention in political science. Professional interest has focused on other systemic approaches some of which, according to Oran Young, "are ultimately derivatives of general systems theory in an analytic, if not an historical, sense":[8] structural functionalism, Easton's input-output model, and cybernetics and communications theory.

Deriving from anthropological sources, structural functional theory has been developed chiefly by Talcott Parsons and Marion Levy. In recent years, the theory has been adopted by political scientists, primarily (but not exclusively) for purposes of comparative analysis. The starting point and basic unit of analysis of structural functionalism is commonly a system or a set of interlocking systems. As its name indicates, the theory tries to explicate the operation of a system by means of certain basic "functional" and "structural" patterns—terms which, unfortunately, are not devoid of ambiguity. Some writers have tended to define "function" as any consequence or effect of a pattern of action; but, as critics have noted, this definition could lead to strange or spurious conclusions.[9] More careful partisans of the approach, therefore, have limited the term to effects relevant to or required for the operation and continued existence of the system. As Marion Levy points out, structural functional analysis involves a series of basic steps or pro-

[6] Morton A. Kaplan, "Systems Theory," in *Contemporary Political Analysis,* James C. Charlesworth, ed. (New York, 1967), p. 150. Compare also his "Systems Theory and Political Science," *Social Research* 35 (1968), 30–47; Peter Nettl, "The Concept of System in Political Science," *Political Studies* 14 (1966), 305–338; Ludwig von Bertalanffy, "General System Theory," *General Systems* 1 (1956), 1–10; A. Hall and R. Fagen, "Definition of a System," ibid., 18–28.

[7] Burkhart Holzner, "The Concept of 'Integration' in Sociological Theory," *The Sociological Quarterly* 8 (1967), 53.

[8] Young, *Systems of Political Science,* p. 14; compare also his "The Impact of General Systems Theory on Political Science," *General Systems* 9 (1964), 239–255.

[9] Thus, the heartbeat might be assigned the function of producing heart sounds; see Carl G. Hempel, "The Logic of Functional Analysis," in *Symposium on Sociological Theory,* Llewellyn Gross, ed. (New York, 1959), p. 279.

cedures: determination of the unit of analysis and of the general limits of its variability; identification of functional requisites or of the conditions necessary for the unit's persistence; and finally some indication of the structural arrangements or patterns of action through which functions are performed.[10] Functionalists differ in their treatment of requisite conditions. Following Parsons' example, Robert Holt has identified four major requisites: pattern maintenance, related primarily to "maintenance of conformity to the prescriptions of the cultural system"; goal attainment, concerned largely with system survival; adaptation to environmental influences; and integration or the promotion of solidarity and cohesiveness among system elements. Other writers have produced more elaborate schemes; but the emphasis is commonly on system stability and integration.[11]

In contrast to structural functionalism, political input-output analysis is largely a homegrown product of our own discipline; but there are significant linkages between the two approaches. As in the functional model, the focus of input-output theory is on the "system" as the basic unit of analysis. According to David Easton, political life can be viewed as "a system of behavior operating within and responding to its social environment as it makes binding allocations of values." Opting against a reliance on concrete or physical criteria, Easton presents the political arena as an "analytic" structure operating within the overall membership system of society, and more particularly as "that system of interactions in any society through which binding or authoritative allocations are made and implemented." [12] Input-output analysis implies that the political community is embedded in an environment

[10] Marion J. Levy, Jr., "Some Aspects of 'Structural-Functional' Analysis and Political Science," in *Approaches to the Study of Politics,* ed. Roland Young (Evanston, 1958), p. 53. According to a slightly different formulation, structural-functional analysis (as distinguished from eclectic and empirical functionalism) involves "first, an emphasis on the whole system as the unit of analysis; second, postulation of particular functions as requisite to the maintenance of the whole system; third, concern to demonstrate the functional interdependence of diverse structures within the whole system." William Flanigan and Edwin Fogelman, "Functional Analysis," in Charlesworth, *Contemporary Political Analysis,* p. 76. Compare also Martin Landau, "On the Use of Functional Analysis in American Political Science," *Social Research* 35 (1968), 48–75; A. James Gregor, "Political Science and the Uses of Functional Analysis," *American Political Science Review* 62 (1968), 425–439.

[11] Robert T. Holt, "A Proposed Structural-Functional Framework," in Charlesworth, *Contemporary Political Analysis,* pp. 86–107; Talcott Parsons, "Some Highlights of the General Theory of Action," in Roland Young, *Approaches to the Study of Politics,* pp. 282–301; a similar scheme was used by William C. Mitchell in *The American Polity* (New York, 1962) and "The Polity and Society: A Structural-Functional Analysis," *Midwest Journal of Political Science* 2 (1958), 403–420. For other schemes see, for example, Marion J. Levy, Jr., *The Structure of Society* (Princeton, 1952), pp. 149–197; Gabriel A. Almond and James S. Coleman, eds., *The Politics of the Developing Areas* (Princeton, 1960), pp. 3–64; Almond, "A Developmental Approach to Political Systems," *World Politics* 17 (1965), 183–214.

[12] David Easton, *A Framework for Political Analysis* (Englewood Cliffs, N.J. 1965), pp. 21, 50.

of diverse components, that it receives stimuli and challenges both from intra- and extrasocietal sources, and that its major task is to transform and convert this stream of inputs into authoritative outputs involving rewards and sanctions. Again akin to functionalism, the system focus of this model is coupled with a stress on system stability. Easton in any event has left little doubt about his preoccupation with systemic persistence—an aspect, to be sure, which need by no means be equated with immobility or stagnation. As he has pointed out, the basic objective of his framework is to uncover "the life processes of political systems—those fundamental functions without which no system could endure—together with the typical modes of response through which systems manage to sustain them. The analysis of these processes, and of the nature and conditions of the responses, I posit as a central problem of political theory." [13] A corollary of Easton's preoccupation with system persistence is his concern with stress avoidance or regulation. Severe stress or disturbance is said to occur whenever the system or its essential processes are pushed beyond their critical range of variability; one of the means of obviating disturbance consists in circular connections or "feedback" mechanisms through which output performance becomes available as information to the system for purposes of readjustment. . . .

As can be seen, systemic approaches share a series of common accents and preferences which differentiate them from other theoretical postures; as a rule, leading exponents have been quite explicit about such accents. Talcott Parsons, for example, has persistently maintained that the functioning of social and political communities should be explained in systemic terms, rather than from an individual or group perspective. Reserving the concept of "political system" to value allocations on the level of whole societies, Easton has relegated internal subgroups to a secondary or "parapolitical" status; he has also criticized theoretical efforts proceeding from an actor focus as a partial if not parochial enterprise.[14] Similarly, systemic theorists have not been greatly attracted to questions of power and domestic conflict. In Deutsch's theory, power appears as but one of the currencies of politics, while conflict is explained largely in terms of information and "switchboard" pathologies.[15] A

[13] Easton, *A Systems Analysis of Political Life* (New York, 1965), p. 17. Compare also his statement (p. 475) that "persistence and change of systems, or rather, persistence through change has seemed to be the most inclusive kind of question that one might ask about a political system."

[14] See, for example, Parsons, "Some Highlights of the General Theory of Action," in Roland Young, ed., *Approaches to the Study of Politics* (Evanston, 1958), p. 291; Easton, *A Framework for Political Analysis* (Englewood Cliffs, N.J., 1965), pp. 36, 52; *A Systems Analysis of Political Life*, p. 380.

[15] Deutsch, *The Nerves of Government* (Glencoe, Ill., 1963), pp. 94–95, 124. Compare also Oran Young's statement: "Various questions concerning patterns of control, power, and influence do not play an important part in input-output analysis. Most of the systemic approaches share this pattern of deemphasis to some extent since they focus on the operation of a system in fairly abstract terms rather than on the behavior patterns of human beings. To continue, input-output analysis has little to say about

frequently voiced objection to systemic approaches concerns their presumed static character; in this general form, however, the stricture seems unwarranted. From his earliest writings, Parsons has been attracted to the concepts of equilibrium and homeostasis; but the terms were said to apply both to static, repetitive operations and to "orderly" patterns of development. In recent years, he has paid increasing attention to processes of social "evolution" and "growth," processes defined largely in terms of a system's expanding faculties of adaptation and integration. Both Easton and Deutsch have attacked the narrow restrictions of equilibrium models; through feedback and other homeostatic devices, both have sought to incorporate adaptive change and growth into their theoretical frameworks. Nevertheless, apart from leaving the impulses of change somewhat opaque, evolution and growth are usually conceived as quasi-biological or teleological processes involving an enhanced capacity of survival; in any event, major cleavages and upheavals tend to be neglected.[16] In a recent study of empirical theories, Oran Young has assessed the strengths and weaknesses of systemic approaches; while prolific in discussions of system stability and moderate change, such approaches in his view are relatively mute on questions of power, goal selection, and radical transformation.[17]

Due to their particular focus, systemic models seem to be equally silent on questions of human motivation and personality. Is it nevertheless possible to discern some human features behind the imposing but abstract edifice? Fortunately, systemic theorists have provided many clues for such an enterprise. Easton, it is true, has disclaimed any implication of his theory for a conception of human behavior and motivation; but his empirical studies of political socialization are indicative of his main concerns.[18] Moreover, as Young has noted, Easton's model displays a significant tendency or bias. "Since the political system is a consciously analytic construct," he writes, "roles and patterns of roles are much more nearly the basic unit of analysis than individuals and groups of individuals. And even in the discussion of

---

the politics of decline, disruption, and breakdown in political systems." *Systems of Political Science,* p. 45.

[16] See Parsons, "Some Highlights of the General Theory of Action," p. 283, and "Evolutionary Universals in Society," *American Sociological Review* 29 (1964), 339–357; Easton, *A Framework for Political Analysis,* p. 99; *A Systems Analysis of Political Life,* pp. 19–21; and "Limits of the Equilibrium Model in Social Research," *Behavioral Science* 1 (1956), 96–104; Deutsch, *The Nerves of Government,* pp. 88–91, 248–254, and "Communication Models and Decision Systems," in James C. Charlesworth, ed., *Contemporary Political Analysis* (New York, 1967), pp. 279–282, 293–297.

[17] *Systems of Political Science,* Young, pp. 5–8, 33–36, 44–48, 56–59.

[18] Easton, *A Systems Analysis of Political Life,* p. 409, n. 6; Easton's main objection is to a "neo-Benthamite" or "utilitarian" conception of human behavior according to which individuals rationally calculate and pursue their interests. See also David Easton and Jack Dennis, "The Child's Acquisition of Regime Norms: Political Efficacy," *American Political Science Review* 61 (1967), 25–38; Easton and Robert D. Hess, "The Child's Political World," *Midwest Journal of Political Science* 6 (1962), 229–246.

roles, the flow of analysis is directed toward the contribution of various role patterns to the persistence of the system, rather than toward the contribution of the system to the well-being of the role holders. . . ." [19] The mechanisms of role compliance have been specified in considerable detail by Talcott Parsons. For purposes of systemic stability, he observes, individuals have to be inducted into the common culture and motivated to conform with expected behavior patterns. This task is accomplished largely through "internalization," a process through which "the norms or values (or role-expectation goals) defined in a culture come to be constitutive parts of the personality" of individuals. "Once socialized," he writes, "and making due allowance for elements of conflict and malintegration on both the personality and the social system levels, a person cannot act otherwise than in conformity with his internalized values." [20]

What we have discovered so far are some intriguing fragments or glimpses of human features; what seems needed at this point is an attempt to combine these fragments into a coherent and compelling human profile. Such an attempt has already been made. As it seems to me, many of the above arguments can be fitted, with some adjustments, into an image of man delineated with great care by Ralf Dahrendorf: the image of *homo sociologicus,* of man the role-player and compliant social actor. As Dahrendorf observes, most research and theoretical work in modern sociology proceeds implicitly or explicitly from the assumption that "man behaves in accordance with his roles," that man becomes relevant for analysis "only to the extent that he complies with all the expectations associated with his social positions. This abstraction," he adds, "the scientific unit of sociology, may be called *homo sociologicus.*" [21] According to Dahrendorf, there are two central sociological concepts which pinpoint the intersection between individual and society: "It is by positions and roles that the two conceptually distinguishable facts, the individual and society, are mediated; and it is in terms of these two concepts that we describe *homo sociologicus,* sociological man, the basic unit of sociological analysis." Of the two concepts, however, role in his view is by far the more crucial. Positions "merely identify places in fields of reference," while roles "tell us about how people in given positions relate to people

[19] Young, *Systems of Political Science,* p. 47. Compare also Deutsch, "Communication Models and Decision Systems," p. 286.

[20] Parsons, "Some Highlights of the General Theory of Action," pp. 288–291. As Mancur Olson, Jr., comments on Parsonian theory: "The central preconception of this type of theory is that people do what they are brought up to do. It holds in effect that the hand that rocks the cradle does indeed rule the world." See "The Relationship Between Economics and the Other Social Sciences: The Province of a 'Social Report,'" in *Politics and the Social Sciences,* ed. Seymour M. Lipset (New York, 1969), p. 146. Compare also Alfred L. Baldwin, "The Parsonian Theory of Personality," in *The Social Theories of Talcott Parsons,* ed. Max Black (Englewood Cliffs, 1961), pp. 153–190.

[21] Ralf Dahrendorf, "Sociology and Human Nature," in *Essays in the Theory of Society* (Stanford, 1968), pp. 90–91.

in other positions in the same field." Basically, social roles "represent society's demands on the incumbents of social positions"; they are "bundles of expectations" whose violation entails a variety of sanctions and deprivations. Yet, before an individual can comply with these expectations, he must know them; thus, "like an actor, man as a social being must learn his roles, become familiar with their substance and the sanctions that enforce them." Role learning constitutes a "process of socialization by the internalizing of behavior patterns." The individual, Dahrendorf writes, "must somehow take into himself the prescriptions of society and make them the basis of his behavior; it is by this means that the individual and society are mediated and man is reborn as *homo sociologicus*."[22]

There can be little doubt that Dahrendorf's image of sociological man pervades much of contemporary social science. Yet, the argument could be made that the profile is still somewhat vague, that—at least with reference to systemic approaches—some of its lines need to be sharpened. Above all, "role-playing" is a rather complex and generic concept, a concept which seems applicable to many human masks and images, above and beyond *homo sociologicus*. What distinguishes systemic approaches from other current theories is their treatment of man as a relatively docile ingredient of a larger unit, their emphasis on man as "role-taker" rather than "role-maker."[23] An argument along these lines has been advanced primarily by Dennis Wrong. Attentive to sociological convention, Wrong agrees that "the sociologist's point of departure is an established social structure," that his initial concern is "with those attributes of human nature which sustain consensus, conformity, and role behavior"; he even finds it acceptable to equate "major attention to psychological processes sustaining social conformity with the sociological perspective *per se*." However, in his view, some current approaches have excessively narrowed this perspective; in particular, "the tendency of structural functional sociologists to stress the primacy in society of consensus on values over conflicts of interest and to define society itself as a 'boundary-maintaining system' with built-in processes preserving its equilibrium, inclines them to reliance on a generalized view of man as a thoroughly oversocialized, conformist creature." As Wrong observes, all social theory is prompted by

[22] Dahrendorf, "Homo Sociologicus," ibid., pp. 33–36, 56. More strongly than Parsons, Dahrendorf insists on the normative character of role expectations, on the fact that "social roles are a constraining force on the individual, whether he experiences them as an obstacle to his private wishes or a support that gives him security" (p. 38). Moreover, in contrast to some systemic writers, he argues that role expectations are established not so much by a nondescript "society," but by "reference groups," that is, groups "to which a person has a necessary relation" by virtue of his social positions (pp. 46, 49).

[23] Compare Ralph E. Turner, "Role-Taking: Process versus Conformity," in *Human Behavior and Social Processes*, ed. Arnold M. Rose (Boston, 1962), pp. 20–38. On role theory see, for example, Heinrich Popitz, *Der Begriff der sozialen Rolle als Element der soziologischen Theorie* (Tübingen, 1967); Bruce J. Biddle and Edwin J. Thomas, eds., *Role Theory, Concepts and Research* (New York, 1966); Michael P. Banton, *Roles: An Introduction to the Study of Social Relations* (London, 1965); Neal Gross, Ward S. Mason and Alexander W. McEachern, *Explorations in Role Analysis* (New York, 1958).

vital questions, especially by the "Hobbesian question" of how social order is at all possible. Confronted with the Hobbesian query, much of current theory has taken refuge not only in an "overintegrated" view of society, but also in an "oversocialized" model of man, a model which depicts human beings as dominated by internalized social norms and as "essentially motivated by the desire to achieve a positive image of self by winning acceptance or status in the eyes of others." [24] Wrong's assessment is supported by the argument of Hans Zetterberg that the quest for social approval comes close to qualifying as "the major motivational theorem in sociology"; against this background, the maximization of approval or of "favorable attitudes from others" could be viewed as "the counterpart in sociological theory to the maximization of profit in economic theory." [25]

EXCHANGE THEORIES

While occupying a predominant position, systemic theories have not been unchallenged in contemporary political thought. Champions of alternative theoretical avenues are by no means in full agreement on premises or conclusions; but most tend to place greater weight on the initiative of participant actors or social groups than is customary in systemic approaches. To be sure, by itself a focus on the individual actor as primary unit of analysis is hardly sufficient for the development of a coherent "empirical theory," even under a liberal construction of this term.[26] To produce researchable propositions, the actor focus has to be modified and refined through the introduction of additional parameters and stipulations, especially the stipulation of human interaction in a social context. This emphasis on human interaction is one of the central features of current "exchange" theories or approaches, theories which have been developed primarily, but not exclusively, by politically concerned economists. In a recent address to the political science fraternity, William Mitchell announced good tidings for partisans of such views by presenting exchange models as "the shape of political theory to come" and by predicting an impending shift "from political sociology to political economy." As Mitchell explained, the starting point of the "new political economy" is a conception of politics as an exchange process not very different from economic exchange. This conception, he added, involves a focus on the choices

[24] Dennis H. Wrong, "Human Nature and the Perspective of Sociology," *Social Research* 30 (1963), 304–306, and "The Oversocialized Conception of Man in Modern Sociology," *American Sociological Review* 26 (1961), 184–185. Compare also Paul F. Kress, "Self, System, and Significance: Reflections on Professor Easton's Political Science," *Ethics* 77 (1966), 1–13.

[25] Hans L. Zetterberg, "Compliant Actions," *Acta Sociologica* 2 (1957), 189.

[26] This reservation seems to apply primarily to the so-called "decision-making" framework; compare James N. Rosenau, "The Premises and Promises of Decision-Making Analysis," in Charlesworth, *Contemporary Political Analysis,* pp. 189–211.

and decisions of interacting individuals, groups, and organizations as they are engaged in the more or less rational pursuit of their subjective self-interests; such decisions, moreover, are assumed to be made under varying degrees of uncertainty concerning the goals of others, their strategies and the rules of the game.[27] While concentrating on the pursuit of subjective self-interest, however, exchange theory commonly does not anticipate cleavage and chaos as the result of this pursuit; rather, competitive interaction is viewed as the harbinger of progress leading to higher levels of happiness, social harmony, and integration. In this respect at least, the new political economy rejoins the perspective of systemic approaches. The peculiarity of exchange models, as Mitchell noted, resides not so much in their views on equilibrium and consensus, but in their method of explanation: instead of deriving from agreement on common values, integration is assumed to emerge from bargaining and limited competition.[28]

In its recent rise to prominence, the new political economy has animated a variety of conceptual formulations and substantive concerns; a relatively pure example of the approach can be found in the work of James Buchanan and Gordon Tullock, especially in *The Calculus of Consent*.[29] As Buchanan and Tullock observe, the adoption of a political exchange model is justified by the fact that economic and political interaction "represent cooperation on the part of two or more individuals," that "the market and the state are both devices through which cooperation is organized and made possible." In defending their choice, the two authors are also relatively careful in identifying competing approaches or counter models. One of these counter models is the "organic conception" of the state in which the political system has "an existence, a value pattern, and a motivation independent of those of the in-

[27] William C. Mitchell, "The Shape of Political Theory to Come: From Political Sociology to Political Economy," in Lipset, ed., *Politics and the Social Sciences*, p. 105. (The paper was first presented at the 1967 Annual Meeting of the American Political Science Association.)

[28] "More recent political sociology has followed the lead of Lipset, Parsons and Kornhauser in emphasizing consensus. In so doing they have furnished a potential linkage with the new political economy which I hope both schools will perceive and develop to their mutual benefit." Ibid., p. 106; compare also his "The New Political Economy," *Social Research* 35 (1968), 76–110.

[29] James M. Buchanan and Gordon Tullock, *The Calculus of Consent, Logical Foundations of Constitutional Democracy* (Ann Arbor, 1962). Mitchell describes this book as "perhaps the best single statement by economists of their version of the political system"; Lipset, ed., *Politics and the Social Sciences*, p. 133, n.13. For other examples of the political economy genre see, for example, Robert L. Curry and Lawrence Wade, *A Theory of Political Exchange: Economic Reasoning in Political Analysis* (Englewood Cliffs, 1968); Mancur Olson, Jr., *The Logic of Collective Action* (Cambridge, 1965); James M. Buchanan, *Fiscal Theory and Political Economy* (Chapel Hill, 1960); Duncan Black, *The Theory of Committees and Elections* (Cambridge, 1958); Anthony Downs, *An Economic Theory of Democracy* (New York, 1957); Robert A. Dahl and Charles E. Lindblom, *Politics, Economics, and Welfare* (New York, 1953); Kenneth Arrow, *Social Choice and Individual Values* (New York, 1951); also George E. G. Catlin, *The Science and Method of Politics* (New York, 1927).

dividual human beings claiming membership." Despite a certain limited usefulness, the organic view is rejected as "essentially opposed to the Western philosophical tradition" and as largely irrelevant to a theory of modern democracy. Although they refrain from doing so, the authors' argument could easily have been extended to some systemic approaches where persistence is postulated as a goal inherent in the collectivity.[30] The other major counter model identified by Buchanan and Tullock places the spotlight of attention on domination, coercion, and conflict. "In quite similar fashion," they write, "we shall also reject any theory or conception of the collectivity which embodies exploitation of a ruled by a ruling class. This includes the Marxist vision, which incorporates the polity as one means through which the economically dominant group imposes its will on the downtrodden." As the authors make clear, their objection applies to coercion in every form "whether the ruling class is supposed to consist of Marxist owners of productive factors, the party aristocracy, or the like-minded majority." Equally proscribed are notions of class struggle and class-based motivation: "The point that has been largely overlooked is that it remains perfectly appropriate to assume that men are motivated by utility considerations while rejecting the economic determinism implicit in the whole Marxian stream of thought." [31]

Having rejected the notions of organic collectivity and of class dominance, Buchanan and Tullock are left with an individualistic premise. As they explain, their model is "methodologically individualistic" in the sense that, for purposes of analysis, it "begins with the acting or decision-making individual as he participates in the processes through which group choices are organized." In analogy to the economic theory of the market, the individual entering the political arena is expected to follow his self-interest in a more or less rational fashion; rationality, moreover, is assumed to apply not only to the choice of means but also to the selection of ends to the extent that the individual is able to rank alternative goods according to a consistent scale of preferences. To be sure, in political life rational behavior is handicapped by risk and uncertainty, especially in view of the absence of "one-to-one correspondence between individual choice and final action." Nevertheless, according to Buchanan and Tullock, the significance of this handicap is greatly reduced once political choice is seen as a continuous process in which risk is evenly distributed among all participants. This aspect of reciprocity points to another central feature of the authors' model: their emphasis on harmony and mutual gain. Consensus, in fact, appears as the cornerstone of their political edifice. In agreement with versions of the social contract theory, all individuals are viewed as initially "free and equal"—or at least as

[30] Buchanan and Tullock, *The Calculus of Consent,* pp. 11, 19. For a more direct attack on systemic approaches, especially structural functionalism, see John C. Harsanyi, "Rational-Choice Models of Political Behavior vs. Functionalist and Conformist Models," *World Politics* 21 (1969), 513–538.

[31] Buchanan and Tullock, *The Calculus of Consent,* pp. 12, 26.

equally free to participate in the adoption of basic political decision-rules. Similarly, changes or improvements in such decision-rules are predicated on the possibility of general acceptance—an arrangement loosely akin to the economist's rule of "Pareto-optimality." These and related stipulations support the authors' conclusion that, instead of engendering cleavage and strife, the political market is primarily a cooperative and integrative enterprise. Arguing against the hypothesis of exploitation, Buchanan and Tullock assert that the perspective of the new political economy "does not require that one individual increase his own utility at the expense of other individuals. This approach incorporates political activity as a particular form of *exchange;* and, as in the market relation, mutual gains to all parties are ideally expected to result from the collective relation." In the terminology of modern game theory, the political process thus appears largely as a "positive-sum" game, rather than a "zero-sum" contest in which the winnings of one party are the losses of the opponent. . . .[32]

Apart from the contributions of political economists and sociologists, some affinities with exchange models can be detected in versions of interest group theory. According to Buchanan and Tullock, the economic "conception of democratic process has much in common with that accepted by the school of political science which follows Arthur Bentley in trying to explain collective decision-making in terms of the interplay of group interests." In their opinion, a group calculus could be substituted for an individual calculus "without significantly affecting the results." [33] An important parallel between exchange theory and such a group calculus consists in the conception of pressure politics as an integrative process resulting in harmony and

[32] Ibid., pp. 3, 23–24, 33, 37, 171 ff. (on Pareto-optimality). As the authors add, however, their discussion does not mean "to suggest that in modern political process, as it operates, elements that are characteristic of the zero-sum game are wholly absent" (p. 344, n.13). In another context (p. 266) they observe that "our conception of the political process, as such, is surely more congenial to those seeking 'sweetness and light,' 'peace' and all such good things than the conception usually implicit in political discourse. We view collective decision-making (collective action) as a form of human activity through which mutual gains are made possible. Thus, in our conception, collective activity, like market activity, is a genuinely *cooperative* endeavor in which *all* parties, conceptually, stand to gain." Compare also James M. Buchanan, "An Individualistic Theory of Political Process," in *Varieties of Political Theory,* ed. David Easton (Englewood Cliffs, 1966), pp. 25–37; James G. March, "The Power of Power," ibid., pp. 39–70.

[33] Buchanan and Tullock, *The Calculus of Consent,* p. 9. As they add: "The essential difference between our 'economic' approach to political choice and that approach represented by the Bentley school lies in our attempt to examine the results of political activity in terms of simplified analytical models and, in this way, to suggest some of the implications of the theory that might be subjected to empirical testing." For a more critical appraisal of interest group theory compare Charles E. Lindblom, *The Intelligence of Democracy* (New York, 1965), pp. 12–16; Olson, *The Logic of Collective Action,* pp. 111–131; Harsanyi, "Rational-Choice Models," 516–517.

mutual adjustment; instead of reflecting a conflict between rulers and ruled, the political system in this view appears as a conglomeration of specialized interests whose strength corresponds roughly to group size. As is well-known, exchange in this sense was a central feature of Bentley's theory, which treated government "as the adjustment or balance of interests"; a similar emphasis on balance and adjustment is characteristic of many neo-Bentleyan arguments.[34] Some of the premises of group theory have also been injected into community power studies and empirical analyses of democracy. Thus, a recent student of community power pictured American society as "fractured into a congeries of hundreds of small special interest groups, with incompletely overlapping membership, widely differing power bases and a multitude of techniques for exercising influence on decisions salient to them."[35] The limits or limitations of this vision have not gone unnoticed. In the words of Elmer Schattschneider, "the vice of the groupist theory is that it conceals the most significant aspects of the system. The flaw in the pluralist heaven is that the heavenly chorus sings with a strong upper-class accent." As he added, the overwhelming majority of the people" cannot get into the pressure game." [36]

The human features underlying the above arguments and models are not very hard to discern. Underneath its formulas and equations, exchange theory presents to us a relatively familiar human profile: the profile of *homo economicus,* of man the gain seeker and maximizer of utilities. To be sure, portions of this profile have been redrawn and its sharp contours tempered in most contemporary writings. As Buchanan and Tullock observe, even orthodox economic theory does not depend for its validity on the assumption of an individual propelled by a single-minded ambition for private gain. By the same token, the calculus of political exchange does not rely for its logical coherence "upon any narrowly hedonistic or self-interest motivation of individuals"; rather, the basic requisites of this calculus are satisfied as long

[34] Compare Arthur F. Bentley, *The Process of Government* (Evanston, 1949), p. 264; David B. Truman, *The Governmental Process* (New York, 1951), pp. 510–516; also Bernard Crick, *The American Science of Politics, Its Origins and Conditions* (Berkeley, 1964), pp. 123–125.

[35] Nelson W. Polsby, *Community Power and Political Theory* (New York, 1963), p. 118. Compare also Heinz Eulau's comment that, in *Who Governs?,* Robert A. Dahl created a "complex model of the democratic order in a competitive environment —a political system in which the politics of influence is not a zero-sum game, but a function of highly fragmented patterns of more or less direct influence, of reciprocal relations between leaders, sub-leaders and constituents, of shifting coalitions and bargaining between more or less overlapping networks of influentials who specialize in different issue areas." *American Political Science Review* 56 (1962), 144.

[36] Elmer E. Schattschneider, *The Semisovereign People* (New York, 1960), p. 35. See also William E. Connolly, ed., *The Bias of Pluralism* (New York, 1969), pp. 3–34; Peter Bachrach, *The Theory of Democratic Elitism, A Critique* (Boston, 1967), pp. 35–46; Olson, *The Logic of Collective Action*, pp. 126–130.

as different individuals are assumed to pursue different goals or interests in both their private and their social actions.[37] Similar sentiments are expressed in Anthony Downs' *An Economic Theory of Democracy*. In his view, the behavioral premises of traditional economics are not tailored to "a man whose thought processes consist exclusively of logical propositions, or a man without prejudices, or a man whose emotions are inoperative"; what is postulated in market theory is simply an individual "who moves toward his goals in a way which, to the best of his knowledge, uses the least possible input of scarce resources per unit of valued output." As Downs adds, the behavioral dimension of his own model does not claim to embrace the whole personality of an individual, the "rich diversity of ends served by each of his acts" or the "complexity of his motives." Moreover, in view of ineradicable uncertainties about the future, the individual of his model is bound to display a less "calculating-machine-brained character" than the personality construct of traditional economic theory.[38]

Despite initial qualifications or disclaimers, however, the characteristic features of *homo economicus* still emerge vividly in contemporary political economy. Downs' model carefully replicates the "two major steps" of orthodox economic analysis: discovery of a decision-maker's ends, and explanation of the most reasonable means of attaining these ends. With regard to the first step, Downs by and large accepts the self-interest axiom of economic theory; only the content or direction of self-interest is modified. While in market relations the individual participant is assumed to maximize material benefits, the actor in the political arena is expected to calculate his advantages in the selection of governments in the same manner as governments and political parties seek to formulate policies which will maximize political support. The most rational means of reaching these goals, according to Downs, are actions which are efficient in the sense of "maximizing output for a given input, or minimizing input for a given output." More particularly, rational behavior in both the economic and the political arena refers to an individual's ability to arrange his preferences in a transitive rank order and to choose consistently the most advantageous alternatives. Through a more protracted line of reasoning Buchanan and Tullock reach almost identical results. . . .

CONFLICT THEORIES

Among contemporary theoretical preoccupations in political science, power and political conflict occupy a relatively subordinate if not obscure position. This obscurity is puzzling both in view of the history of social science and

[37] Buchanan and Tullock, *The Calculus of Consent*, pp. 3–4, 14, 17.
[38] Anthony Downs, *An Economic Theory of Democracy*, pp. 5, 7.

of the concrete lessons of experience. At least since the dawn of the modern age, the attention of leading social theorists has been absorbed by the dilemmas of power. The "Hobbesian question" of how society is at all possible was posed against the stark background of conflict and destruction.[39] The political experiences of our own age would seem to lend support to this formulation of the question. Yet, during recent decades, social scientists have tended to elude the Hobbesian query and to concentrate almost exclusively on the quasi-organic functioning of society or the rational behavior of its participants. To be sure, despite this temporary shift in focus, the more disquieting features of political life have not gone unnoticed. As Robert Dahl observed some time ago, because of the absence of complete homogeneity "an important element of coercion" is liable to exist in human society; "government by unanimity" seems unattainable. More recently, there has been a growing stress on the importance of such elements and on the need to reincorporate them in the study of politics. Among others, Francis Wormuth has exhorted political science to return "to its proper theme, the study of power." As he added: "The dangers and the promises of the future are the dangers and the promises of power." [40]

Statements to a similar effect could be multiplied without difficulty; in fact, the literature of political science abounds with references to the themes of power, domination, and conflict. Nevertheless, the use of this vocabulary alone is insufficient evidence of a coherent theoretical framework. By and large, the development of contemporary conflict theory has been the work of sociologists, aided by some political scientists conversant with the theory of games.[41] In the terminology of game theory, political conflict can be formulated as a "zero-sum" contest, in contrast to cooperative encounters involving mutual gain; William Riker's study of political coalitions is built

[39] Horowitz traces the ancestry of the conflict approach back to antiquity when he writes: "The roots of conflict theory reach back in time to Hobbes and the formation of the modern nation-state, Marsilius of Padua in the medieval world and Thrasymachus, Socrates and Plato in ancient Greek society." See "Consensus, Conflict and Cooperation: A Sociological Inventory," p. 179.

[40] Robert A. Dahl, *Congress and Foreign Policy* (New York, 1950), 223; Francis D. Wormuth, "The Politics of George Catlin," *Western Political Quarterly* 14 (1961), 811. Compare also Robert Presthus' comment: "However difficult it may be to develop a higher toleration for ambiguity on a national scale, criticism and conflict must again become fashionable." *The Organizational Society* (New York, 1962), p. 294.

[41] This statement, of course, requires qualification; for elements of a conflict perspective in political science literature compare, for example, Robert A. Dahl, *Pluralist Democracy in the United States: Conflict and Consent* (Chicago, 1967); J. David Singer, "The Political Science of Human Conflict," *The Nature of Human Conflict,* ed. Elton B. McNeil (Englewood Cliffs, 1965), pp. 139–154; Robert E. Agger, Daniel Goldrich and Bert E. Swanson, *The Rulers and the Ruled* (New York, 1964); Kalman H. Silvert, *The Conflict Society* (New York, 1961); Harold D. Lasswell and Abraham Kaplan, *Power and Society, A Framework for Political Inquiry* (New Haven, 1950); Charles E. Merriam, *Political Power* (New York, 1934).

solidly on this theoretical basis. In his study, Riker concentrates on the "authoritative allocation of values" by decision-makers, focusing on groups as primary units of analysis; as he explains, conscious decision-making in groups is essentially "a process of forming coalitions." For the examination of this process, Riker adopts the parameters of game theory, especially two basic assumptions. The first of these is the postulate of "rationality." In his formulation, rational behavior in the political arena consists in the effort to maximize power or, more precisely, in the adoption of a "winning" strategy. Although such conduct may not be characteristic of all individuals, those "institutions that work by coalitions" select and reward behavior which is rational in the specified sense. The second major assumption is the zero-sum axiom—the requirement that the gains of the winners equal the losses of their opponents. Riker readily admits that political life is not always a condition of pure and unrelieved conflict and that bargaining in particular "involves some sort of gain for both parties." However, although in the long run all participants stand to gain from society and civilization, there are occasions when winning is the paramount objective. In contrast to money, which can be divided and distributed among the contestants, victory in the political arena is frequently "an indivisible unit." Thus, "by emphasis on winning what is often an indivisible prize in these matters, as in games, the common imagination abstracts pure conflict for which the zero-sum model is entirely appropriate." [42]

While impressive in its mathematic elegance, Riker's study is circumscribed by its formal axioms and its focus on coalition formation. The broader connotations of social conflict have been elaborated by contemporary sociologists, most notably by Ralf Dahrendorf. The contribution of sociologists in this area is not surprising in view of the heritage of their discipline; Dahrendorf is quick to acknowledge his debt to this tradition. "From Marx and Comte to Simmel and Sorel," he writes, "social conflict, especially revolution, was one of the central themes in social research." [43] It may be instructive to note some parallels between the arguments of the game theorist and the sociologist. Like Riker, Dahrendorf concentrates on social groupings or

[42] William H. Riker, *The Theory of Political Coalitions* (New Haven, 1962), pp. 10–12, 21–22, 28–31. The passage acknowledging the positive-sum character of bargaining situations refers explicitly to the work of Buchanan and Tullock; on power see Riker's "A Test of the Adequacy of the Power Index," *Behavioral Science* 4 (1959), 120–131. Compare also William T. Bluhm, *Theories of the Political System: Classics of Political Thought and Modern Political Analysis* (Englewood Cliffs, 1965), pp. 290–299.

[43] Dahrendorf, "Toward a Theory of Social Conflict," in *Social Change,* ed. Amitai and Eva Etzioni (New York, 1964), p. 98. In another context, he describes the work of Vilfredo Pareto, Gaetano Mosca, and Raymond Aron as "the proximate origin" of his thought; however, at least with regard to Pareto and Mosca, he notes a "crucial difference between elite theories and conflict theories." *Class and Class Conflict in Industrial Society,* pp. 194, 199.

"structural elements" of society as primary targets of his analysis;[44] these groupings, in his case, are the product of the differential distribution of power and authority, of the fact that all societies are divided into positions of dominance and subordination. Also like Riker, Dahrendorf stresses the "zero-sum" element implicit in the power relationships of the political arena. While income and money can be divided and distributed throughout society in a continuum ranging from the lowest to the highest rank, power remains recalcitrant to complete diffraction. "Wealth is not and cannot be conceived as a zero-sum concept," he asserts. "With respect to authority, however, a clear line can at least in theory be drawn between those who participate in its exercise in given associations and those who are subject to the authoritative commands of others. . . ." [45]

Against this background, the rudiments of Dahrendorf's own approach can now briefly be sketched. This approach is formulated as a counter model to prevailing integration or consensus schemes. While the latter rely on the assumption of stability, integration, value consensus, and functional coordination of elements, conflict theory is based on the ubiquity of social change and conflict, the "dysfunctionality" of all the elements of social structure, and the constraining character of social unity. The element of constraint is particularly significant because of its dynamic implications. "Power," writes Dahrendorf, "always implies non-power and therefore resistance. The dialectic of power and resistance is the motive force of history." This means that every political organization exhibits a differential and in fact dichotomous distribution of power and authority; in Max Weber's terminology, the political community is an "imperatively coordinated association." The dichotomous distribution of power in society gives rise to at least two opposing social groups: the groups of the powerful and the powerless, the carriers of "positive" and "negative dominance roles." From this starting point, conflict theory proceeds to the exploration of group formation and group conflict. Initially, the carriers of positive and negative dominance roles constitute merely two structurally defined quasi-groups with opposite "latent interests." In certain situations, however, the bearers of these roles organize themselves into groups properly speaking with "manifest interests"; among the factors which promote or obstruct this transition are technical, social, and political conditions of organization. Once organized, interest groups generated in this manner engage in conflict over the preservation or change of the *status quo,* with the form and intensity of the conflict being determined by empirically variable circumstances. Subject to variations in speed and extent,

[44] However, Dahrendorf opposes the reduction of sociological explanation to psychological factors or individual behavior. Compare "Homo Sociologicus," in *Essays in the Theory of Society,* pp. 24, 64; also *Class and Class Conflict in Industrial Society,* pp. 145–149.

[45] Dahrendorf, *Class and Class Conflict,* pp. 160–170.

the conflict among interest groups produces changes in the structure of social positions, through changes in dominance relations.[46]

As in previous instances, the question which I want to raise now concerns the behavioral implications of the discussed perspective. What human features can we discern in the stipulations of struggle and constraint? Despite the usual need of extrapolation, the profile presented to us in this theory is no stranger to political scientists: it is the image of *homo politicus,* of man the power seeker and maximizer of self-determination. While seemingly simple and straightforward, this image is by no means one dimensional. Of the epithets which I have selected, the latter referring to self-determination is probably the more significant. As has frequently been observed, power is a somewhat elusive possession which is rarely sought for the sake of its own pleasure; but this objection does not touch the central issue. The image of political man reminds us that politics is not simply or not only a matter of convention or rationality, but a matter of will and action. Yet, though all human beings are endowed with some will power, not all are equally capable of implementing their wills and thus determining the courses of their lives. In all known political communities, at least, some layers have had an advantage over others in shaping both their own lives and the direction of society; in other words, social positions granting this kind of autonomy have traditionally been scarce. From this scarcity arises a struggle of wills, a struggle which is primarily a contest over the extent and direction of self-determination and self-realization.

While he is reluctant to resort to behavioral arguments, Dahrendorf's analysis provides at least some glimpses of political man. As a sociologist, Dahrendorf tends to explain social conflict primarily in terms of structurally defined social positions and corresponding role expectations; the major conflict groups in his theory are the carriers of positive and negative dominance roles. Yet, his concept of roles points beyond the strictly structural domain. As he emphasizes, social roles are a constraining force on individuals due to the availability of sanctions attached to role expectations. Since sanctions, however, are decreed by ruling groups and since conflict theory postulates imperfect compliance, Dahrendorf's role-player would seem to acquire some of the troubled features of *homo politicus.*[47] Despite the limiting parameter

[46] Ibid., p. 227; Dahrendorf, "Toward a Theory of Social Conflict," in *Social Change,* ed. Etzioni and Etzioni, pp. 103–109; *Class and Class Conflict in Industrial Society,* pp. 157–240. For additional sociological literature compare Lewis Coser, *The Functions of Social Conflict* (Glencoe, Ill., 1956) and *Continuities in the Study of Social Conflict* (New York, 1967); Irving L. Horowitz, *The New Sociology* (New York, 1965), pp. 3–48; T. B. Bottomore, *Elites and Society* (New York, 1964); Barrington Moore, Jr., *Political Power and Social Theory* (Cambridge, Mass., 1958); James S. Coleman, *Community Conflict* (New York, 1957); C. Wright Mills, *The Power Elite* (New York, 1956).

[47] Compare Dahrendorf, "Homo Sociologicus," *Essays in the Theory of Society,* p. 38; also "On the Origin of Inequality Among Men," ibid., 167; and Dahrendorf, *Class and Class Conflict in Industrial Society,* pp. 177–178.

of "rationality," traces of these features can also be found in Riker's model; the prime ambition of political man in this model is to win over others. "Politically rational man," Riker comments, "is the man who would rather win than lose, regardless of the particular stakes." This formulation, he adds, is quite consonant with definitions of power prevalent in social science: "The man who wants to win also wants to make other people do things they would not otherwise do, he wants to exploit each situation to his advantage, and he wants to succeed in a given situation." [48] The darker, nonrational forces operative in this quest have not escaped the attention of political scientists. In a study contrasting scientific and political man, Hans Morgenthau asserted that political conflict cannot be dissolved through rational adjustment or scientific formulas. "The failure of the dogmatic scientism of our age to explain the social and, more particularly, the political problems of this age and to give guidance for successful action," he wrote, "calls for a re-examination of these problems in the light of prerationalist Western tradition. This re-examination must start with the assumption that power politics, rooted in the lust for power which is common to all men, is for this reason inseparable from social life itself." [49]

Morgenthau's statement alluded to motivational constants, to a psychological infrastructure of political conflict; concern with this infrastructure has been shared by many social scientists. In fact, political man on this level shades over into and blends with another image or profile of social science, the image of "psychological man. . . ."

The convergence of psychological and political man is exemplified nowhere better than in the writings of Harold Lasswell. Integrating Eduard Spranger's notion of the power seeker with Freudian personality theory, Lasswell in *Psychopathology and Politics* sketched a developmental physiognomy of *homo politicus*. The core of his conception was the stipulation that political man is propelled by private motives which he displaces onto public objects and rationalizes in terms of public interest.[50] More detailed features of this physiognomy were presented in *Power and Personality*. As Lasswell endeavored to show in this study, the basic idea underlying the notion of political man was "that some personalities are power seekers, searching out the power institutions of the society into which they are born and devoting themselves to the capture and use of government"; moreover, the political individual had to be grasped as a "developmental type who passes through a distinctive career line in which the power opportunities of each situation are

[48] Riker, *The Theory of Political Coalitions*, p. 22.

[49] Hans J. Morgenthau, *Scientific Man vs. Power Politics* (Chicago, 1946), p. 9.

[50] Harold D. Lasswell, *Psychopathology and Politics* (Chicago, 1930; new ed. with afterthoughts by the author; New York, 1960), p. 75. According to Lasswell, Spranger's power seeker was characterized primarily by "desire to control the motives of others; methods varying from violence to wheedling; and success in securing communal recognition" (p. 52).

selected in preference to other opportunities." The driving motive of the power seeker was identified as an intense craving for deference which remains unsatisfied in the private sphere. Political man, in other words, was said to pursue power as a means of compensating for psychological deprivations, such as lack of respect and affection, suffered during childhood. This quest was not necessarily conscious or deliberate; but yearning had to be accompanied by at least a minimum degree of skill and effectiveness. The human profile which thus emerged was that of an individual who accentuates power, demands influence for himself or those with whom he identifies, possesses and inspires confidence in his capabilities, and acquires at least a minimum proficiency in the skills of power.[51]

The preceding journey through our discipline leaves us in a discomforting condition. We started from an examination of empirical or scientific political theory, and we soon discovered that there is a variety of such theories or frameworks in contemporary political science. Investigating these theories and their human dimensions, we found again that our discipline is populated not by one, but a diversity of human images and models of man. One after the other, we saw *homo sociologicus, homo economicus,* and *homo politicus* enter the limelight of our profession and deliver their prepared monologues. What are we to make of these stylized performers, of these familiar yet elusive characters whom Dahrendorf calls the "glass men of social science"? As it seems, we have entered a difficult labyrinth, a complex cabinet of mirrors whose oddly bent surfaces confront us with a procession of Doppelgänger. How can these divergent images be reconciled with each other? And more important: what is our relationship to them? Can we still recognize ourselves in the mirrors of contemporary science?

Clearly, the divergence of images is a manifestation of the identity crisis of modern man, a result of his alienation from the world and his products. Against this background the models of empirical theory reveal themselves as the projections and reflections of man in an estranged universe.[52] While the symptoms of the crisis are relatively evident, however, the remedy is not.

[51] Lasswell, *Power and Personality* (New York, 1948; new ed. New York, 1962), pp. 20–21, 37–41, 57. Compare also Gordon J. DiRenzo, *Personality, Power and Politics* (Notre Dame, 1967); Arnold A. Rogow and Harold D. Lasswell, *Power, Corruption, and Rectitude* (Englewood Cliffs, 1963); Robert A. Dahl, *Modern Political Analysis* (Englewood Cliffs, 1963), p. 67; Marc, "What Image of Man for Political Science," *Western Political Quarterly* 15 (1962), 600–601.

[52] As Dahrendorf notes in "Homo Sociologicus," *Essays in the Theory of Society,* 44: "Society is the alienated persona of the individual, homo sociologicus a shadow that has escaped the man to return as his master." Compare also Julian N. Hartt, *The Lost Image of Man* (Baton Rouge, 1963); Fritz Pappenheim, *The Alienation of Modern Man* (New York, 1959); Allen Wheelis, *The Quest for Identity* (New York, 1958); Maurice Natanson, "Alienation and Social Role," *Social Research* 33 (1966), 375–388; Peter L. Berger, "Identity as a Problem in the Sociology of Knowledge," *European Journal of Sociology* 7 (1966), 105–115; Carl J. Couch, "Self-Identification and Alienation," *The Sociological Quarterly* 7 (1966), 255–264.

How can man's alienation be overcome and his sense of identity restored? At least two sweeping solutions have been suggested to this query; both, one might say, consist in the destruction of the mirror relationship. According to one argument, the dilemma itself is illusory: we are the glass men of science. In a strictly logical sense, we are told, there is no reality, at least no intelligible reality outside the scientist's mirrors. Therefore, what can be known or said about human beings is portrayed and explained in these mirrors, an explanation which is potentially complete. This ambition of completeness seems to be the scientist's peculiar temptation; most of the approaches discussed in these pages claim or aspire to be "general theories" of society and human behavior.[53] However, at least if generality is meant to suggest comprehensive coverage, the claim is demonstrably spurious. Ever since social disciplines have decided to emulate the sciences of nature, man's practical strivings have been slipping from their grasp. The dichotomy of facts and values—a distinction which "empirical" political theory is bound to support—imposes an irremediable restriction on the scientist's legitimate range of explanation; for the same reason, his models cannot hope to absorb the man of common sense experience. Where this limitation is ignored, social science quickly deteriorates into ideology, a doctrine in which prescription masquerades as analysis and empirical propositions assume normative control over human behavior.[54]

The other solution acknowledges the dilemma of alienation but puts the blame on the scientist's doorsteps. As we are told by enthusiasts—some of them members of our profession—the identity crisis of modern man was precipitated by scientific mirrors and will be cured with their demolition. In this view, the glass men of social analysis are simply arbitrary disfigurements; their removal, we are assured, will quickly restore man's pristine integrity. There is little point here in embellishing the artifacts of scientific imagination; their blemishes and incongruities have been noted even by their friends. Yet on closer inspection, some of these defects may turn out to be virtues. His artificiality, for example, has not prevented *homo economicus* from strengthening the explanatory arsenal of economic theory; a similar intellectual service may be performed by his companions. Viewed in this manner, the glass men of science are not merely distortions, but Doppelgänger whose stylized profiles reveal and magnify some of the traits of our complex physiognomy. Little would be gained in this case from the destruction of mirror images. Although

[53] Compare, for example, Talcott Parsons and Edward A. Shils, eds., *Toward a General Theory of Action* (Cambridge, Mass., 1951); Gordon Tullock, *A General Theory of Politics* (U. of Virginia, 1958, private circulation); George C. Homans, *The Nature of Social Science* (New York, 1967).

[54] As Jürgen Habermas points out: "As soon as the attitude of objectivity is turned into an ideological affirmation, the difficulties of the methodologically unconscious individual distort themselves into the doubtful virtue of a scientistic creed." See "Knowledge and Interest," *Inquiry* 9 (1966), 298.

an urgent task, the restoration of man's identity can hardly be accomplished through amputation and truncation; instead of promoting human wholeness, such a method can only result in the forced poses of a petty dogmatism.

If we reject amputation, we will somehow have to live with our stylized artifacts; in the absence of compulsion, the acquisition of human wholeness can only be the work of dialogue and patient interrogation. One phase of this dialogue is of an intramural character, involving as participants the glass men of empirical theory. Probably not all these artifacts possess equal stature and explanatory capacity. It can plausibly be argued, I think, that conflict theory has special significance for some crucial problem areas of our discipline; *homo politicus* seems to speak with particular cogency to an age of upheaval and rapid transformation.[55] However, I want to forego invidious comparisions at this point and concentrate on the prospect of amicable relationships. One way of conceptualizing these relationships is through reliance on Freudian imagery. In this imagery—passingly invoked by both Wrong and Dahrendorf—sociological man appears as the representative of man's conscience or "superego," while economic and political man are expressions of his "ego" and "id" components. Advancing beyond the level of suggestive metaphors, Mancur Olson has reflected on the interrelationships of scientific models, especially models of sociological and economic provenance; as he explains, sociology is primarily concerned with "the formation and transmission of wants and beliefs of all kinds," while economics explores the means through which people strive to obtain their goals most efficiently. The diversity of available models, he adds, is bound to broaden and enrich our discipline; since different perspectives imply divergent strategies and conclusions, we should hope not only "for a great deal of disciplinary overlap" and communication, but for a similar confrontation inside the domain of political science.[56]

The dialogue to which I am referring, however, cannot be restricted to the glass men of science; in this intramural setting, their discourse would be empty and pointless. If they are to be more than crisis symptoms, our artifacts have to face not only each other, but also their moral counterpart, the man without mirrors. This man—integral and free despite the testimony

[55] For a listing of some of the advantages of conflict theory see Horowitz, "Consensus, Conflict and Cooperation: A Sociological Inventory," *Social Forces* 41 (1962), 184–185.

[56] Olson, "The Relationship Between Economics and the Other Social Sciences," pp. 147, 160–161. On the Freudian concepts see Wrong, "The Oversocialized Conception of Man in Modern Sociology," 186–187, and "Human Nature and the Perspective of Sociology," 315; Dahrendorf, "Homo Sociologicus," 57, 75; also Harold D. Lasswell, "The Triple-Appeal Principle: A Contribution of Psychoanalysis to Political and Social Science," *American Journal of Sociology* 37 (1932), 523–538. For attempts at a closer amalgamation of approaches compare Gerhard E. Lenski, *Power and Privilege, A Theory of Social Stratification* (New York, 1966), pp. 14–23; Pierre L. Van den Berghe, "Dialectic and Functionalism: Toward a Theoretical Synthesis," *American Sociological Review* 28 (1963), 695–705.

of his detractors—has been described by Robert Musil as the "tenth character," a character marked by "the passive fantasy of unfilled spaces." [57] Although relatively silent and elusive, this individual is yet the most influential partner in our dialogue; in fact, our glass men have to remain poised in his direction, unless they are to degenerate into the phantoms of closed societies and a closed universe. Thus, the models of empirical theory are neither self-sufficient nor eternal; their profiles resemble the rough contours of a statue still in the making. Underneath their stylized masks and awkwardly frozen gestures there are glimpses of an unfinished man—an individual embarked on a fantastic adventure, the adventure of reassembling a broken creation.

[57] Robert Musil, *Der Mann ohne Eigenschaften* (Reinbek, 1952), p. 35; quoted in Dahrendorf, "Homo Sociologicus," *Essays in the Theory of Society,* p. 74. Compare also Helmuth Plessner, *Die Stufen des Organischen und der Mensch* (2nd ed., Düsseldorf, 1964); Ruth Wylie, *The Self-Concept* (Lincoln, 1961); Anselm Strauss, *Mirrors and Masks* (New York, 1959); Eduard Urbanek, "Roles, Masks and Characters," *Social Research* 34 (1967), 529–562; Robert R. Ehman, "Two Basic Concepts of the Self," *International Philosophical Quarterly* 5 (1965), 594–611; Gajo Petrovic, "Man as Economic Animal and Man as Praxis," *Inquiry* 6 (1963), 35–56; Richard A. Schermerhorn, "Man the Unfinished," *The Sociological Quarterly* 4 (1963), 5–17.

12

Alienation and Anomie

Steven Lukes[1]

Both Marx and Durkheim were profound critics of industrial society in nineteenth-century Europe. What is striking is the markedly different bases of their criticisms of the ills of their societies, which can best be brought out by a careful consideration of the different assumptions and implications that belong to the two concepts of alienation and anomie, which they respectively employed.[2] These concepts were elaborated by the two thinkers in their earliest writings and remain implicit as basic and integral elements in their developed social theories. Thus a study of the differing perspectives which they manifest should be fruitful. I shall argue: first, that they are both socio-psychological concepts, embodying hypotheses about specific relationships between social conditions and individual psychological states; second, that they differ precisely in the sorts of hypotheses they embody; and third, that this difference derives in part from a fundamental divergence in the views of human nature they presuppose. Fourthly, I shall examine the nature of that divergence, and in particular the extent to which the dispute is an empirical one. I shall conclude by asking to what extent such approaches to the analysis of society remain relevant and important today.

First, however, I need to make the negative point that contemporary uses of the notions of alienation and anomie, while claiming to derive from Marx and Durkheim, are not for our purposes a useful starting-point. "Alienation" in particular has achieved considerable and widespread contemporary

Source: *Philosophy, Politics and Society,* ed. Peter Laslett and W. G. Runciman (Oxford: Basil Blackwell and Mott Limited, 1967). Reprinted by permission of the author and A. D. Peters and Company.

1 My thanks are especially due to Dr. S. Avineri, Professor Sir I. Berlin and Mr. J. P. Plamenatz for their kind and helpful comments on an earlier draft of this article.

2 For other discussions of these concepts, treating them together but in ways rather different both from one another and from that adopted here, see J. Horton, "The Dehumanisation of Anomie and Alienation," *British Journal of Sociology,* XV, 4 (December 1964), and E. H. Mizruchi, "Alienation and Anomie," in *The New Sociology: Essays in Social Science and Social Theory,* ed. I. L. Horowitz (New York, 1964).

currency, but it has become debased in consequence. Its evident resonance for "neo-Marxist" thinkers, in both the West and the East, for existentialist philosophers and theologians, for psychiatrists and industrial sociologists, for *déraciné* artists and intellectuals and student rebels, has meant that it has been widely extended and altered in the interests of a number of contemporary preoccupations; as a result the core of Marx's concept has been lost.[3] "Anomie" has been less widely used, but it too has achieved a new life, within American social science. In particular, Robert Merton's paper "Social Structure and Anomie" [4] (published 1938) has led to an extensive literature of conceptual refinement and empirical research, chiefly concerned with "deviance" in all its forms.[5] But here too, much of the original meaning of the concept has been lost: in particular, most writers have followed Merton in discarding Durkheim's theory of human nature.

Furthermore, modern versions of these concepts vary widely in the range of their empirical reference. In the work of sociologists they are often taken as synonymous or else one is taken to be a subtype of the other. Thus Nettler, Seeman and Scott in recent attempts to develop typologies of alienation count anomie as a variant, while Srole[6] counts alienation as a variant of anomie. Worse, there has been endless dispute in the case of both concepts about whether they are to be taken as sociological or psychological or as socio-psychological and, if the last, in what sense. Thus Merton defines "the sociological concept of anomie" as "a breakdown in the cultural structure, occurring particularly when there is an acute disjunction between the cultural norms and goals and the socially structured capacities of members of the group to act in accord with them," [7] and Robin Williams observes that "Anomie as a social condition has to be defined independently of the psychological states thought to accompany normlessness and normative conflict";

[3] Robert Nisbet writes: "The hypothesis of alienation has reached an extraordinary degree of importance. It has become nearly as prevalent as the doctrine of enlightened self-interest was two generations ago" (*The Quest for Community,* New York, 1953, p. 15). There is even an "alienation reader" (E. and M. Josephson, *Man Alone,* New York, 1962).

[4] R. K. Merton, *Social Theory and Social Structure* (Glencoe, revised edition, 1957), Ch. IV.

[5] According to a recent article on the subject (H. McClosky and J. H. Schaar, "Psychological Dimensions of Anomy," *American Sociological Review* 30, 1965) there have been since Merton's paper first appeared about 35 papers on "anomy." "In addition, the concept has been used in a large number of books and essays and applied to discussions of an astonishing variety of topics, ranging from delinquency among the young to apathy among the old, and including along the way such matters as political participation, status aspirations, the behaviour of men in prisons, narcotics addiction, urbanization, race relations, social change, and suicide." (p. 14.)

[6] G. Nettler, "A Measure of Alienation," *American Sociological Review* 22, 1957. M. Seeman, "On the Meaning of Alienation," *American Sociological Review* 24, 1959. M. B. Scott, "The Social Sources of Alienation," *Inquiry* 6, 1963. L. Srole, "Social Integration and Certain Corollaries," *American Sociological Review* 21, 1956.

[7] Merton, *Social Theory,* Ch. V, p. 162.

while, for example, Riesman, MacIver, Lasswell and Srole[8] take it to refer to a state of mind. Similarly, "alienation" is sometimes taken to refer to an objective social condition, which is to be identified independently of people's feelings and beliefs, as in the work of Lukacs and those who follow him: men live within "reified" and "fetishist" social forms and the task is precisely to make them *conscious* of their history, which is "in part the product, evidently unconscious until now, of the activity of men themselves, and in part the succession of the processes in which the forms of this activity, the relations of man with himself (with nature and with other men) are transformed";[9] on the other hand, very many writers take alienation to be a state of mind (e.g., existentialist writers, theologians, psychiatrists, American sociologists). One writer even takes alienation to be synonymous with frustration of any kind, arguing that it "lies in every direction of human experience where basic emotional desire is frustrated." [10]

Concepts can embody hypotheses and, in the case of these two concepts, when the focus is sociological there is frequently assumed to be a psychological correlate, and vice versa. Thus, e.g., Merton classifies the psychological states resulting from sociological anomie, while others make assumptions about the social causes of psychological anomie; similarly Marxist sociologists make assumptions about the psychological effects of alienated social forms, while, e.g., Erich Fromm sees the psychological state of alienation as a function of market society.

A basic unclarity thus exists about the range of reference of each of these concepts and, even where the concepts are clearly used to embody hypotheses about relationships between social conditions and mental states, the very diversity of such hypotheses makes an analytical comparison of the concepts in their modern forms unmanageable in a short space. Where "alienation" can mean anything from "bureaucratic rules which stifle initiative and deprive individuals of all communication among themselves and of all information about the institutions in which they are situated" [11] to a mode of experience in which the person experiences himself as an alien," [12] and where "anomie" can extend from the malintegration of the cultural and social structure to "the state of mind of one who has been pulled up by his moral roots," [13] then the

[8] R. Williams, *American Society* (New York, 1951), p. 537. D. Riesman, *The Lonely Crowd* (New Haven, 1950), pp. 287. R. MacIver, *The Ramparts We Guard* (New York, 1950), pp. 84–5. H. Lasswell, "The Threat to Privacy" in *Conflict of Loyalties* ed. R. MacIver (New York, 1952), and Srole, "Social Integration," p. 712.

[9] G. Lukacs, *Histoire de Classe et Conscience de Classe* (Paris, 1960), p. 230.

[10] L. Feuer, "What Is Alienation? The Career of a Concept," *New Politics*, 1962, p. 132.

[11] C. Lefort in "Marxisme et Sociologie," *Les Cahiers du Centre d'Etudes Socialistes* 34–5 (1963), p. 24.

[12] E. Fromm, *The Sane Society* (New York, 1955), p. 120.

[13] MacIver, *The Ramparts We Guard*, p. 84.

time has come either to abandon the concepts or return to their origins for guidance.

I

Marx distinguishes four aspects of alienated labor: (1) "the relationship of the worker to the *product of labor* as an alien object which dominates him." Thus, "the more the worker expends himself in work the more powerful becomes the world of objects which he creates in face of himself, the poorer he becomes in his inner life, and the less he belongs to himself"; (2) "the relationship of labor to the *act of production,*" with the result that "the work is *external* to the worker, that it is not part of his nature; and that, consequently, he does not fulfil himself in his work but denies himself, has a feeling of misery rather than wellbeing, does not develop freely his mental and physical energies but is physically exhausted and mentally debased. The worker, therefore, feels himself at home only during his leisure time, whereas at work he feels homeless. His work is not voluntary but imposed, *forced labor.* It is not the satisfaction of a need, but only a *means* for satisfying other needs"; (3) The alienation of man from himself as a "species-being," from "his own active function, his life-activity", which is "free, conscious activity." Man is thus alienated from "his own body, external nature, his mental life and his *human* life"; (4) The alienation of man "from other *men.* When man confronts himself he also confronts other men . . . in the relationship of alienated labor every man regards other men according to the standards and relationships in which he finds himself placed as a worker." Social relations "are not relations between individual and individual, but between worker and capitalist, between farmer and landlord, etc." Further, men's lives are divided up into different spheres of activity, where conflicting standards apply: "The nature of alienation implies that each sphere applies a different and contradictory norm, that morality does not apply the same norm as political economy, etc., because each of them is a particular alienation of man; each is concentrated upon a specific area of alienated activity and is itself alienated from the other."

"Alienation" thus refers to the relationship of the individual to elements of his social and natural environment and to his state of mind, or relationship with himself. Marx contends that "the division of labor . . . impoverishes the worker and makes him into a machine," that "the division of labor offers us the first example of how . . . man's own deed becomes an alien power opposed to him, which enslaves him instead of being controlled by him. For as soon as labor is distributed, each man has a particular exclusive sphere of activity, which is forced upon him and from which he cannot escape." In conditions where men must work for the increase of wealth, labor is "harmful and deleterious"; the division of labor, which develops in such conditions, causes the worker to become "even more completely dependent . . . upon a particular, extremely one-sided mechanical kind of labor." All the aspects of alienation are seen to derive from the worker's role in production: his view of his work, his products, the institutions of his society, other men and himself. In general, the capitalist economic system "perfects the worker and degrades the man." Thus Marx's socio-psychological hypothesis concerning alienation is that it increases in proportion to the growing division of labor under capitalism, where men are forced to confine themselves to performing specialized functions within a system they neither understand nor control.

Durkheim uses "anomie" in *The Division of Labor* to characterize the pathological state of the economy, "this sphere of collective life (which) is, in large part, freed from the moderating action of regulation," where "latent or active, the state of war is necessarily chronic" and "each individual finds himself in a state of war with every other." In *Suicide* it is used to characterize the pathological mental state of the individual who is insufficiently regulated by society and suffers from "the malady of infinite aspiration": "unregulated emotions are adjusted neither to one another nor to the conditions they are supposed to meet: they must therefore conflict with one another most painfully." It is accompanied by "weariness," "disillusionment," "disturbance, agitation and discontent," "anger" and "irritated disgust with life." In extreme cases this condition leads a man to commit suicide, or homicide. It is aggravated by sudden crises, both economic disasters and "the abrupt growth of power and wealth": with increased prosperity, for instance, anomie ". . . is heightened by passions being less disciplined, precisely when they need more discipline." Anomie is the peculiar disease of modern industrial man, "sanctified" both by orthodox economists and by extreme socialists. Industry, "instead of being still regarded as a means to an end transcending itself, has become the supreme end of individuals and societies alike." Anomie is accepted as normal, indeed "a mark of moral distinction," and "it is everlastingly repeated that it is man's nature to be eternally dissatisfied, constantly to advance, without relief or rest, toward an indefinite goal." Religion, governmental power over the economy and occupational groups have lost their moral force. Thus "appetites have become freed of any limiting authority" and "from top to bottom of the ladder, greed is aroused without knowing where to find ultimate foothold. Nothing can calm it, since its goal is far beyond all it can attain." The lives of "a host of individuals are passed in the industrial and commercial sphere," where "the greater part of their existence is passed divorced from any moral influence . . . the manufacturer, the merchant, the workman, the employee, in carrying on his occupation, is aware of no influence set about him to check his egoism." [14]

[14] Durkheim, *Professional Ethics and Civic Morals*, tr. C. Brookfield (London, 1957),

"Anomie," like "alienation," thus also refers first to the relationship of the individual to elements of his social environment and second to his state of mind. Durkheim initially thought that the division of labor itself has a "natural" tendency to provide the necessary regulative force, that it produces solidarity because "it creates among men an entire system of rights and duties which link them together in a durable way," for "functions, when they are sufficiently in contact with one another, tend to stabilize and regulate themselves." Anomie is prevalent because of the rapid growth of the market and big industry, for since "these changes have been accomplished with extreme rapidity, the interests in conflict have not yet had time to be equilibrated"; also there is the harmful existence of "the still very great inequality in the external conditions of the struggle." Later he came to believe that it was primarily due to the lack of occupational groups which would regulate economic life by establishing "occupational ethics and law in the different economic occupations": anomie "springs from the lack of collective forces at certain points in society; that is, of groups established for the regulation of social life." Both explanations are consistent with Durkheim's socio-psychological hypothesis concerning anomie, which is that it is a function of the rapid growth of the economy in industrial society which has occurred without a corresponding growth in the forces which could regulate it.

II

Alienation and anomie have in common the formal characteristic that they each have a multiple reference to: (1) social phenomena (states of society, its institutions, rules and norms); (2) individual states of mind (beliefs, desires, attitudes, etc.); (3) a hypothesized empirical relationship between (1) and (2); and (4) a presupposed picture of the "natural" relationship between (1) and (2). Thus, whereas Marx sees capitalism as a compulsive social system, which narrows men's thoughts, places obstacles in the way of their desires and denies the realization of "a world of productive impulses and faculties," Durkheim sees it as a state of moral anarchy in the economic sphere, where men's thoughts and desires are insufficiently controlled and where the individual is not "in harmony with his condition." We will later notice the extent to which (3) is related to (4) in the two cases. Let us here concentrate on (3), and in particular on the difference between the hypotheses in question.

Compare what the two thinkers have to say about the division of labor. For Marx it is *in itself* the major contributing factor in alienation, in all its

p. 12. This quotation, incidentally, confirms that, despite Durkheim's attempt to distinguish "anomie" from "egoism" in *Suicide,* they are not in the end conceptually distinct. See B. D. Johnson, "Durkheim's One Cause of Suicide," *American Sociological Review* 30, 6 (1965), pp. 882–6.

forms, and not just for the worker but for all men. All men are alienated under the division of labor (for, as he says, "capital and labor are two sides of one and the same relation" and "all human servitude is involved in the relation of the worker to production, and all the types of servitude are only modifications or consequences of this relation"). Men have to enter into "definite relations that are indispensable and independent of their wills," they are forced to play determined roles within the economic system, and, in society as a whole, they are dehumanized by social relations which take on "an independent existence" and which determine not only what they do, but the very structure of their thought, their images of themselves, their products, their activities and other men. Alienated man is dehumanized by being conditioned and constrained to see himself, his products, his activities and other men in economic, political, religious and other categories—in terms which deny his and their human possibilities.

Durkheim sees the division of labor as being (when properly regulated) the source of solidarity in modern industrial society: the prevalence of anomie is due to a lag in the growth of the relevant rules and institutions. Interdependence of functions (plus occupational groups) should lead to growing solidarity and a sense of community, although the division of labor in advanced societies is also (ideally) accompanied by the growth of the importance of the individual personality and the development of values such as justice and equality. For Durkheim the economic functions of the division of labor are "trivial in comparison with the moral effect it produces." By means of it "the individual becomes aware of his dependence upon society; from it comes the forces which keep him in check and restrain him." When educating a child, it is "necessary to get him to like the idea of circumscribed tasks and limited horizons," for in modern society "man is destined to fulfil a special function in the social organism, and, consequently, he must learn in advance how to play this role." The division of labor does not normally degrade the individual "by making him into a machine": it merely requires that in performing his special function "he feels he is serving something." Moreover, "if a person has grown accustomed to vast horizons, total views, broad generalities, he cannot be confined, without impatience, within the strict limits of a special task."

By now it should be apparent that alienation, in Marx's thinking, is, *in part,* what characterizes precisely those states of the individual and conditions of society which Durkheim sees as the solution to anomie: namely, where men are socially determined and constrained, when they must conform to social rules which are independent of their wills and are conditioned to think and act within the confines of specialized roles. Whereas anomic man is, for Durkheim, the unregulated man who needs rules to live by, limits to his desires, "circumscribed tasks" to perform and "limited horizons" for his thoughts, alienated man is, for Marx, a man in the grip of a system, who "cannot escape" from "a particular, exclusive sphere of activity which is forced upon him." [15]

Whence does this difference derive? In part, obviously, from the fact that Marx and Durkheim wrote at different periods about different stages of industrial society. Also it is clear that Marx was concerned chiefly to describe the alienated worker, while Durkheim saw economic anomie as primarily characterizing employers. But there is also a theoretical difference that is striking and important: these concepts offer opposite and incompatible analyses of the relation of the individual to society.

Compare Marx's statements that "it is above all necessary to avoid postulating 'society' once again as an abstraction confronting the individual" and that communism creates the basis for "rendering it impossible that anything should exist independently of individuals" with Durkheim's that society is "a reality from which everything that matters to us flows," that it "transcends the individual's consciousness" and that it "has all the characteristics of a moral authority that imposes respect." Marx begins from the position that the independent or "reified" and determining character of social relationships and norms is precisely what characterizes human "pre-history" and will be abolished by the revolutionary transition to a "truly-human" society, whereas Durkheim assumes the "normality" of social regulation, the lack of which leads to the morbid, self-destructive state of "non-social" or Hobbesian anarchy evident in unregulated capitalism. Social constraint is for Marx a denial and for Durkheim a condition of human freedom and self-realization.

III

It is my contention that one can only make sense of the empirical relationships postulated between social conditions and individual mental states which are held to constitute alienation and anomie by taking into account what Marx and Durkheim see as the "natural" (or "human" or "normal" or "healthy") condition of the individual in society. Alienation and anomie do not identify themselves, as it were, independently of the theories from which they derive: witness the diversity of contemporary uses of the terms, discussed above. They are, in fact, only identifiable if one knows what it would be *not* to be alienated or anomic, that is, if one applies a standard specifying "natural" states of institutions, rules and norms and individual mental states. Moreover, this standard must be external. That is, neither the individual mental

[15] But Durkheim obviously did not want to see men treated as commodities or as appendages to machines. (See *Division of Labour,* pp. 371–3), and Marx had much to say, especially in Vol. III of *Capital,* about avarice and unregulated desires prevalent under capitalism (see also his account of "raw communism" in the 1844 manuscripts).

states nor the social conditions studied can provide that standard, for they themselves are to be evaluated for their degree of alienation and anomie.

Thus despite recent attempts to divest these concepts of their non-empirical presuppositions,[16] they are in their original form an inextricable fusion of fact and value, so that one cannot eliminate the latter while remaining faithful to the original concepts.

The standard specifying the "natural" condition of the individual in society involves, in each case, a theory of human nature. Marx's view of man is of a being with a wide range of creative potentialities, or "species powers" whose "self-realization exists as an inner necessity, a need." In the truly human society there will be "a new manifestation of *human* powers and a new enrichment of the human being," when "man appropriates his manifold being in an all-inclusive way, and thus is a whole man." Man needs to develop all his faculties in a context where neither the natural nor the social environment are constraining: "objects then confirm his individuality . . . the wealth of subjective human sensibility . . . is cultivated or created" and "the practical relations of everyday life offer to man none but perfectly intelligible and reasonable relations with regard to his fellow men and to nature." With the end of the division of labor, there will be an end to "the exclusive concentration of artistic talent in particular individuals and its suppression in the broad mass." The "detail worker of today," with "nothing more to perform than a partial social function," will be superseded by "an individual with an all-round development, one for whom various social functions are alternative modes of activity." [17] Furthermore, with the end of the social determination of "abstract" individual roles, man's relationship with man and with woman will become fully human, that is, fully reciprocal and imbued with respect for the uniqueness of the individual. As Marx says, "the relation of man to woman is the most *natural* relation of human being to human being. . . . It also shows how far man's needs have become human needs, and consequently how far the other person, as a person, has become one of his needs, and to what extent he is in his individual existence at the same time a social being." Thus Marx assumes that the full realization of human powers and "the return

[16] See, e.g., B. F. Dohrenwend, "Egoism, Altruism, Anomie and Fatalism: A Conceptual Analysis of Durkheim's Types," *American Sociological Review* 24, 1959, p. 467, where anomie is described as "ambiguous . . . indistinct . . . and infused with value judgments about what is 'good' and 'bad,' " and, e.g., Seeman, "On the Meaning of Alienation," *American Sociological Review* 24, 1959.

[17] Cf. the famous passage from the *German Ideology* in which Marx writes of "communist society, where no one has one exclusive sphere of activity but each can become accomplished in any branch he wishes" and where it is "possible for me to hunt in the morning, fish in the afternoon, rear cattle in the evening, criticize after dinner, just as I have a mind, without ever becoming hunter, fisherman, shepherd or critic." See also *Capital* (Moscow, 1959), I, pp. 483–4 and Engels, *Anti-Dühring* (Moscow, 1959), pp. 403 and 409. On the other hand, Marx seems to have changed his attitude at the end of his life to a concern with leisure in the "realm of freedom."

of man himself as a *social*, i.e., really human, being" can only take place in a world in which man is free to apply himself to whatever activity he chooses and where his activities and his way of seeing himself and other men are not dictated by a system within which he and they play specified roles.

Durkheim saw human nature as essentially in need of limits and discipline. His view of man is of a being with potentially limitless and insatiable desires, who needs to be controlled by society. He writes: "To limit man, to place obstacles in the path of his free development, is this not to prevent him from fulfilling himself? But . . . this limitation is a condition of our happiness and moral health. Man, in fact, is made for life in a determinate, limited environment. . . ." "Health" for man in society is a state where "a regulative force" plays "the same role for moral needs which the organism plays for physical needs," which makes men "contented with their lot, while stimulating them moderately to improve it" and results in that "calm, active happiness . . . which characterizes health for societies as well as for individuals." Durkheim's picture of a healthy society in modern Europe is of a society that is organized and meritocratic, with equality of opportunity and personal liberty, where men are attached to intermediary groups by stable loyalties rather than being atomized units caught in an endemic conflict, and where they fulfil determinate functions in an organized system of work, where they conform in their mental horizons, their desires and ambitions to what their role in society demands and where there are clear-cut rules defining limits to desire and ambition in all spheres of life. There should be "rules telling each of the workers his rights and duties, not vaguely in general terms but in precise detail" and "each in his sphere vaguely realizes the extreme limit set to his ambitions and aspires to nothing beyond . . . he respects regulations and is docile to collective authority, that is, has a wholesome moral constitution." Man must be governed by "a conscience superior to his own, the superiority of which he feels": men cannot assign themselves the "law of justice" but "must receive it from an authority which they respect and to which they yield spontaneously." Society alone "as a whole or through the agency of one of its organs, can play this moderating role." It alone can "stipulate law" and "set the point beyond which the passions must not go"; and it alone "can estimate the reward to be prospectively offered to every class of human functionary, in the name of the common interest."

IV

The doctrines of Marx and Durkheim about human nature are representative of a long and distinguished tradition of such doctrines in the history of political and social theory. The difference between them is also representative of that tradition (and parallel differences can be traced back to the Middle Ages). Doctrines of this general type can be seen to underlie, for example, the work of Hobbes, Rousseau, the Utopian Socialists and Freud; and it is evident that, in large measure, Durkheim sides with Hobbes and Freud where Marx sides with Rousseau and the Utopians. For the former, man is a bundle of desires, which need to be regulated, tamed, repressed, manipulated and given direction for the sake of social order, whereas, for the latter, man is still an angel, rational and good, who requires a rational and good society in which to develop his essential nature—a "form of association in which each, while uniting himself with all, may still obey himself alone. . . ." [18] For the former, coercion, external authority, and restraint are necessary and desirable for social order and individual happiness; for the latter, they are an offence against reason and an attack upon freedom.

I want here to ask two difficult questions. First, how is one to understand Marx's and Durkheim's theories of human nature, and, in particular, what is their logical and epistemological status? And, second, how is one to account for their divergence?

(A) Statements about human nature can be construed in many different ways. They commonly include such terms as "need," "real self," "real will," "basic desires," "human potentialities," "human powers," "normal," "healthy," and so on. Statements of this sort might be taken to refer to: (1) man as existing before or apart from society, (2) man considered analytically, with those factors due to the influence of society abstracted, (3) man considered in an a priori manner, i.e., according to some a priori definition, (4) man considered from the point of view of features which seem to be common to men in all known societies, (5) man considered from the point of view of features which are held to characterize him in certain specifiable social conditions as opposed to others.[19]

My suggestion is that very often, and in particular in the cases I am discussing, the last is the most accurate way to read statements about human nature. It is, in general, not absurd to take statements about human needs, "real" wants, potentialities and so on as asserting that individuals in situation S are unable to experience satisfactions that situation S_1 is held to make possible for them and which they would experience and value highly. Now, it is, in my view, not necessary that such statements refer to actual *discontents* of individuals in situation S: both Marx and Durkheim, for example, were clear that individuals could acquiesce in and even value highly their alienated or anomic condition. What is required is that, once they are in S_1, they experience satisfactions unavailable in S.

Thus far it is evidently an empirical matter. It is an empirical and testable question (1) whether the satisfactions in question are precluded in S; (2)

[18] J. J. Rousseau, *The Social Contract,* tr. G. D. H. Cole (London, 1913), p. 12.

[19] These possibilities are distinguished for analytical purposes. Clearly, in most actual cases they are combined. Rousseau, for instance, combines (1) and (2), while Pareto combines (2) and (4). I shall in the end argue that Marx and Durkheim combine (4) and (5).

whether they would be available in S_1, and (3) whether they would be actually experienced by individuals in S_1 and would be important and valuable to them. (1) can in principle be investigated directly. To take easy examples, it is not difficult to show that work on the assembly line precludes work-satisfaction or that the life of the highly ambitious businessman precludes a mental condition of harmonious contentment. (2) and (3) can be investigated indirectly or directly. To do so indirectly would involve looking at evidence available in S and, indeed, in other societies, which provides a strong presumption in their favor. Thus Marx can write of what happens when "communist artisans form associations." When "French socialist workers meet together," he writes, "society, association, entertainment which also has society as its aim, is sufficient for them: the brotherhood of man is no empty phrase but a reality, and the nobility of man shines forth upon us from their toil-worn bodies." And he writes in *The Holy Family* that one "must be acquainted with the studiousness, the craving for knowledge, the moral energy and the unceasing urge for development of the French and English workers to be able to form an idea of the *human* nobleness of that movement." Durkheim can appeal to countless examples of cohesive social groups—primitive tribes, medieval guilds, rural Catholic communities, the Jews, and to the evidence of, e.g., differential suicide rates. He compares, for instance, the poor with the rich and argues that "everything that enforces subordination attenuates the effects of (anomie). At least the horizon of the lower classes is limited by those above them, and for this same reason their desires are more modest. Those who have only empty space above them are almost inevitably lost in it. . . ." *Direct* investigation of (2) and (3) can be pursued only by social experiment. Thus the final test for Marx's theory of human nature is the communist revolution; and that for Durkheim's is the institution of a kind of centralized guild-socialism.

We have analyzed statements about human nature as empirical statements (in this case, hypothetical predictions) about the condition of man in S_1. But our analysis is as yet incomplete, for they also involve the affirmation that this condition is privileged—that it is evaluated as preferable to all other conditions. How is one to analyze this evaluation: is it also empirical, that is, a ranking in accordance with what men actually want, or is it nonempirical—a mere exhortation to look at the world in one way rather than another?

If it is empirical, the question arises: by *whom* is the condition of man in S_1 said to be preferred—which men's wants are relevant here? If one believes, as Marx and Durkheim did, that man is largely conditioned by social circumstances, that new needs are generated by the historical process, that his very picture of himself and others is a function of his situation, then the problem becomes even more acute, for no one is in a position genuinely to compare and evaluate alternatives, like Mill's wise man deciding between higher and lower pleasures. An appeal to men in S_1 is self-defeating, for it carries the presumption that their evaluations are privileged, which is what is at issue. An appeal to men in S will not do either, for they would not ordinarily have the necessary evidence, and, again, why should their judgments be privileged? Worse still, what criteria are appropriate? If men in S_1 are satisfied, fulfilled, contented in certain ways, what is privileged about judgments which value these states rather than others?

Both Marx and Durkheim *thought* that they had found solid empirical ground upon which to base statements about human nature. They both had a picture of history as a process of the progressive emergence of the individual and both thought that man's potentiality for individual autonomy and for genuine community with others (both of which they envisaged differently) was frustrated by existing social forms. They thought that they had found conclusive evidence for their respective views of human nature in present and past societies: they assumed that, despite the continual generation of new needs throughout history, men's fundamental aspirations, more or less hidden, and the conditions of their ultimate happiness had always been and would continue to be the same. They were both impressed by the growth of industrialism and by the possibilities it had opened up for human fulfilment [20] and they believed that men were, despite the present, and temporary, obstacles, increasingly becoming (and would continue to become) what they had it in them to be; one could identify *this* by looking at their miseries and sufferings, as well as at their strivings and aspirations towards "human" or "healthy" forms of life, and at historical examples of societies or institutions in which alienation or anomie were less severe or even absent. Yet this evidence about men's wants is itself selected and interpreted, and that requires a prior perspective, providing criteria of selection and interpretation.

It would seem, therefore, that statements about human nature, such as those examined here, are partly empirical and partly not. One can often get a long way with support of the empirical part, for evidence of all kinds is relevant to the question of what men's lives would be like in alternative circumstances. The hypothetical prediction about S_1 may be verifiable; at least one would know how to verify it, and one could in principle point to evidence which strongly supports it. The claim, however, that life in S_1 is to be judged superior, though it may rest on an appeal to evidence about men's wants, is ultimately nonempirical, for that evidence has been selected and interpreted in the light of the claim. Which men's wants and which of their wants has already been decided. Moreover, the claim of superiority does not follow logically from the evidence: one must add the premise that certain wants and

[20] As Marx says, "The history of *industry* and industry as it *objectively* exists is an *open* book of the *human faculties*" (*Early Writings*, ed. T. B. Bottomore, London, 1963, p. 162); and, as Durkheim says, "society is, or tends to be, essentially industrial" (*Division of Labour*, ed. G. Simpson, Glencoe, 1933, p. 3) and what characterizes its morality is "that there is something more human, and therefore more rational" about modern, organized societies (ibid., p. 407).

satisfactions are more "human" or "healthy" than others. In the end what is required is a perspective and an initial set of evaluations.

(B) It is precisely here that Marx and Durkheim differed radically. Marx wrote that the "socialist perspective" attributed importance to "the wealth of human needs, and consequently also to a *new mode of production* and to a new *object* of production" as well as to a "new manifestation of human powers and a new enrichment of the human being." He began from an image of man in society, where a morality of duty would be unnecessary because irrelevant, an image in which *aesthetic* criteria were of predominant importance in assessing the quality of man's relationship with the natural and social world.[21]

Yet where Marx wrote in the *Theses on Feurbach* from "the standpoint of . . . human society," Durkheim argued in the *Rules of Sociological Method* that it was "no longer a matter of pursuing desperately an objective that retreats as one advances but of working with steady perseverance to maintain the normal state, of re-establishing it if it is threatened, and of rediscovering its conditions if they have changed." He was haunted by the idea of man and society in disintegration. Here he appealed to the remedy of moral rules, defining and prescribing duties in all spheres of life, especially where men's anarchic and unstable desires had the greatest scope. This is a moral vision, for, as he said, "the need for order, harmony and social solidarity is generally considered moral." [22]

Where Marx valued a life in which in community with others "the individual" has the means of "cultivating his gifts in all directions," and where the relations between men are no longer defined by externally imposed categories and roles—by class and occupation—and men freely come together in freely chosen activities and participate in controlling the conditions of their social life, Durkheim held that "we must contract our horizon, choose a definite task and immerse ourselves in it completely, instead of trying to make ourselves

21 This image is, I would argue, ultimately Romantic in origin. Compare the following from Schiller's *Briefe ueber die aesthetische Erziehung des Menschen:* " . . . enjoyment is separated from labor, the means from the end, exertion from recompense. Eternally *fettered* only to a single little fragment of the whole, man fashions himself only as a fragment; ever hearing only the monotonous whirl of the wheel which he turns, he never displays the full harmony of his being . . ." *(Sixth Letter).* For Schiller, and, I believe, for Marx it is "the aesthetic formative impulse" which "establishes . . . a joyous empire . . . wherein it releases man from all the fetters of circumstance, and frees him, both physically and morally, from all that can be called constraint" (ibid., *Twenty-Seventh Letter*).

22 *Division of Labour,* p. 63. Whereas Marx's model of disalienated work is artistic creation, Durkheim writes that "art is a game. Morality, on the contrary, is life in earnest" and "the distance separating art and morality" is "the very distance that separates play from work" (*Moral Education,* New York, 1961, p. 273). This is the Protestant ethic transposed into Kantian terms: "the categorical imperative is assuming the following form: Make yourself usefully fulfil a determinate function" (*Division of Labour,* p. 43). As to self-realization, Durkheim writes, "As for a simultaneous growth of all the faculties, it is only possible for a given being to a very limited degree." (*Division of Labour,* p. 237, amended translation, S. L.)

a sort of creative masterpiece," and hoped to see men performing useful functions in a rationally organized society, in accordance with clearly defined roles, firmly attached to relevant groups and under the protective discipline of rules of conduct at home, at work and in politics. They both sought liberty, equality, democracy and community, but the content which they gave these notions was utterly different.

V

What is the relevance of these concepts today? This question needs to be subdivided into three more specific questions, which follow the lines of the preceding argument. First, how valid is the empirical hypothesis which each embodies? To what extent do they succeed in identifying and adequately explaining phenomena in modern industrial societies? Second, how plausible is the theory of human nature which each presupposes? What does the evidence from past and present societies, from sociology and psychology, suggest about the plausibility of their respective hypothetical predictions, and about the nature of the changes which men and institutions would have to undergo to attain the conditions they predict and advocate? And third, how desirable is the ideal, how attractive is the vision to which each ultimately appeals? How today is one to evaluate these ideals: what degree of approximation to either, or both (or neither), are we to think desirable?

These questions are challenging and far-reaching. Here I shall raise them and offer tentative suggestions as to how one might begin to answer them.

One problem in answering the first question is to know at what level of generality it is being posed. How *specifically* is one to read Marx's account of alienation and Durkheim's of anomie? Marx and Durkheim identified certain features of their own societies and offered explanations of them. But they may also be seen to have identified features characteristic of a number of societies including their own; indeed, one may even see them, to some extent, as having identified features which may be said to characterize any conceivable society. Is it a specific type of technology, or form of organization, or structure of the economy, or is it the existence of classes or of private property, or the accumulation of capital, or the division of labor, or industrial society, or the human condition which is the crucial determinant of alienation? Is it the lack of a specific type of industrial organization (technical or administrative?), or the absence of appropriate occupational groups, or an economy geared to the pursuit of profit, or the cultural imperatives of a "success ethic," or the fact of social mobility, or the erosion of a traditionally stable framework of authority, or social change, or industrial society, or the human condition, that is the major factor leading to anomie? Alienation and anomie are phenomena which have particular aspects, unique to particular forms of society or institution, other aspects which are more general and still others which are universal.

We may attempt to identify new forms of these phenomena, using these concepts and the hypotheses they embody in the attempt to describe and explain them. They are in this sense concepts of "the middle range." They allow for specific new hypotheses to account for particular new forms, or they may account for them by means of the existing, more general hypotheses. In general, the contemporary forms of alienation and anomie are best approached on the understanding that their causes are multiple and to be sought at different levels of abstraction. A systematic investigation of alienation and anomie would range from the most particular to the most universal in the search for causes.

Marx and Durkheim attributed, as we have seen, certain types of mental condition (specified positively, in terms of what occurs, and negatively, in terms of what is precluded) to certain types of social condition. Marx pointed to meaninglessness of work and a sense of powerlessness to affect the conditions of one's life, dissociation from the products of one's labor, the sense of playing a role in an impersonal system which one does not understand or control, the seeing of oneself and others within socially imposed and artificial categories, the denial of human possibilities for a fully creative, spontaneous, egalitarian and reciprocal communal life. He attributed these, in particular, to the form taken by the division of labor under capitalism and, more generally, to the fact of class society. Durkheim pointed to greed, competitiveness, status seeking, the sense of having rights without duties, the concentration on consumption and pleasure, the lack of a sense of community with others, of a feeling of limits to one's desires and aspirations, and of the experience of fulfilling a useful function and serving a purpose higher than one's own self-interest, and the denial of human possibilities for an ordered and balanced life, where everyone knows his station and its duties. He attributed these, in particular, to the industrial revolution and the failure of society to provide appropriate groups to adjust to it, and, more generally, to social disorganization.

We are familiar with countless examples of these phenomena, though in many cases not all the features isolated by the concepts are necessarily present. Let me give just two examples.

Alienation is found today in perhaps its most acute form among workers in assembly-line industries, such as the motor-car industry, where, as Blauner writes in his sensitive study of workers' alienation, "the combination of technological, organizational and economic factors has resulted in the simultaneous intensification of all the dimensions of alienation." Here, in the extreme situation, "a depersonalized worker, estranged from himself and larger collectives, goes through the motions of work in the regimented milieu of the conveyor-belt for the sole purpose of earning his bread," "his work has become almost completely compartmentalized from other areas of his life, so that there is little meaning left in it beyond the instrumental purpose," and it is "unfree and unfulfilling and exemplifies the bureaucratic combination of the highly rational organization and the restricted specialist. In relation to the two giant bureaucracies which dominate his life, he is relatively powerless, atomized, depersonalized, and anonymous." [23]

Likewise, anomie is noticeably evident and acute among "the Unattached," well described by Mary Morse, especially those in "Seagate"—the drifting, purposeless and unstable teenagers, who felt no connection with or obligation to family, work, school or youth organization, the children of *nouveau riche* parents, suffering from "a sense of boredom, failure and restlessness" and refusing "to accept limitations, whether their own or external." Often there was "a failure to achieve unrealistic or unattainable goals they had set for themselves or had had set for them"; also there was "a general inability to postpone immediate pleasure for the sake of future gain," there was "a craving for adventure," and "leisure-time interests were short-spanned, constantly changing and interspersed liberally with periods of boredom and apathy." Finally, they showed "pronounced hostility towards adults," adult discipline was quite ineffective and, in general, "all adults in authority were classed as 'them'—those who were opposed to and against 'us'." [24]

These are merely two instances, but they illustrate the general point made above. The causes of alienation and anomie must be sought at different levels of abstraction. At the most specific level, all sorts of special factors may be of primary importance. In a case of alienation, it may be the technical or organizational character of an industry or the structure of a bureaucracy; in a case of anomie, it may be a combination of personal affluence and a breakdown, rejection or conflict of norms of authority at home, at school and at work. But clearly, too, the nature of the wider society is of crucial importance. The extent and nature of social stratification, the structure of the economy, the character of the political system, the pace of industrialization, the degree of pluralism, the nature of the predominant social values—all these will affect the nature and distribution of alienation and anomie. Again, one can plausibly argue that *some* degree of alienation and of anomie is inseparable from life in an industrial society, characterized as it is, on the one hand, by the ramifying growth of organization and bureaucracy in all spheres of life, by economic centralization and by the increasing remoteness and technical character of politics; and, on the other, by built-in and permanent social changes, by the impermanence of existing status hierarchies and the increasing role given to personal ambition and career mobility. And at the most general level, they may each be seen to relate to the most universal features of social structure and social change. In this sense, some alienation must exist wherever there are reified social relations, socially given roles and norms; while some anomie must exist wherever hierarchies disintegrate and social control is weakened.

What about the plausibility of Marx's and Durkheim's theories of human

[23] R. Blauner, *Alienation and Freedom: The Factory Worker and His Industry* (Chicago and London, 1964), pp. 182 and 122.

[24] M. Morse, *The Unattached* (Penguin Books, London, 1965), pp. 75–6 and 28–9.

nature? They each had definite views about men's needs, which they believed to be historically generated and empirically ascertainable. How plausible today is the picture of mutually cooperative individuals, each realizing a wide range of creative potentialities, in the absence of specific role-expectations, lasting distinctions between whole categories of men and externally imposed discipline, in conditions of inner and social harmony, where all participate in planning and controlling their environment? What, on the other hand, is the plausibility of the view of human happiness, in which men are socialized into specific roles, regulated, and to some extent repressed, by systems of rules and group norms (albeit based on justice, equality of opportunity and respect for the individual), serving the purposes of society by fulfilling organized functions—all of which they accept and respect as constituting a stable framework for their lives?

These questions confront all those who hold versions of these ideals today. One cannot begin to appraise either, or compare them with one another, until one has come to some view about the likelihood of either being realized. What evidence is there that if the social conditions are constituted in the way Marx and Durkheim wanted, men would experience and would value highly the satisfactions of which they speak? Here one would, for example, need to examine all the accumulated evidence throughout history of experiments in community living and in workers' control, of communes, collective farms and kibbutzim, on the one hand; and of experience in "human relations" and personnel management, of professionalism and of life in organizations, on the other. There is a vast amount of such evidence available, but it has never been systematically reviewed in this light.

Let us look at two examples in this connection. In the opinion of Friedmann the Israeli kibbutz represents "an original and successful application, on a limited scale, of communist principles," nearer to "the ethical ideal defined by the philosophy of Marx and Engels (for instance, with regard to the role of money, the distinction between manual and intellectual labor, family life)" than life in Moscow or on a kolkhox. "The kibbutz movement," he writes, "despite its limitations and its difficulties, constitutes the fullest and most successful 'utopian' revolutionary experiment, the one which approximates most closely to the forms of life which communism has assigned itself as an aim. It is in the kibbutzim that I have met men of ample culture, and even creators, artists, writers, technicians, among whom the contradiction between intellectual and manual work, denounced by Marx, is truly eliminated in their daily life." Friedmann goes on, of course, to qualify and elaborate this: in particular, he outlines the perpetual confrontation between the kibbutzim and the wider society, devoted to economic growth and "imbued with models of abundance, where, with the development of the private sector, there is proclaimed a sort of material and moral New Economic Plan." [25] He examines the attempts of the kibbutzim to reduce to a minimum the tensions and frustrations

[25] G. Friedmann, *Fin du Peuple Juif?* (Paris, Gallimard, 1965), pp. 95, 99, 96.

of community life and asks the crucial questions: whether the kibbutz will be able to adapt to the economic and technical demands of an industrial society, while retaining its essential values; and whether the wider society will evolve in a direction that is compatible or incompatible with these values.

Let us take a second example, which relates to the plausibility of Durkheim's ideal, the overcoming of anomie. Perhaps the best instance is the evidence accumulated and interpreted by the theorists of modern managerialism, concerned to remedy "the acquisitiveness of a sick society" [26] and treating the factory, the corporation and the large organization as "a social system." Particularly relevant are the writings of the "organicists," whose aim is to promote "the values of social stability, cohesion and integration" [27] and to achieve, within the "formal organization" (the "explicitly stated system of control introduced by the company") the "creation and distribution of satisfactions" among the members of the system.[28] Selznick, who typifies the attempt to explore communal values within large corporations and administrative organizations, argues that the organization requires "stability" in its lines of authority, subtle patterns of informal relationships, "continuity" in its policies and "homogeneity" in its outlook.[29] Another writer describes its reification and normative significance for those who participate in it in the following terms, terms of which Durkheim might well have approved. "One might almost say that the organization has a character, an individuality, which makes the name real. The scientist will not accept any such reification or personalizing of an organization. But participants in these organizations are subject to no such scientific scruples, and generations of men have felt and thought about the organizations they belonged to as something real in themselves." [30] For Selznick, social order and individual satisfaction are reconciled when "the aspirations of individuals are so stimulated and controlled, and so ordered in their mutual relations, as to produce the desired balance of forces." [31]

I have merely suggested two areas in which one might look for evidence that is relevant to the plausibility of the hypothetical predictions which partially constitute Marx's and Durkheim's theories of human nature. Clearly there is much else that is relevant in, for instance, the work of industrial sociologists, social psychologists, in community studies and the writings of organization theorists. It is also important to look at what evidence there is about the prevalence of existing tendencies in modern societies which favor or hinder

[26] E. Mayo, *The Human Problems of an Industrial Civilization* (New York, Macmillan, 1933), pp. 152–3.

[27] I am particularly indebted in the discussion of this example to the pages on this subject in S. S. Wolin, *Politics and Vision* (London, Allen and Unwin, 1961), pp. 407–14.

[28] F. J. Roethlisberger and W. J. Dickson, *Management and the Worker* (Cambridge, Mass., Harvard University Press, 1939), p. 551.

[29] Wolin, *Politics and Vision,* p. 412.

[30] E. W. Bakke, *Bonds of Organization,* quoted in Wolin, *Politics and Vision,* p. 506.

[31] P. Selznick, *Leadership in Administration,* quoted in Wolin, *Politics and Vision,* p. 413.

the sorts of changes which would be necessary in order to approach these ideals. Here it would be necessary to look, for example, at the changes in the nature of occupations brought about by automation—the replacement of the detail worker by the more educated and responsible technician; at the effects of economic planning on small-scale decision-making; at the effects of the growth of organizations on status aspirations; at contemporary trends in consumption patterns. All this, and much else, is relevant to an assessment of the costs of approaching either ideal in our societies. Without these detailed inquiries, it is hardly possible to state firm conclusions, but it would appear that Durkheim's ideal is much nearer to and easier of realization in the industrial societies of both West and East than is that of Marx.

Finally, how is one to evaluate these ideals? To do so involves a commitment to values and an assessment of costs. Either may be seen to conflict with other values or may not be considered to be worth the cost of its realization. Both sociological evidence and conceptual inquiry are relevant in the attempt to decide these matters, but in the end what is required is an ultimate and personal commitment (for which good, or bad, reasons may, none the less, be advanced). One may, of course, hold, as both Marx and Durkheim in different ways did, that one's values are, as it were, embedded in the facts, but this is itself a committed position (for which, again, good, or bad, reasons may be advanced).

This is no place to argue about these matters at the length they require. Let it be sufficient to say that these two quite opposite and incompatible ideals represent in a clear-cut form two major currents of critical and normative thinking about society, to be found throughout the whole tradition of political and social theory in the West and still very much in evidence.

It is becoming increasingly common for that tradition to be attacked, by the advocates of a "scientific" social and political theory, as being rudimentary and speculative, and lacking in scientific detachment. It is all rather like Sir James Frazer's view of primitive religion as "bastard science." What is required, it is argued, is the abandonment of concepts which are internally related to theories of the good life and the good society. Evaluation of this sort should be kept strictly apart from the process of scientific inquiry.

Yet the desire for scientific rigor is not in itself incompatible with the sort of inquiry which is concerned precisely to put to the task of empirical analysis concepts which have the type of relation I have outlined to theories of human nature and thereby to prior evaluative perspectives. This type of inquiry is exactly what has primarily characterized social and political theory in the past (under which heading I include the writings of the classical and many modern sociologists). The case for eliminating it necessarily involves advocating the abandonment of the application of models of alternative and preferred forms of life to the critical analysis of actual forms. That case has yet to be made convincing.

13

Some Notes on the Concept of Power

P. H. Partridge

I

Talcott Parsons, in a review article attacking Wright Mills's *The Power Elite,* rejects many of Mills's empirical conclusions about the distribution of power in the U.S.A. He gives as one of his reasons that Mills works with a defective concept of the nature of power; Parsons goes on to remark that "unfortunately the concept of power is not a settled one in the social sciences, either in political science or in sociology"; [1] no one who has read the recent literature of the subject could disagree with him. The same uncertainty attaches to other closely related concepts. Thus, in the *Encyclopedia of the Social Sciences,* Michels defines "authority" as "the capacity innate or acquired, for exercising ascendency over a group"; but Bierstedt,[2] an American sociologist who has written a good deal on these matters, says that this is wrong in every one of its terms: authority is not a capacity, it is not innate, and it is not a matter of exercising ascendency. He argues that what Michels has done is to confuse authority with something quite different, viz. "competence." We need not illustrate further; in the writing about power (as about freedom) there is no end to the disputes about definition and usage. And these are not merely disputes about usage; as I have briefly hinted by referring to the differences between Wright Mills and Parsons, they are sometimes connected with the different conclusions that different writers reach in their studies of the exercise and distribution of power in actual societies.

Source: *Political Studies* 11 (1963). Reprinted by permission of the Clarendon Press, Oxford, England.

[1] Talcott Parsons, "Distribution of Power in American Society," *World Politics* 10 (Oct. 1957).

[2] Robert Bierstedt, "The Problem of Authority" in *Freedom and Control in Modern Society,* ed. M. Berger, T. Abel and C. H. Page (New York: Van Nostrand, 1954).

It is not hard to see why these differences should persist. We have a series of terms which are obviously very closely related: such terms as freedom, power, influence, coercion, constraint, force, compulsion, authority, leadership, prestige, and so on. In ordinary language, each of these words has an indeterminate use: they are pretty loosely used to stand now for one relationship, now for another. Most of them are open-ended terms: as regards each one of them we know that at a certain point we would at last draw the line and refuse to employ it, but usually we are not able to say at all exactly where we would draw the line. In other words, in almost every case, the situations to which we apply the terms form a continuum (as we shall see in more detail later on in the case of "power") and we do not precisely know at what point on the continuum our use of the term would stop. Thus, there are many situations to which we would not hesitate to apply the description "coercion": but suppose that one man controls the actions of another by offering him bribes which his psychological constitution makes it virtually impossible for him to resist (for instance, plying him with alcohol): is this a denial or impairment of the latter's freedom? (Political moralists have often written as if "bribing the electorate" were an illegitimate way of exercising power.) Again, since we are referring to situations which form a continuum, pairs or groups of the terms with which we are concerned overlap at the edges. Yet again, though we are dealing here with series of different situations or relationships between persons which shade into one another, for the purposes of ordinary life we are not concerned to identify and distinguish the quite different sorts of interpersonal relationships to all of which we may apply such words as "freedom," "power," "influence" or "constraint." One of the purposes of this paper is to point to a few of the different interpersonal relations all of which are frequently described as being examples of the exercise of "power."

These, then, are some of the reasons why it is not surprising that there should be no agreement about usage, or even a very high degree of consistency in the writing of a single writer. And, of course, it goes without saying that there is no set of definitions or usages which should prevail over all others for all purposes. In these "Notes" I am proposing certain ways of viewing the concept of power; but I do not recommend my usages (and my ways of distinguishing "power" from other very closely connected concepts) as being equally valid for all theoretical purposes; as a matter of fact, I have come at the subject of power in this way mainly because it has seemed to me to be useful in illuminating certain questions about freedom. . . .

But there is one point on which it is important to be clear. However we may decide to employ the terms that are available from ordinary language, we must deal faithfully with the facts. In speaking of power, freedom, coercion, and the like, we are concerned with relations between persons and groups of persons; and different types of relations differ subtly from one another, although, as I have mentioned, some shade into others. Whatever system of nomenclature we may find it convenient to adopt, we must ensure that we do not do violence to the qualitative differences between the different sorts of relationships we are really referring to; and especially that we do not treat as being identical relationships which differ from each other in subtle but important ways. . . .

In these "Notes" I shall refer only incidentally to the organized and institutionalized manifestations of power; my examples will be almost always of relations between two persons. . . . I do not want to deny that institutionalization brings with it additional important elements and complexities; but I would want to maintain that the "primitive" relationships are also present; and further, and most important, that we cannot understand or judge the more complex structures unless we can identify the simpler forms of relations that are involved therein and determine some of their relevant qualitative features.

II

I shall begin with a proposal and work from it. I propose to take "power" as being the most inclusive term, and, within this wider concept, I shall distinguish two poles, the pole of "influence" and the pole of "domination." These will mark the ends of the scale: I shall suggest how we might arrange a number of situations all involving the exercise of power in order along the scale: and I shall also want to mark somewhere on the scale a point that I take to be of especial importance—the point at which a *conflict situation* between the person exercising power and the person over whom it is exercised begins to manifest itself.

First, as regards "power." Russell says that "power is the production of intended effects." [3] According to this definition, A has power over B when A can produce certain effects that he intends to produce in B's behavior. It will be convenient to accept this formulation to begin with; however, later on I shall point out that it brushes aside certain complications that it is very necessary to take into account. The complications mainly concern the notion of power as the *production* of effects, and the requirement that the effects are *intended* effects. However, postponing those matters for the time being, it will be noted that Russell's definition of power is in some respects a very wide one: we could be said to have power over inanimate material like wood or iron because we have the power to produce certain intended effects on those materials. When we use the word in reference to the relations between human beings, we certainly give it a rather narrower reference: thus, the surgeon has power over my body in that he can produce intended effects upon it, but we should not say that this is an example of his power over *me*. As a concept employed in the discussion of interpersonal relations and social affairs, we give "power" a more restricted range. I shall not try to state

[3] Bertrand Russell, *Power: a New Social Analysis* (New York: W. W. Norton, 1936), p. 35.

exactly what the restriction is: it is sufficient for my purposes to say that A has power over B when A can affect B's acts or behavior in ways intended by A.

At one end of the continuum of relationships involving the exercise of power we may place "influence." A teacher may have influence over a pupil or a parent over a child; a painter like Cézanne may influence a generation of painters; or a great thinker, everyone who subsequently writes about a subject. It will already be apparent that some of these examples raise questions about intended and unintended effects, but we may postpone these: let us assume that the effects are intended effects. At the extreme end of the scale I wish to place the type of situation in which it can be said that A affects the behavior of B in intended ways, *without its being true that B is required to subordinate his own wishes, inclinations, beliefs, interests, etc. to those of A*. These will be cases in which a conflict situation does not appear at all. Now, it may well be that this is an "ideal" case, never in fact realized, because it may be argued that, wherever influence exists, there is some element of conflict present, some degree of subordination of one man's desires or interests to those of another. This, also, is a matter that will have to be considered more fully later. Nevertheless, it is sufficiently obvious that we can readily distinguish situations which approximate to that which I have defined from those at the other end of the scale which I have arbitrarily called "domination." This, of course, is the type of situation in which A directs or controls the behavior of B and where A's wishes prevail over those of B: B acts as he does only because he is compelled so to act by A, and would not do so but for A's ability to make him act in ways that he does not want to act. There is manifestly a conflict situation. As an example of the pole of "influence," we may take the example of a scientist who takes a young man into his laboratory, communicates to him his own passion for scientific research, some of his own qualities of mind and character, passes on his own skills, and perhaps by the exercise of the influence that he has, enables the student to become the independent scientist that he wanted to become. Or perhaps it is only gradually that the pupil comes to feel the spell of the master: what initially had elements of conflict or resistance in it may be changed as the situation develops. At the other end of the scale, the gunman's intimidation of his victim manifestly involves a conflict situation.

Now, it is equally obvious that if we begin with the Rutherford-pupil type of relationship, we can slightly vary the conditions and produce a series of relationships which lie along a continuum, getting nearer and nearer to the pole of "domination" or pure coercion. In the Rutherford-pupil relation we can introduce a slight element of domination: teachers are not unknown who, in order to bind disciples to themselves, use certain advantages they enjoy in order to restrain the natural inclinations or "bent" of their pupils: again (and we must not forget that power is generated by the beliefs, feelings, and attitudes of *both* parties to the relationship) pupils are not unknown who yield to the supposed wishes of teachers because of sanctions that they suppose teachers to possess—for instance, the disposal of good jobs. It is unnecessary to multiply examples: it will be evident that, as one "goes down" the scale, different types of relationships involving the presence of power shade into one another. Of course, this geometrical mode of representation is a very crude expository device; as a matter of fact, as we look more closely at a number of these very complex situations, it is perhaps not so much a matter of one sort of situation being followed by, and shading into, another, but rather of the presence in varying degrees of many different psychological and other components. For this reason, the notion of a continuum may after all be rather misleading, but I can think of no simpler method of exposition.

As you "move down" the scale, sanctions (inducements and penalties to induce compliance with the wishes of one party) begin to appear, but at first in such subtle ways that it is very difficult to determine whether sanctions are operating at all. The difficulty is not only that of the observer; it is often impossible for the actor or patient to know whether his action is affected by consideration of real or possible sanctions, or whether, in conforming to the wishes of another, he is acting "on his own initiative." Later, of course, sanctions become more obvious and assume increasing severity. Again as we examine types of situations arranged along the scale in relation to the absence and presence of a conflict situation, we observe differences concerning the "bases" or "sources" of the influence or domination that A enjoys over B, and also as regards the "mechanisms" by means of which power is exercised. It is not always easy to distinguish "bases" and "mechanisms." Thus, the influence of a Rutherford over his pupil may flow in part from his known standing in his science and the authority he enjoys by virtue of his achievement (and these, I suppose, would be examples of what many writers now call "bases" of power); but also in part from felt superior qualities of mind or imagination, and these may perhaps be regarded as mechanisms by means of which influence is exerted. Moving further down the scale, we know that many rulers have managed to dominate subjects not by employing manifest sanctions (either penalties or inducements) but by subtle and hidden means of manipulation—causing the subjects to want what the ruler wants them to want and think what he wants them to think. This is an example of the "shading into" of which I have spoken, and of the extraordinary difficulty often in recognizing the kind of power situations we are dealing with: it is often impossible to say with any confidence whether we are observing a situation in which B "freely" subordinates himself to an imposed discipline or accepts the authority of a leader or whether his compliance has been secured by means of manipulation by A. Yet, tricky, subtle, and arguable as such distinctions often are, they are the distinctions we are compelled to try to make if we want to describe the structure of power within a social group, the qualitative features of the power relationships that are present, and their significance for the freedom of members of the group.

In ordinary talk, and in much of the writing of political scientists and sociologists, assertions about power, its distribution, its consequences, etc. are often very confidently made; one of the objects of the points I have been making is to suggest that this confidence is usually unjustified. Even in a simple relation between two persons, it is frequently extremely difficult to identify the kind of relationship it is, the motives, the psychological mechanisms, and so on, of the parties in the relation; this difficulty is, of course, very much greater when we are dealing with complex groups and institutions. The position is clearer when the patient in a power relation is aware of a conflict situation, and when overt sanctions are present. In our ordinary talk about power, I imagine that we usually apply the term to situations of this kind, and this is also the practice of many political scientists. I shall return to this point also at a later stage. This does not seem to be a very convenient restriction of the application of the term "power," and, as we shall see, it can lead to misleading results in the empirical study of social groups and communities. In the political relationships of actual societies, relations of the "influence" type and those of the "domination" type are frequently so much intertwined, are causally so closely interconnected, that it is not very sensible to make an analysis of a political structure which leaves on one side the relationships which I have called "influence." For example, in the analysis of many examples of political "leadership," it would be impossible not to bring into the reckoning relations both of "influence" and "domination," and the manner in which they interact with one another.

III

Let me now return to Russell's "Power is the production of intended effects." If we confine our attention to situations down towards the "domination" end of our scale, we shall emphasize *intended* effects: the power of the gunman is certainly his production of intended effects—for instance, the handing over of the contents of the till. But if we look at relations of influence, the position is more difficult: the influence A has on B is sometimes intended, sometimes unintended; furthermore, A may be either conscious or unconscious of the influence he has upon B, and similarly B may be conscious or unconscious of the fact that he is being influenced. Towards the end of these "Notes" I want to suggest some reasons why a realistic or adequate study of political or social power cannot afford to discount unintended effects. On the other hand, it is easy to see why the majority of social scientists agree with Russell in connecting power with intended effects only. In the first place, intended effects are much easier to deal with empirically: we can observe A expressing a wish or demand or a policy: we can observe B's disagreement or reluctance: and we can observe B's final compliance with A's demand. In the case of unintended effects, it is often more difficult to establish the fact that there has been influence at all, and not merely a coincidence of decisions. Moreover, the concept of unintended influence is a tricky one to deal with; clearly, it would be impossible to claim that A is influencing B whenever he produces unintended effects on B. Mr. Menzies produces unintended effects on *The Sydney Morning Herald*: we should scarcely say that he is influencing *The Sydney Morning Herald.* (Actually he is, but not in the sense that is relevant to this discussion.) Apparently, it is not simply a matter of A producing unintended effects on B; it appears, roughly speaking, that unintended effects are equated with being influenced when B becomes more like A, adopts his opinions, or his preferences, or his way of living: the once much-discussed "embourgeoisement" of the working class is perhaps a sociological example of influence in the form of unintended effects, and one that supports the point already made that a realistic account of social power can hardly afford to ignore influence as the production of unintended effects. On the other hand, if the unintended effect the parent has on the child is to stiffen the child's determination to be as different from the parent as possible, such influence would not be taken as an instance of power.

What has been said of unintended influence illustrates again the manner in which any one of these power relationships becomes a whole family of relationships as soon as we inspect it closely. Let us separate out just two or three of the relationships that we may call unintended influence. A may influence B in the sense that B repeatedly imitates A, adopts his opinions or his style, acts as he acts, and so on. We may say that A has power over B in the sense that he, albeit unconsciously, decides for B, is the dominant character of the pair. At the same time, it may be in no way to A's advantage that this should be so; there may be no interest of A's that is furthered by this situation; on the contrary, if B is a lieutenant from whose advice A wishes to profit, it may be a defect in him from A's point of view. But, secondly, we may have a situation which is identical with the first except for this, that B's "reflection" of A may have the effect of supporting or strengthening some interest of A's, of helping to secure him in some position or way of life that he enjoys. Now, obviously, this is a very important type of situation for the analysis of political power or the power structure of a society: the tendency of the members of a society to imitate or take their color from ruling groups or elite groups has often been one of the most important factors in maintaining the political and social position of such groups. Some of the things Marx says about the absorption of the ideology of a ruling class give examples of this mechanism. Or, thirdly, if we say that Joyce exercised a great influence upon many subsequent writers, what is the analysis of this relationship? The influence is not only a matter of conscious or unconscious imitation; some writers rather developed and exploited in their own way techniques that he taught them; but, although they were original and independent writers, Joyce's influence is apparent, and they could not have written as they did but for him. We may hesitate to class this example of unintended influence as a form of power; yet in principle it is not very different from forms of power or influence in the field of political and social action; political and social leadership can be sometimes partly a matter of unusual power of imagination and inventiveness. The chief difference seems to be this: unlike the influence exercised by a book, political leadership is a reciprocal relation persisting over a considerable period of time; and the leadership is, so to speak, being repeatedly renewed by fresh acts of inventiveness. But often it is a form of influence identical neither with the first nor with the second of the other two forms I have also pointed to.

IV

Russell says "the *production* of intended effects." But, of course, sociologists and political scientists, when they speak of power, wish to include, not only the actual production of effects, but also a capacity to produce effects if and when the power holder should decide to produce them. . . .

Suppose we are deciding whether to launch a revolt against the dictator who now rules us. We try to estimate the power he now has. The estimation of his present power is not the same as observing the effects he now produces or has produced in the past; our task is to estimate what effects he will be able to produce when we challenge him. In other words, the concept of power does not *always* refer to a process between persons that is actually in train; power is not something that is present only when the process of producing effects is actually going on (in the way that life can be said to be present only while certain chemical and other processes are occurring); the concept may *also* refer to the capacity to produce effects in the future. We say sometimes that a man has the power to do so and so even though we believe that he will never in fact act to produce the effects in question. The identification of power with the production of effects would make nonsense of much of what we habitually say about power in social affairs.

Thus, we encounter another difference of meanings which writers often fail to notice. When I was discussing the scale from "influence" to "domination," I had in mind interactions or transactions actually occurring between persons; it would have been meaningless to speak of such things as voluntary acceptance of discipline, manipulation, sanctions, a conflict situation, etc. if that were not so. Similarly, it would be meaningless to speak (as we have done) about qualitative differences between different sorts of power relation unless we are thinking of power as an interaction, a process actually in train. If, however, the power we are referring to is the present power to produce effects in the future, *part* of what we are talking about must be a man's control over the means sufficient to produce the effects—as when we say that "wealth is power." In recent writing the distinction is sometimes made between power itself and the "power base" (whatever it is in virtue of which a man can exercise power);[4] but it now appears that, so far as one of the most common and important conceptions of power is concerned, the "power-base" is itself part of the power we attribute to the power holder. . . .

Summing up this part of the discussion, we may conclude that attributions of power always (or almost always) involve future reference. Assertions about the power that an individual or a group possesses are assertions about *both* an existing structure or system of processes and also about future effects. Influence, and other concepts of power, refer to continuing structures; they refer to systems of causally related actions which are constantly repeated; and they are often used in a way that involves a projection into the future. So far as this is so, the empirical analyses of social power structures which are undertaken by sociologists and political scientists are not purely contemporary or purely descriptive exercises; they will include rather complicated predictions about the future, assumptions which it will be very difficult to make explicit about effects that will follow if certain decisions are made or certain other events occur.

V

Let us now glance briefly at another complication. What are the future events we have in mind when, at this moment, we attribute power to A? I have said that we are referring, not only to future events, but also to other persons (usually unspecified). But we can easily see that this is an over-simplification. In addition to the aspects of power we have already pointed to—the character of the interrelated motives and desires of the actors, the presence or absence of a conflict situation, the mechanisms and bases of power—we must introduce still another aspect in order to explicate the concept, what we may call the "field"; that on which the power holder operates or within which he produces his effects. Attributions of power are incomplete, and strictly meaningless, unless there is at least some specification of the "field."

Between persons and within social groups, power is, of course, distributed and diffused in infinitely complicated ways. And even with simple relations between two persons it will not be easy to find a case where the weaker is literally *powerless* in relation to the stronger. It seldom happens that B is so weak that he cannot compel A to pay a price he would rather not pay for the sake of enforcing his will. Because of the virtual omnipresence of power in human relations, our attributions of power to particular persons are comparative more often than we realize; they are quantitative judgments. A

[4] R. A. Dahl, "The Concept of Power," *Behavioral Science* 2 (July 1957), 201–15.

powerful man is like a moneyed man; most of us have some money, but not as much as the moneyed man. And when we look more closely at what these quantifications involve, we see the relevance of what I have called the "field."

There are a number of different dimensions that we are (usually implicitly) quantifying. I shall mention three by way of example. First, the power of a "powerful" man may relate to the number of men he can influence or coerce: Billy Graham is a more influential lecturer than I am, Menzies a more powerful man, because they can affect the behavior of far more men than I can. This dimension may be called the "range" of power. Second, the power that A has over B is relative also to the particular set of B's interests, desires, or activities that are amenable to A's influence or control. If I try to influence the views my students have about Marx, I may succeed; if I try to influence, still more to prescribe, their choice of wives, they will ignore me. Following Simon,[5] we call this dimension the "zone of acceptance"; and clearly it is of fundamental importance in describing the distribution of political and social power; a government may have very great power within some "zone of acceptance," but its power can quickly evaporate if it attempts to operate outside that zone. Thirdly, we find also that within the "zone of acceptance," and with respect to *one* particular segment of a man's interests or activities, there is a limit to the extent that another can influence or control this segment. A Fagin may have established a great influence or domination over an apprentice in crime, but the apprentice may rebel rather than be induced to attempt certain particular crimes. This dimension we call the "intensity" of power; it, too, is an extremely important one in the analysis of political power.[6] A commander may be able to compel his troops to endure a certain amount of suffering; but perhaps there is a limit beyond which mutiny will occur.

Thus, when we attribute power to a man, and especially when our attribution is comparative (as it usually is), we were referring to a "field" in which the power holder operates, and we are giving quantitative values to these and no doubt to other dimensions. There is no reason, of course, to suppose that these dimensions are commensurable. For this reason, it does not seem likely that measurements of political and social power, including judgments about the distribution of power, have, or can ever have, any very exact meaning. In particular cases we might try to increase comparability by restricting

[5] H. A. Simon, "Notes on the Observation and Measurement of Political Power," *Models of Man* (New York: John Wiley, 1957).

[6] In *one* popular usage, the distinction between "influence" and "power" seems to be related to a difference in "intensity." A man will often say about another: "I know that I cannot control him but I think I may be able to influence him—that is, I know that I cannot get him to act exactly as I want him to act, but I can perhaps get him to come part of the way to meet my wishes. This, of course, is quite different from my own use of "influence."

comparisons to positions on a single dimension; but this will not often be very illuminating in dealing with the extremely intricate power relations of a political system or a complex social group.

VI

Thus, it is usually easy to pick holes in empirical studies of the power structure of actual societies. Wright Mills's book, *The Power Elite,*[7] has been attacked on the ground that Mills does not define the criteria which in his opinion would have to be met before one could say that a particular group of men (say, the top men in the Pentagon) have the predominance of power in the U.S.A., and that consequently the assertions he makes about the distribution of power in the U.S.A. cannot be verified. As we have suggested, it is probably impossible for "logical" reasons for any global study of the structure of power within a society to meet these requirements.

R. A. Dahl, in an article which criticizes Mills's book on these grounds, outlines a method for the study of the distribution of power.[8] To abridge fiercely, what he proposes is something like this: one must start with a conflict situation, or a cluster of conflict situations. One must identify in advance the conflicting interests and demands within the situation or situations. And one must then be able to show, over a period of time and in a specified proportion of cases, that the demands or interests of one group have prevailed or predominated in the decisions that are finally taken.

No doubt, some such method will often be applicable, yet there is much that could be said about this recipe for the empirical study of the distribution of power. In the first place, it will be noticed that Dahl has especially in mind what I have called the "domination" sector of the power continuum: his procedure would not be applicable to what I have called the "influence" sector, where there is no clearly identifiable conflict situation, and where the defining characteristic of the situation is not that one man's demands or interests are forced to yield to those of another. In the second place, we must recognize that this is a rather important exclusion, because of the concept of political and social change that is presupposed. Dahl concerns himself with cases in which *decisions* are debated and made. But social change is not only a matter of the taking of a series of discrete and distinguishable decisions. Equally important is slow, nondeliberate, unforeseen and unintended change; and in *this* sort of change the influence that is exercised by elites or pace-setting minorities on the masses of men may be a crucial factor; here, however, we cannot begin by identifying opposing interests or assume that power

[7] C. Wright Mills, *The Power Elite* (New York: Oxford University Press, 1956).

[8] R. A. Dahl, "A Critique of the Ruling Elite Model," *American Political Science Review* 52 (June 1958), 463–9.

is expressed in the solution of a conflict situation. At those points where, for instance, "power" and "prestige" interact, the methods of empirical analysis which may help in the study of situations of the "domination" type may be entirely useless.

But, thirdly, suppose that we *do* confine ourselves to those cases where deliberate, discrete decisions are taken. Even so, the method we are examining will secure greater empirical rigor only at the cost of a great over-simplification of social reality. One thing that Mills appears to be saying is this: that certain groups (for instance, the military, the industrialists, and the top political men) constitute the "power elite" in the U.S.A. because the decisions *they* make affect most deeply, and throughout a very wide "zone," the lives of all the citizens of their country. This statement introduces all three of the dimensions I have just distinguished. But its interest for us at this point is that it brings us back to the question of *unintended* effects. I do not understand Mills to imply that all the effects of the decisions of his "power elite" are intended effects; it is quite intelligible to say that men whose decisions alter the lives of a great number of other men, continuously, deeply, and through a wide range of their interests and activities, are far more powerful than you and I whose decisions have effects in a very restricted "field." Thus, it is plausible to suppose that sometimes when we attribute great power to an individual or group, we have in mind the range, the intensity, the extent of the zone of influence of the power that is exercised, but we may not think it highly relevant to consider whether the effects of decisions are intended or unintended. Political scientists and sociologists might well find it convenient to distinguish pretty sharply between power as the production (or ability to produce) *intended* effects and all other forms or senses of power (including power to produce effects that are not intended); in studies of the distribution and mechanisms of political power, it might be convenient for them to concern themselves only with the first. Still, this would be at variance with the history of the term "power." For many important social theorists have habitually employed the concept as meaning simply power to produce effects on other men (intended *or* unintended); for instance, Marxist-inspired analyses of the power structure of capitalist society, with their emphasis on the power of the capitalist, the entrepreneur, and the investor, have certainly implicitly included the effect of their decisions in "determining" the fate of other men, not necessarily in intended or expected ways, in the calculation of the sum of their power. Similarly, the arguments which have been advanced in the present century in support of what is called "economic democracy"—bringing the operation of the economy within the system of democratic control—have also usually appealed as much to the assumed power of "big business" to produce *unintended* effects as to its power to impose deliberate decisions. And it seems to me that no study of the nature of power and of its political and social significance can afford to exclude this meaning from its inquiries.

VII

I remarked earlier that one problem for an empirical study of a power structure is the problem of "identification"—to recognize the qualitative characters of the power relations present in the situation we are studying. I remarked also that we shall find, in any political system or social group, a great number of qualitatively different power relations most intricately intertwined. . . . We shall find relations which do involve conflict situations of different sorts and degrees, and sanctions of different sorts. And we shall find decisions having both intended and unintended effects. It is not easy to make the necessary discriminations; it is so difficult in fact that very often the participants themselves, the man who exercises power and the man over whom it is exercised, do not themselves know whether sanctions are being employed, or whether there is an element of what I have called "domination" in the relationship. That the quality of the relationship is often concealed from the actors themselves is often enough illustrated by interpersonal relations within the family—for instance, in the relations between husbands and wives, between parents and children: this is a commonplace with which psychoanalysts and novelists are very familiar. It is clear that the psychoanalytical theory of "internalization" or "introjection" would introduce some very nasty problems for analysts of power. It is a still more difficult problem to identify relationships within political or social situations. Abundant examples of this difficulty can be found in discussions of democracy; political scientists do not agree, nor are they likely ever to agree, concerning the role of "domination" in democratic societies like our own, the extent to which sanctions are brought into play in maintaining the stability of democracies, the extent to which the pattern of power (or structure of "powers") depends upon the consent of the governed, the voluntary acceptance of leadership, an ingrained respect for legitimate or constituted authority, and so on. Within recent years, political scientists and sociologists have been giving some attention to the problems connected with the *measurement* of power.[9] It appears to me, however, that a prior problem, and perhaps an even more important one, is what I call the problem of identification. At any rate it is a difficult enough task, apart from quantification, to discover what *kinds* of relationship confront us in any complex social situation; unless we can make these qualitative identifications and discriminations, we cannot begin to consider the significance of a power structure, its relation to problems about freedom and many other issues.

I want to amplify this last point a little further by returning in conclusion to the "influence" pole of the continuum. Talcott Parsons, in another article

[9] J. G. March, "Introduction to the Theory and Measurement of Influence," *American Political Science Review* 49 (June 1955), 431–51 and references in Dahl's article, "Concept of Power."

attacking Mills's book about the power elite of the U.S.A.,[10] asserts that Mills works with a "zero sum" conception of power; that is, that Mills assumes, or tends to assume, that an increase in power at one point within a social system implies its diminution at another. I shall not ask whether this criticism really applies in this case; nevertheless, in our ordinary talk about power it is certainly true that the assumption is often made that there is, so to speak, a finite sum of power, and that if A has become more powerful, then there is a B who has become less powerful. Yet it is easy to see that this is an assumption that cannot generally be made without considerable amplification and qualification.

Now, we can observe in many power relations that a man who enjoys power over others is endowed with the power that he has by those over whom it is exercised. One of the simplest and most familiar examples of this is the leadership situation—the situation where a group of men endow another man with power (including power over themselves) because they expect that by so doing their own power to satisfy some desire, demand, or interest they want to satisfy will be augmented. The power of the leader often survives (or continues to grow) so long as the expectations of those over whom power is exercised continue to be satisfied. Of this situation there are many variants; for instance, the power that the leader or ruler has conferred upon him by the followers or subjects may be the result of a conscious calculation of advantage, or it may come from nonrational belief or sentiment of one kind or another, such as a belief in the magical or nonnatural gifts of the leader. Some instances of what Weber calls "charismatic authority" belong here.

But there are features of all the variants that are worth pointing to. First, A's power does not flow merely from *his* exclusive possession of some power base (wealth, superior strength of knowledge, or whatever it may be); it is an aspect of the interaction between A and those over whom he has the power. Second, sanctions may be completely absent, or quite secondary. Third, and this is here the most relevant point, the power with which A is endowed need not entail what B, C, and D would consider to be a significant loss of power; on the contrary, the increase of A's power can contribute to an increase in their own power to satisfy certain of their own demands. In fact, one of the main functions of social power, one of the purposes of creating power structures and reservoirs of power, and of experimenting with possible distributions of power, is to enlarge the available volume of power—the volume of power that is available not only to the leaders or governors of a group but to all its members.

And this appears with particular clarity in relationships at the extreme end of the "influence" pole of the continuum. We sometimes say of thinkers, writers, painters or musicians that they possess unusual power; we appear to mean that they can produce effects in their work, or that they have a control

10 Talcott Parsons, "Distribution of Power in American Society."

over their medium, beyond the power of ordinary men—this is power simply as the "production of (intended?) effects." Now, a painter may not possess "by nature" the power of a Picasso, or a thinker the power of a Marx or a Freud; but it is not uncommon for them to develop a power that they could not otherwise have acquired by subordinating themselves to a master, following a discipline imposed upon them, and learning to work with the other man's skill and technique, to master his style. And in politics, as in all other forms of cooperative working, there are close analogies to this particular relationship.

But if we want to argue that a man can in certain circumstances increase his own power by subordinating himself to the authority or the power of another person, we can avoid paradox only by admitting further complexities in the power relation. During the war the English, let us say, increased their own power by conferring on Churchill an unusual degree of power and a set of unprecedented "powers": thereby they may be said to have increased their power to achieve ends they were pursuing in common, the defeat of Germany. To build up their power to achieve this end, they surrendered their power to act in certain other ways or to achieve certain other ends. The essential point is that the individuals who participate in a power relation possess many different interests and motives and are engaged in different sets of activity concurrently. Moreover, each person will often give different values to his different interests and activities; at least, he may in many cases rank them in an order of importance to himself.

It is at this point that one of the dimensions I distinguished, "the zone of acceptance," becomes of some importance. It is seldom that A who is said to have power or influence over B has the same power over all of B's interests or activities. In simple interpersonal relations it often happens that A's power to control certain of B's desires or activities (even sometimes to the point of being able to prevent their expression or indulgence) is a necessary or a sufficient condition of B's being able to satisfy other desires or carry out other activities. This, of course, is one of the familiar relationships between parents and children, and between teachers and pupils; the ordinary commonsense justification of the power of parents and of teachers assumes that this does happen. The influence or control which A exercises over B within the "zone of acceptance" may be experienced by B as unalloyed frustration or domination, without any compensating satisfaction or enlargement of potency (as of course it often is by children and school pupils); or B may rank his interests, desires, etc. in such an order that he may feel that the interests which gain in potency or facility are more important to him than those that are blocked. And, although I have spoken only of cases where these judgments are made by the actors themselves, we also habitually make such judgments for other persons; just as we do not make a rule of consulting the wishes of young children when we require them to submit themselves to educational discipline, so as political philosophers and as citizens we habitually make such judgments for other men; we do so whenever we take a position on questions of the legitimacy and illegitimacy of forms, distributions, modes of exercise, etc. of power. And, indeed, with power as with freedom, evaluations of the kind I have been referring to often affect our use or nonuse of the term "power" as a proper description of concrete situations.

VIII

A survey of a few only of the different relations that may be intermingled and confused within any power situation warns us that the connections between one man's power and another's, between one form of power and another, or between power and freedom, may be extremely obscure, and their unravelling a very hazardous enterprise. One conclusion that is possibly suggested by these "Notes" is that the concept of power, for reasons implicit in this discussion, is not likely to be a fruitful concept in the explication of the "power structures" of actual societies; perhaps what is called for is a great deal of analysis in the sense of breaking up and discrimination, and the substitution of more manageable concepts for the portmanteau concept of power. I cannot pursue this question here. It is fair to say, I think, that both in ordinary discussion, and in the discussions of social scientists, there is a tendency to concentrate very heavily on certain manifestations of "power," and to ignore or minimize others. The power relations which lie towards the lower end of the scale tend to be emphasized; those lying towards the pure "influence" end tend to be played down. Furthermore, common sense does tend to assume a "zero sum" concept of power; everyday discussions (for instance, of the growth of the state's power or of the power of the bureaucracy) not only pay scant regard to the "dimensions" I have shown to be highly relevant, but also tend to assume that if there is a building up of power at one point within the system there must be a diminution at others. Again, in thinking about power as a social phenomenon, we tend to be too much obsessed with problems of distribution; and perhaps we operate with very crude notions of distribution to boot. No one would be in danger of assuming that the wealth of a society is a fixed quantity; or that the effects of a reallocation of wealth could be calculated by simple operations of addition and subtraction. Or, again, if we happen to be interested in moral issues connected with power and its operation, it is very obvious that such well-worn assertions as Acton's "power tends to corrupt and absolute power corrupts absolutely," or Reinhold Niebuhr's theme of the persistent tension between power and morality, are not in an undissected form either illuminating or interesting. With power as with many other things, as Oakeshott has reminded us, *la verité reste dans les nuances.*

14

On Interests in Politics

William E. Connolly[1]

THE IMPORT OF CONTESTS OVER "INTERESTS"

To say that a policy or practice is in the interests of an individual or group is to assert both that the recipient would somehow benefit from it and that there is, therefore, *a reason* in support of enacting that policy. Of course the reason may be overridden by other considerations. But it is important to see that, as it is used in our society, "interest" is one of those concepts which connects descriptive and explanatory statements to normative judgment.

One way of seeing the connection between talk about interests and normative appraisal is suggested by Charles Taylor.[2] That is, although to say "*x* is in *y*'s interest" is not *equivalent* to saying it is good, it is one of the licenses for making the prima-facie judgment that *x* is good or desirable. Another route to understanding this connection is to note the role that wanting, choosing, and preferring play in the concept of interests. For although the latter concept has been variously defined, all definitions seriously advanced make an important reference to the wants, preferences, and choices of agents somewhere in the definition. We generally accept the principle that people ought to be able to do what they choose or want to do unless overriding considerations intervene. And talk about interests carries that presumption into political discourse; indeed it strengthens the presumption, since the sort of wants, preferences, and choices which enter into the meaning of interests are exactly those which are deemed to be somehow important, persistent, basic or fundamental in politics. Disagreements about where and how these conative states are included in the concept of interests reflect, I want to suggest,

Source: Reprinted in revised form from *Politics and Society* (Summer 1972), 459–477.

[1] My thanks to Glen Gordon, George Kateb, David Kettler, and Felix Oppenheim for their insightful criticisms of an earlier draft of this essay.

[2] "Neutrality in Political Science," in this volume.

disagreements about which conative states under what conditions deserve the normative sanction "interests" provides.

It is obvious and notorious that social theorists have disagreed extensively about proper meaning to assign to "interests" in political and social life, but the participants in these disputes have typically tried to limit themselves to lines of argument permitted by a positivist disjuncture between descriptive statements and normative appraisals. The debates, thereby, take the form of arguments over which proposed definition is more "operational" or, vaguely, of greater "theoretical importance." But when we state explicitly what even positivist social scientists have tacitly known—that talk about interests has a *normative function* in our discourse—we can understand more profoundly just why disagreements about the descriptive conditions or *criteria* of its application are so intense and persistent.[3] For one set of criteria will draw our attention to one set of conative states formed under certain conditions, while other proposals will divert our attention from these conditions and toward others. The effect of such definitional proposals is to privilege certain actual or potential conative states for purposes of normative appraisal in politics, and, often, to blind us to possible considerations operating outside of those boundaries.

Now if the very *notion* of our interests shapes our normative priorities in the way suggested, an explanatory theory employing that notion will generate more definite and detailed normative conclusions. For such a theory purports to tell us what interests citizens in various settings have, how the political system nourishes some interests, protects others, and dampens or suppresses yet others; it tells us as well why and how particular segments of the society fail to recognize some of their interests, whether and to what extent some of these unrecognized interests could be revealed and promoted through political pressure; it tells us what costs are likely to be incurred by efforts to reveal and promote these suppressed interests; and finally, it purports to tell us to what extent some of the existing demands and pressures on the political system reflect not the identifiable interests of citizens but their projection of unattainable fantasies and wishes onto public arenas. The explanatory theory, in short, "sets the crucial dimensions through which the phenomena (of interests) can vary" and through its assessment of the possibilities, costs, and risks of satisfying the interests it identifies, it informs us "how we are to judge of good and bad." [4]

I certainly do not want to suggest that the concept of interests is the only concept in political inquiry which serves as a bridge between explanatory

[3] See the distinction between the "material" and "formal" elements of a concept drawn by Julius Kovesi in *Moral Notions* (London: Routledge and Kegan Paul, 1967). Kovesi's approach to conceptual analysis suggests a profound critique of the approach conventionally adopted by political scientists.

[4] Taylor, "Neutrality in Political Science" (pp. 30 and 40 of original text).

theory and normative judgment, but it is one of those concepts performing this crucial function.[5] Our inquiry into the various efforts to prescribe criteria for the application of this concept will be more self-conscious and illuminating if we keep its normative function in mind. In this way, we will grasp the extent to which debates about the *criteria* of "interests" are a part of larger debates about the structure and style of the good society. When we judge proposed definitions in this way, we will be able to confront directly factors and considerations which typically remain in the shadow of contemporary debates.

I will explore four alternative efforts to elucidate the criteria of "interests," arguing that the notions improve successively as we move from the first to the last.[6]

INTERESTS AS POLICY PREFERENCE

Most American political scientists, working largely within the confines of a pluralist theory of politics, do not explicitly define "interests," but tend to equate the notion in practice with the political pressure an individual or group brings to bear on government. Often too, the investigator locates "interests" so understood by identifying the policy preferences of the agents. Since the criticisms advanced here apply to either of these formulations, I will treat them as interchangeable, speaking in general of interests defined as the policy preferences of individuals and groups.[7]

Typically the tendency to define interests as policy preference is sharpened when the scholar is presenting a methodological critique of explanatory theories that purport to find "false consciousness" among some segments of society. Thus Nelson Polsby rejects on methodological grounds C. Wright

[5] For examples of essays that explicitly place "interests" in the center of moral discourse, see Stanley Benn, "Egalitarianism and the Equal Consideration of Interests," in *Justice and Equality,* ed. Hugo A. Bedau (Englewood Cliffs, N.J.: Prentice-Hall, 1971), pp. 152–167 and John Rawls, "Justice as Fairness," *The Philosophical Review* (1958), 164–194.

[6] I omit reference here to "explications" of the following sort, that seek to bypass the issues involved: "Well, what is an *interest* then? . . . But for our purposes in this volume at least that is exactly the kind of question we have tried to avoid. The *scientific procedure* is to observe and isolate certain acts (or behaviors) and actions, and connect these into 'bundles' whose interconnections may prove fruitful. 'Interest group' being just a convenient label for one such 'bundle,' it need have no connection at all with the meaning of its two constituent terms." (!) Graham Wootton, *Interest Groups: Foundations of Modern Political Science Series* (Englewood Cliffs, N.J.: Prentice-Hall, 1970), p. 18.

[7] Probably because the concept has received increased attention lately in philosophical literature, few political scientists today argue as confidently for interest as policy preference. But the concept is still commonly *employed* that way, largely on the grounds of operational rigor. For earlier statements, see David Truman, *The Governmental Process* (New York: Alfred A. Knopf, Inc., 1951), pp. 50–51; Glendon Schubert, *The Public Interest* (New York: The Free Press, 1960).

Mills' assertion that "false consciousness" is "the lack of awareness of and identification with one's objective interests." Polsby's alternative view holds, "at least presumptively, that decisions affect people's interests differentially, and that people participate in those areas *they care about the most.* Their values, eloquently expressed by their participation, cannot, it seems to me, be more effectively 'objectified.' "[8]

The notion of interest as policy preference is open to several telling criticisms.[9]

1. The debate between pluralist theorists and their critics hinges in strong measure on the extent to which specific groups in the society fail to identify and press policy proposals which could substantially improve their well-being. But by defining interests merely as policy preference, pluralists help to push the issue dividing them and their critics outside the reach of empirical inquiry. For given that definition of interest, there simply cannot be "unarticulated interests"; those without particular policy preferences in certain areas must be viewed as not having an interest in a given policy result. If it is possible to formulate a concept of interest, meeting reasonable methodological standards, that does enable us to ask questions such as "Does group *Q* have unarticulated interest *y*?" that explication will be preferable on the grounds that it avoids settling by definitional fiat an important question that might be studied empirically.
2. Equating "interest" with policy preference collapses an important distinction, sanctioned in ordinary discourse, between one's support for a policy because of a perceived moral obligation and his support

[8] Both quotations are from Nelson Polsby, "The Sociology of Community Power," *Social Forces* (1959), 235, my emphasis. I should note that in private correspondence Polsby has denied that he defines interest as policy preference and has suggested that "interest" is not a central category in his work on community power. While it is not central to my argument whether he does or does not employ the term that way and while he has not given an explicit definition of the term in the works considered here, the following two points are relevant: 1) "Interests" must be a central category for Polsby, for "proposition" 4 of the "stratification theory" that he is out to refute holds that "The upper class power elite rules in its own interests." (*Community Power and Political Theory* [New Haven: Yale University Press, 1963], p. 11). 2) Statements such as the following are found at several junctures in his book when he is criticizing "stratification theorists" for imputing to groups interests that the groups themselves don't acknowledge: "However, 'real' conflicts apparently can take place in the view of stratification analysis without overt disagreements .... For the moment, rejecting this presumption of 'objectivity of interests,' we may view instances of intra-class disagreement *as* intra-class conflicts of interest and interclass agreement as interclass harmony of interest. To maintain the opposite seems perverse." (Ibid., p. 22, my emphasis.)

[9] I deal with the criticisms briefly here in order to get to more intriguing notions. For other criticisms with which I largely agree, see Isaac Balbus, "The Concept of Interest in Pluralist and Marxian Analysis," *Politics and Society* (1971), 151–178; Brian Barry, *Political Argument* (New York: The Humanities Press, 1965), Ch. X; Richard Flathman, *The Public Interest* (New York: John Wiley and Sons, 1966).

for it solely on the grounds of self-interest. Failure to sustain this distinction clearly in political inquiry lends illicit (because unargued) support to the view that political man must act only, or at least primarily, in his self-interest. The pernicious effects of such an unexamined assumption, both for political inquiry and for the considerations governing the political commitments of citizens, can hardly be overstated.[10]

3. If, as suggested above, to say 'policy *x* is in *A*'s interest' is to provide a prima-facie justification for that policy, defining interests in terms of policy preferences, and then viewing actual political participation as the best indicator of policy preference, combine to sanction perverse normative judgments. Since a high level of participation is correlated with high socio-economic status, this view of interests supports the claims of the various segments of society in inverse proportion to their need. By thus restricting the application of the concept while tacitly retaining its conventional function in normative assessment, a significant bias is insinuated into materials from which normative conclusions are forged.[11]

Yet such criticisms, impeccable as they may be, fail to speak to the central counter-argument wheeled out by those adopting this notion of interests. The argument, suggested by Polsby's statement quoted above, is that most alternative notions of interest incorporate the possibility of attributing false consciousness to citizens, thereby encouraging researchers to impute arbitrarily to groups interests that the groups themselves do not acknowledge. The more modest notion of interest as policy preference forces the investigator to confront the hard facts about the preferences and behavior of people in political life. It is a more operational definition.

It is not my intention here to argue generally against the myth of opera-

[10] Pernicious for inquiry because, accepting that assumption, students of political "socialization," for example, forget to explore the central question perplexing Rousseau: Under what conditions of social life and education do citizens develop the capacity to support justice and the public interest even when that support requires a sacrifice of private advantage? Pernicious for political conduct because the assumption that political acts (almost always) will be self-interested helps to justify particular acts of *selfishness* as part of the human condition. For an intriguing effort to raise the Rousseauian question, see Lawrence Kohlberg, "Moral Development," *International Encyclopedia of the Social Sciences* (New York: Macmillan, 1968) Vol. 10, pp. 483–494.

[11] There are many arguments for the presumption to remain close to ordinary discourse in explicating conceptions such as "power," "interest," and "politics." One argument stands out sharply here: Concepts, as vehicles for thought and action, have complex rules governing their use that are never fully stated. Since a particular concept receives its full meaning only in relation to the entire conceptual system in which it is embedded, a change in one of its dimensions is likely to produce unnoted implications for its ability to perform its several conventional functions. Such a consideration does not militate against conceptual revision, but against such revision lightly undertaken. Concept revision is more analogous to a heart transplant than to a watch repair.

tionalism which has unjustifiably confined the scope of contemporary political inquiry.[12] Two points, though, are particularly pertinent to the question at hand. 1) Even if the notion of interest as policy preference is more operational than alternative explications, this advantage might well be outweighed by its other manifest deficiencies. 2) That notion of interest, when elaborated more fully, is not as neatly operational as its proponents suggest. Since a reasonable assessment of the first claim must await further arguments in this paper, I will limit my attention here to the second.

There is, initially, the obvious problem of discovering the policy preferences people actually have. The preferences people express do not always converge with their unexpressed and latent preferences. A survey of blacks just prior to the Detroit riots surely would not have detected "preferences" clearly discernible during the riot and in studies shortly thereafter. Also, policy preferences expressed to middle-class investigators by members of maverick groups bearing on legalization of dope, protection of homosexuality, legalized prostitution, etc. may well distort the actual orientations of these groups. Distortions of these types are likely to lead the investigator to overplay the extent and depth of consensus in contemporary politics.

More importantly, the term "preference," used in this way, includes choices of at least two kinds, and these differences must be unsorted in any appraisal of interests. We have noted the distinction between supporting a policy because I prefer it for itself and, alternately, because it seems morally appropriate to do so even though I would choose otherwise if moral considerations did not intervene. Hence, a farmer might prefer to continue using DDT on his crops when considering only his own benefit, but decide, on balance, to vote in favor of making its use illegal. Surely an advocate of interest as policy preference will accept this distinction, once drawn, for otherwise he would allow an important question deserving empirical study (that is, when people's policy preferences are self- or other-regarding) to be obscured by conceptual sloppiness or, more likely, settled by definitional fiat. But then he is forced to distinguish between "self-regarding" and "other-regarding" preferences, and the problem of applying that distinction in research practice will be severe indeed. It will force the dissolution of those crude indicators of interest commonly employed, such as collecting statements from interviewees about their policy preferences and observing the participation of group leaders in support of particular policies. To apply this distinction in research practice will require the subtle assessment of multiple cues in concrete settings.

12 See William Alson, *Philosophy of Language* (Englewood Cliffs, N.J.: Prentice-Hall, 1964), last chapter; Max Black, "Reasoning with Loose Concepts," in his *The Margins of Precision* (Ithaca, Cornell University Press, 1970), pp. 1–13); George Schlesinger, "Operationalism," *Encyclopedia of Philosophy,* Vol. 5 (1967), 543–547; and especially Friedrich Waismann, "Verifiability," in *Logic and Language,* First Series ed. Anthony Flew (Oxford: Basil Blackwell, 1951), pp. 115–145.

Finally, since one always *prefers* something to other specified alternatives, the range of alternatives taken into account is crucial to the preference adopted. I might prefer democracy to communism, communism to death, and death to prolonged torture by the secret agents of a democratic society. But attention to this conceptual point complicates the effort to "operationalize" policy preference as interest. Is the range of alternative preferences to be limited to those issues considered in governmental arenas? If so, the terms of comparison within which policy preferences are stated will be biased in favor of whatever groups benefit the most from existing processes of issue formation. If the range of preferences is broadened beyond these limits, the question of how far must be faced. For surely a policy preference must be distinguished from a mere wish. If a trade union leader lobbied in favor of a policy that would ensure the immortality of blue-collar workers, Professor Polsby, for example, would surely concur in labeling that a pipe dream rather than an interest of the workers. Such distinctions must be made, but no set of *operations* has been specified that enable investigators to determine even roughly the point in contemporary politics where policy preference shades off into political fantasy.

In practice these multiple discriminations are presupposed by research assumptions rather than tested by impersonal operations. Such presuppositions generally go unnoted when shared by a community of scholars. But when the theory of pluralism within which this notion of interests is embedded is challenged, when the props are exposed, the impressionistic status of the discriminations themselves become apparent. Among the central disagreements between, say, a C. Wright Mills and a Nelson Polsby are diverging interpretations of the unexpressed and latent preferences of the underclass in American society, of the occasions when political actors are guided by moral imperatives rather than self-interest in their political conduct, and, especially, of those aspirations within contemporary society that can properly be construed as political preferences rather than mere wishes or pipe dreams.[13] The notion of interest as policy preference does appear moderately operational when appraisals of interest are made within the framework of the theory in which this concept functions. When that context itself is in dispute, the tenuous connection between the concept and any particular set of operations becomes apparent.

UTILITARIAN INTERESTS

Utilitarianism, narrowly defined, takes the wants, desires, and inclinations

[13] Thus, even the equation of interests and policy *preference* makes "false consciousness" of a sort possible. Polsby, *Community Power and Political Theory*; C. Wright Mills, *The Power Elite* (New York: Oxford University Press, 1959). Such comparisons are developed in William E. Connolly, *Political Science and Ideology* (New York: Atherton Press, 1967), Ch. 2.

of persons as given and asks how to maximize their attainment. In this sense, Brian Barry can be said to advance a utilitarian notion of interests. He considers a "policy, law or institution (to be) in someone's interest if it increases his opportunities to get what he wants . . . whatever that may be." [14]

Now this definition, once the term "want" is appropriately clarified, constitutes a clear improvement over the first notion of interest considered. First, in line with usage in ordinary discourse, this definition makes it possible for an agent to be mistaken about his interests. For misinformation, poor calculation, or failure to consider feasible but unarticulated policy alternatives might lead one to prefer a policy that does not, on a comparative basis, maximize his "opportunities to get what he wants." A low-income citizen, for example, might want to maximize his disposable income but then favor a state sales tax over an income tax because of a mistaken view about the relative effects of each tax on the amount of his disposable income. His policy preference, in this instance, would be at odds with his interest.

The definition, as clarified by Barry, also sustains the distinction between supporting a policy because it is in my interest and supporting it because of moral reasons. And since one's interest in a policy, on this view, has no conceptual linkage to participation in the political process, the illicit normative bias built into the first definition is avoided.

The limitations of this notion, though, become more apparent when we probe the phrase "opportunities to get what he *wants.*" With one qualification, Barry takes the prevailing wants of persons as given for purposes of appraising their interests.[15] But the wants we have, as Barry knows, are shaped to a large degree by the society in which we mature. Without regard now to questions of truth or falsity, there is surely a *prima-facie meaningfulness* to the claim that a perfectly adjusted slave or a well-socialized consumer has wants at odds with his real interests. Social theorists as diverse as Karl Marx and Emile Durkheim, as Ortega y Gasset and John Kenneth Galbraith, have advanced interpretations which rest upon just such claimed distortions

14 Quoted from "The Public Interest," in *The Bias of Pluralism* ed. W. Connolly (New York: Atherton Press, 1969), p. 163. Barry is not, of course, strictly a utilitarian. For he considers ideals which are not "want regarding" relevant to the appraisal of public policy. He is utilitarian only in the sense that he makes interest a want-regarding concept. See Barry, *Political Argument,* Ch. III.

15 The qualification is this: It might be in one's interest to sacrifice the satisfaction of a current want if its attainment will impede his ability to satisfy future wants he might have. (Ibid., p. 184.) Thus legalization of heroin might help me to get what I now want but limit my ability to attain future wants (and even affect my future wants themselves?). But a qualification posed along a *purely* temporal dimension is necessary but insufficient to handle conventional uses of interest. We need to specify in addition, conditions that enable us to ask, and bring evidence to bear on, whether it is in the slave's interest to escape slavery even if he now prefers that state to all known alternatives and *always will as long as he remains a slave.* A purely temporal qualification will not handle this paradigm case or the numerous other situations that more or less approximate it.

in processes of interest articulation. We should not accept a notion of interest that excludes such statements unless serious efforts to explicate the concept in ways that accommodate them are shown to be vitally flawed.

Barry's use of "want" limits "interest" in another questionable respect. For the kind of wants Barry considers relevant to ascriptions of interest seem to be egoistic wants. Put more clearly, although Barry emphasizes that persons can consciously choose to act against their interests, the paradigm case of "doing what I want" is that of securing objects and advantages for my *private enjoyment.* When I act as a want-regarding creature, other persons are viewed merely as means or obstacles to my attainment of "life, liberty, health and indolency of body, and the possession of outward things such as money, houses, furniture and the like." [16] As Barry states the point elsewhere while distinguishing an interest from an ideal, "results concerning people other than *A* are not directly relevant" in the ascriptions of an interest to *A*.[17] This restriction, I shall argue, is too confining.

To be clear about interests, we must specify the kinds of persons we are talking about and what aspects of their activity we have in mind. Some definitional statements draw our attention to the "interests" one has when he acts egoistically, but it seems to me that we can also speak sensibly about the interests a person has as a social being. When I act egoistically, I seek such things as food and leisure for myself; the satisfactions (or dissatisfactions) I attain do not themselves involve a reference to other people. They are private gratifications—not in the sense that I am the one who experiences them (for that is true of all *my* states), but in that other people are seen only as *means* or *obstacles* to my states and not as implicated with me in mutually gratifying *relationships.*

When my interests as a social being are at stake, more than private wants are involved. Certain kinds of relationship with others are fostered—relationships that involve trust, friendship, shared conventions, and the like. One who cherishes the social dimension of life may often be willing to sacrifice purely private satisfaction for the mutual benefits of social life. For instance, a person might decide to forgo attaining certain material benefits in the interests of maintaining a relationship of trust with another. He might simply cherish for itself the kind of life implied by sustaining such relationships more than he prizes the sacrificed material benefits. He is surely acting in his interest in this case. There is a *sacrifice* here, of course, but not in the sense that an act of altruism is the sacrifice of one's interest. The person is simply sacrificing a lower-order private interest for his higher-order social interest.

Interests I have as a social being are those which make "essential reference

[16] Barry's quotation from John Locke to illustrate the "kinds of ways in which a policy, law, or institution might impinge on someone before it can be said to be 'in his interest.'" Barry, "The Public Interest," in *The Bias of Pluralism,* p. 163.

[17] Barry, *Political Argument,* p. 182.

to reciprocal states of awareness among two or more persons." [18] Thus workers might, as Marx contends, have an interest in policies supporting a work-life in which they interact creatively in the productive process. Citizens might, as Herbert Morris believes, have an interest in a system of punishment that treats an accused criminal as an agent capable of acting responsibly in his relations with others.[19] Human beings in general might, as Durkheim believes, have an interest in policies enabling each to share with others a set of social norms that give regularity, purpose, and direction to their interaction. It isn't that Marx, Morris, and Durkheim are necessarily correct in their assessments of the interests we have as social beings or in the extent to which those interests override purely egoistic interest, for these three theorists disagree among themselves and one or all of them might indeed be seriously mistaken in his assessment of interests. But if a reasonable notion of "interest" can be advanced that enables us to cope with conflicts between egoistic and social interests, on the same plane, so to speak, we will be able to sharpen and clarify those fundamental issues lying beneath the surface of contemporary debates about political life.[20] We will be able to make sense of the kind of claim advanced when someone says: "John favors that policy because he wants to increase his income, but his real interest would be promoted further if the social conditions of his work life were reformed."

With these distinctions in mind, consider Gerhard Lenski's use of "interest"—a concept crucial to his description and explanation of inequality in complex societies. His identification of "interest" with my category of egoistic interest is exemplified in the following statement: "In time, of course, the normal child learns to take the wishes of others into account. But this does not mean he is any less motivated to maximize his own satisfaction. Rather, it means that the attainment of his goals is inevitably linked with interests of others." [21]

In Lenski's view one needs others primarily as instruments for private satisfactions, and one is generally *motivated* by a desire to maximize these private interests. The pertinent distinction for him is between self-interested action (in the narrowest sense), which is very common, and altruistic action, which is very rare. That concept of interest in conjunction with his theory that human behavior is motivated by self-interest accounts for Lenski's first "law" of distribution: "Men will share the product of their labor to the extent required to insure the survival and continued productivity of those whose

[18] Robert Paul Wolff, *The Poverty of Liberalism* (Boston: Beacon Press, 1968), p. 181. See also Isaac Balbus, "The Concept of Interest in Pluralist and Marxian Analysis."

[19] Herbert Morris, "Persons and Punishment," *The Monist* (1968), 471–501.

[20] Those issues are tapped effectively in Fred Dallmayr, "Empirical Political Theory and Images of Man," in this volume.

[21] Gerhard Lenski, "The Nature of Distributive Systems," in this volume, p. 128.

actions are necessary or beneficial to themselves." [22] And because most people generally pursue their egoistic interests, a society with a large "surplus" will find that surplus distributed to those with the most power.

But this dichotomy between egoistic and altruistic action is too crude to capture the richness of human relationships and motivation. People also have interests, as I have argued, as social beings, and when this dimension of social life is understood, Lenski's theory of motivation and explanation of inequality itself becomes less plausible. For people might have interests in community relationships that, to be attained, require the loss or diminution of possible material benefits for those involved. And in some societies where particular conditions make the mutual gratifications flowing out of such social ties apparent to many, the citizens themselves might be *motivated* by exactly these considerations. In these circumstances, Lenski's central postulate that "man has an insatiable appetite for goods and services" would not apply as stringently as he supposes.[23] Since that postulate flows naturally from Lenski's dichotomy between self-interested and altruistic conduct, we can see how the very concept of interest Lenski adopts impedes his ability to explore patterns of motivation which are neither purely egoistic nor purely altruistic. Forced by his *categories* to assimilate observed conduct to selfishness or altruism, Lenski naturally concludes that the former dominates.

These considerations bear on the difficulties Lenski encounters in explaining why benefits in industrial societies are distributed *less* unequally than his general theory would lead one to expect. He explains this "discrepancy" in large part by reference to a "democratic ideology" that has somehow captured the sentiments of the masses and now operates also as a constraint on privileged elites. Acknowledging difficulty in explaining the rise of this ideology, he thinks its role in industrial society is nevertheless crucial.

Two points are pertinent here: First, the rise of a democratic ideology is more readily explicable if one refuses to assume that human beings must always and everywhere be governed by egoistic impulses, assuming instead that, under appropriate conditions of social life, people can and will be motivated by desires to support their interests as social beings (as well as by a stronger measure of altruistic principle than Lenski allows). Second, if one then concludes that certain communitarian relationships would be fulfilling to participants were they to experience them, a set of questions ignored by Lenski now become pertinent. Do the present distribution of power and prevailing patterns of motivation in our industrial society obstruct citizen awareness of more fulfilling possibilities? Do certain structural arrangements (such as patterns of work life, social mobility, rise of the nuclear family, the isolation and psychological deprivation of older people) encourage egoistic motives and discourage attention both to interests we have as social beings and ideals

[22] Ibid., p. 133.
[23] Ibid., p. 129.

we might otherwise support as moral agents? Could reduction in the existing range of inequality be accomplished if such structural sources of insecurity and narrow self-concern were modified? In this way a revision of Lenski's concept of interest opens one to a reexamination of central postulates in his theory and encourages an exploration of alternative ways to explain prevailing inequalities.

These large issues cannot be explored here, but it should be emphasized that the suggested conceptual revision is not *alone* sufficient to establish an affirmative answer to the new questions posed. It could turn out that the concept of interest offered here is viable, but that in fact most people in most settings almost always subordinate interests they have as social beings to their egoistic interests. Or, maybe certain communal arrangements are in the interests of most people today, but structural requirements of industrial society make these arrangements unattainable. Or maybe the envisaged relationships are in fact compatible with extensive and steep inequalities. Each of these possibilities is debatable—which is exactly the point. For rejection of Lenski's dichotomy between egoistic interest and altruistic action enables one to raise new questions and possibilities bypassed by a theory reflecting Lenski's notion of interests and his postulates about the self-interested motivation people everywhere must have.

To fix more concretely the way in which Lenski's theory of interests loads the conclusions of his analysis, consider his argument that inequalities in job opportunity and salary between men and women are explicable in large part by reference to the opportunities women have for status and material comfort through marriage. In a society where marriage is a way of life, "a woman may obtain half interest in a very substantial income, entree to exclusive circles, and leisure to do most of the things she wishes. Even a woman whose marriage is less successful by economic standards is usually provided with a measure of economic security." [24]

Because *these* satisfactions are available to women, he concludes (1966), it is unlikely that existing inequalities between the sexes "will be eliminated or greatly reduced beyond the present level." [25] Lenski's failure to perceive that women might have interests beyond those enumerated above and might also become motivated to press militantly to fulfill them flows in large part, I contend, from the poverty of his notion of interest and the theory of human nature to which that notion is attached.

INTERESTS AS NEED FULFILLMENT

We can speak rather easily of the interests one has relative to an accepted standard of social life. Thus, given the principle of respect for persons, it

24 Gerhard Lenski, *Power and Privilege* (New York: McGraw-Hill, 1966), pp. 405–406.
25 Ibid., p. 406.

is in the interests of the slave to be freed even if he has been conditioned to accept slavery. But is it in the slave's real interest to be treated with such respect? How could we warrant or undermine such a claim when advanced by another for the slave?

American social scientists who have approached this problem have most often posited a set of universal human "needs" that are thought to stand above and beyond variations in social structure and patterns of socialization and to provide a standard of achievement against which particular social arrangements can be assessed.[26] The term "need" is not always defined carefully in this literature, but Christian Bay's definition typifies a wider usage: A need is "any *behavior tendency* whose continual denial or frustration leads to pathological responses."[27] Needs are not reducible to wants here, for wants are specifically oriented to particular goals, while an unmet need *may* find expression as malaise, vague anxiety, or unfocussed tension. Bay, for example, takes suicide, alcoholism, psychosis, delinquency, and drug addiction to be among the symptoms of need frustration. And he holds that these pathologies sometimes develop when "higher level" needs are frustrated, such as the needs to develop cognitive capacities, to act as responsible agents, and to enter into intimate relationships with others.

Even if this notion of needs were fully serviceable, "need" and "interest" would not be synonomous. For innumerable personalized and localized cases of need frustration might remain beyond the reach of effective public policy. But, on this view, a *policy* would be in someone's interest to the extent that it, by comparison with other alternatives, promoted need fulfillment or increased opportunities to promote need fulfillment.

Such a definition does underline deficiencies in the first two formulations considered. For there are situations where people have, as C. Wright Mills would say, "troubles" not yet translated into firm wants, let alone into a set of political claims. "Instead of troubles defined in terms of values and threats—there is often the misery of vague uneasiness, instead of explicit issues there is often merely the beat feeling that all is somehow not right."[28] To the extent that the first two concepts of interest slide over situations such as this, they divert conceptual attention from possible tensions simmering just

[26] Thus Amitai Etzioni, in his defense of a theory of basic human needs, describes the function of such a theory: "Theories which assume autonomous human needs provide an independent basis with which to compare societies to each other, as more or less consonant with basic human needs." See "Basic Human Needs, Alienation and Inauthenticity," *American Sociological Review* (1968), p. 878. See also: Christian Bay, "Politics and Pseudo-Politics: A Critical Evaluation of Some Behavioral Literature," *American Political Science Review* (1968), 870–884 and James C. Davies, *Human Nature in Politics* (New York: John Wiley, 1963).

[27] Christian Bay, "Needs, Wants, and Political Legitimacy," *Canadian Journal of Political Science* (1968), 242.

[28] C. Wright Mills, *The Sociological Imagination* (New York: Oxford University Press, 1959), p. 11.

below the surface of pluralist politics. Conceptual blinders of this sort help to explain the failure of liberal social scientists of the last generation to anticipate the political crises of the sixties and seventies, to detect those troubles shuffled out of pluralist politics, and to formulate political issues implied by their presence (Mills of course is the exception).

And yet this definition too has serious deficiencies. For a simple test will show, I think, that the suggested conceptual connection between needs and interests may well impose severe limits on the resulting theory of interests. These limits are both contrary to the intentions of those who advance the notion of human needs and, I shall later argue, unwarranted.[29]

Consider a hypothetical situation in which we (as investigators) have full and direct knowledge of the tensions and behavioral inclinations of a subservient population. We find the population to have all its needs met (defined as behavioral tendencies); there are no "pathological" responses, no blockage of felt inclinations, and no vaguely felt tensions. The creatures we are to visualize are well fed and clothed; they exhibit a strong sense of security; they even express a doglike warmth in their personal relationships. What they lack, though, is the ability to choose reflectively among alternative courses of conduct, to act responsibly, to express the complex reactive attitudes of love, resentment, grief, guilt, remorse, and outrage that we associate with the social life of human beings.

I am not concerned to argue that the condition described is likely to occur anywhere. But if it were to occur, we would surely be tempted to say that the population's lack of felt inclinations to develop, say, their deliberative capacities to a high pitch was not conclusive proof that it would not be in their interests to do so. This is not only because they might find such skills necessary to the fulfillment of other vaguely felt inclinations (a consideration need theories could easily accommodate). But human beings might, in some settings, lack inclinations or urgings of any sort to achieve states they would prize for themselves once attained; they might possess strong dispositions to resist the attainment of those very modes of life they would find the most gratifying, once having experienced them; and they might even find that certain arrangements prized for themselves necessarily include tensions and anxieties as part of the prized condition.

Need theories typically start with a plausible statement of primary needs tied to observable behavioral tendencies and inclinations. But as one advances up the hierarchy of postulated needs, a subtle conceptual shift emerges. From "needs" as a noun defined in terms of inclinations, we shift increasingly toward "needs" as a verb construed as those conditions instrumental to the attainment of one's full development as a person. And at the upper end of

[29] The next two paragraphs are a somewhat revised version of my critique of a paper given by Christian Bay at the *Ripon Conference on Rights and Political Action,* Ripon College, October 8–10, 1970. The critique, along with the rest of the conference proceedings, is published in *Inquiry* (1971), pp. 237–243.

the hierarchy, the connection between what one needs to become a person and any set of behavioral inclinations becomes increasingly tenuous. Indeed need theorists display a tendency to tolerate those tensions and anxieties that might accompany attainment of the highest postulated states.

To avoid this tendency toward equivocation—a tendency supported by ordinary usage—it is advisable to treat "need" as a verb in our theoretical work. This form calls attention to the fact that need statements are always triadic: "Person *A* needs *x in order to* (do, be, or become) *y*." And *y* in this triad is always the crucial variable. One might need something in order to survive, to survive comfortably, to develop the capacity to act responsibly, to polish his shoes, or to eliminate all sexual urges. Thus when we translate need statements into this form, we can see that to say "*A* needs *x*" is not necessarily to say either that *A* is inclined towards *x* or that it is a worthy object for him to pursue. Such judgments must await consideration of what *x* is needed for.

My charge, then, is this: The conceptual connection between needs and interests seems plausible only when the equivocal use of "need" in need theories goes unnoted. But when need is defined consistently in terms of behavioral inclinations, we can both imagine inclinations that it might not be in our interests to promote and identify possible interests not manifested by our most inchoate behavioral tendencies. Any view that anchors interest exclusively in felt behavioral tendencies runs the risk of celebrating uncritically those inclinations cultivated by prevailing socialization processes while deflecting conceptual attention from possible gratifying modes of existence bypassed by those same processes. If the intellectual enterprise aims to recover worthy aspirations that have been lost, to render intelligible modes of life that are now only dimly glimpsed, then a definition of interest *restricted* to felt behavioral tendencies can hardly suffice.

REAL INTERESTS

Need theories are informed by the right questions; it is only the answer that is inadequate. Can we, though, articulate a notion of interests that will speak more effectively to these issues? I think we can. But first I must mention a feature of definitional statements too often ignored by analysts of political concepts. As Friedrich Waismann has shown, no concept is ever completely defined; every concept is incorrigibly "open textured." In our definitional statements we limit a concept in particular directions, but there are "always other directions in which a concept has not been defined." [30] The definitional statement I will make, then, is only a first approximation. The accompanying text will help to make the import of the initial definitional gloss clear, but will not "limit the concept" in all important directions. That gloss will be useful

[30] Friedrich Waismann, "Verifiability," p. 126.

if it provides a basis from which further clarifications and adjustments can be made when new circumstances are confronted. To say that is not an apology for my definitional effort, but merely pointing to a little-noted dimension of all such efforts. As a first approximation, then, consider the following: "Policy *x* is more in *A*'s interest than policy *y* if *A*, were he to experience the *results* of both *x* and *y*, would choose *x* as the result he would rather have for himself." [31]

Several clarifying comments are in order.

First, the definition focusses on the results of policy rather than on attitudes toward the policy itself, bypassing problems posed in the first definition considered. Furthermore, following Barry's lead here too, it treats interest as a comparative concept because for "any given proposal there is nearly always one that compared to it is in someone's interest and at least one that compared to it is contrary to someone's interest." [32] Defining the concept in this way encourages people to state explicitly the terms of comparison implicitly adopted when they tell us something is or is not in our interests.

Second, the key criterion is the choice of the agent involved, but the privileged choice is one made after the fact, so to speak, rather than before it. This does require investigators to make difficult judgments, in many situations, about the choices a person would make if he had had the relevant experiences, but such a reference to counterfactual conditions is required by most concepts employed in contemporary political inquiry (such as power). And the definition does enable us, I think, to *say* all of the things about interests we find people in ordinary discourse saying, thereby retaining for political inquiry not only the function that "interests" plays in normative discourse but the full range of activities it covers in performing that function.[33] It allows one to

[31] Since I am especially indebted to S. I. Benn's views about how one should construe interests in political inquiry ("Interests in Politics," *Proceedings of Aristotelian Society* [1960], 123–140), I should specify the point at which I disagree. I agree that "to say something is in a man's interest is not to say that he will be glad of it immediately; but it does seem to imply that one would expect him to be glad of it at some time" (p. 130). But, Benn then suggests, there "may be a sense in which something is in a person's interest even if he doesn't want it, would not want it if he rightly understood the position, or even that, want it or not, he would be pleased if he got it" (p. 130). It would be in his interests, Benn thinks, *relative to a* valid norm of conduct, even if that norm is one the agent could never prize for itself. But if he himself did not, once he understood and "lived up to" the norm, come to be pleased with it for itself, then I don't see how we can appropriately say that policies that help him to see and achieve it are in his interests—even though it might be *right* for him to support such policies.

[32] Barry, "The Use and Abuse of the Public Interest," in *The Public Interest,* ed. Carl Friedrich (New York: Atherton Press, 1966), p. 198.

[33] I do not accept ordinary language as the final court of appeal here, especially since an atomistic view of human nature continues to infect talk about interests. But I do think any definition should at least cover the paradigm cases of "interest" sanctioned by ordinary discourse (remembering that "ordinary discourse" means not the definitions people give out but the rules they actually follow), and then give reasons for any proposed extensions or modifications. To the extent I modify usage, my reason is simply that the

say that something *might* be in another's interests, even though the other does not now (or might never, if prevailing social conditions persist) want it. It allows, further, for the possibility of having an interest in some result that I presently have strong inclinations against. And, as I shall argue next, it allows persons to have interests as social beings as well as interests whose results do not essentially involve reciprocal states of awareness.

Third, clarification of the phrase "the result he would rather have" is required to understand what *kind* of choices made after the fact are relevant to ascriptions of interest. If the phrase is interpreted too loosely, we risk merging "interest-regarding" choices with those that reflect a sense of obligation, selfless benevolence and, perhaps, fear of reprisal. Interpreted too narrowly, it would rule out the kinds of considerations people tacitly have in mind when they counsel us about our "real interests" or our "best interests" as social beings. Thus Erik Erikson clearly thinks that social arrangements and policies that help to nourish relationships of "mutuality" (that is, the sort of relationship that "strengthens the doer as it strengthens the other") are in the real interests of the parties involved, even if neither party fully recognizes that fact. For in a relationship of mutuality between parent and child, "a parent dealing with a child will be strengthened in *his* vitality, in *his* sense of identity, and in *his* readiness for ethical action by the very ministrations by means of which he secures to the child vitality, future identity, and eventual readiness for ethical action." [34]

As I see it, then, the distinction between interest-regarding choices and other kinds of choices social beings might make can be formulated, if roughly, along the following lines: An agent's choice is interest-regarding when or to the extent that (for many choices will reflect several kinds of considerations) it takes into account the quality of the result for the agent himself and includes a reference to others insofar as his relationships to them are of the sort he would choose as gratifying and fulfilling in themselves. Much more could probably be said about the demarcation line I seek to sustain here. For example, I would hope to argue that it is in my interests to develop the *capacity* to act as a morally responsible agent, even though the very perfection of that capacity could, on particular occasions, enjoin me to act against my interests. Even with further clarification, though, boundary problems will persist between those actions that are in my interests in one role or another and those that are indifferent or contrary to them. This, however, is not a problem peculiar to the definition I propose; those definitions couched in terms of pref-

atomistic conception of human nature (partially) reflected in contemporary usage is faulty; when those faults are recognized, we can also see that relationships we prize as social beings have much in common with other conditions and objectives we cover with the language of interests.

[34] Erik Erikson, *Insight and Responsibility* (New York: W. W. Norton and Co., 1964), p. 233.

erences and private wants face, at different junctures, their own boundary problems, as in sorting among "privately oriented," "publicly oriented," and "ideal-regarding" wants.[35]

Fourth, what if a person, after experiencing the results of a policy which legalizes heroin, chooses that as the result he would rather have? Does this apparent counter-example, and others like it, undermine the proposed definition? I think not. It impels us, rather, to clarify the meaning of "choice" further. For if the person regrets those previous actions which now make him an addict, if he wishes he could choose to give up the habit but knows he cannot, or even if we are convinced he would now choose otherwise were he fully capable of choosing freely, then we can properly say that his present capacity to choose freely has been impaired. The appropriate question in this context is not "What does he now want?" but "What would he choose if, knowing what he now knows, he could freely make that choice again?" [36] Situations like this raise difficult questions of judgment which we must approach with some humility, but it is also certain that occasions do arise when we cannot avoid making judgments of this sort, occasions when the question becomes not if, but how and on what grounds. We are focussing here on the grounds.

Indeed, I am inclined to urge here that any current choice the implications of which deeply impairs one's capacity to make future choices—such as the agreement to accept enslavement—always weighs heavily against one's interests. For one of the things we include as part of being a person is the capacity to make choices based upon reasoned deliberation *and* to reconsider those deliberations and those choices on future occasions. We are speaking here, after all, of the interests *persons* have; and reflection about interest regarding choices is part of the process of deliberation about what it means to be a person. To illuminate one of these areas is to shed some light on the other.

[35] See Barry, *Political Argument,* pp. 35–41 and 295–299. For formulations that move in the direction I seek to sustain, see William Alston, "Pleasure," *Encyclopedia of Philosophy,* Vol. 6 (1967), pp. 341–347, and Alasdair MacIntyre, "Egoism and Altruism," *Encyclopedia of Philosophy,* Vol. I (New York: Macmillan Co., 1967), pp. 462–466.

[36] I realize, of course, that the charge of "elitism" will be hurled here. But the charge moves too far too fast. First, all of the definitions adopted finally end up, as I have noted, acknowledging that people might be mistaken about their interests on occasion. And on most usages most people would agree that certain actions that go against the inclinations of individuals are nevertheless in their interests—as in the case of some policies toward children and idiots. One only needs one example to raise the question I pose here *of the grounds for making such judgments.* Second, for me to say that you are mistaken about your interests is not necessarily to imply that I will jam my view down your throat. Only authoritarian types leap to that implication. I might simply try to persuade you or to bribe you. Indeed, persuasion is usually the most justifiable approach to take for one who celebrates cultivating the capacity for choice. Third, there are some occasions in politics when we simply cannot avoid taking positions on issues that affect the interests of others. Here we simply must exercise our best judgment, remembering human fallibility, and privileging to some extent the views of those affected by that judgment.

APPRAISALS OF REAL INTERESTS

Finally, we must confront, if briefly, the question of testability. There are some easy cases where the choice criterion can be applied in ways which would settle the issue for most investigators. Thus the worker who changes his preference scale as between more income and a more creative work life after having experienced benefits produced by the latter can be said to provide solid evidence in support of the view that the policies promoting a more creative work life were more fully in his interest after all. Even here the contextual setting within which the "test" is made would have to be understood thoroughly by the investigator. Perhaps the worker would choose the second option if he could, but he is now so deeply in debt that he must opt for the first. A test, then, which overlooked this factor, and hundreds like it, would run the risk of mistaking a choice reflecting contingent, immediate constraints for one representing the more basic and stable interests of the agent. Or perhaps the worker "chooses" the second option after experiencing both, but his choice reflects in part the tacit pressure of the group to which he is attached. Even in this apparently simple situation, then, appraisals of interest require the careful assessment of the social context within which the appraisal is made. And this is true of all the notions of interest considered.

Surely with regard to the broadest and fundamental questions about the higher order interests of persons and classes of persons, the conclusions we reach will rest necessarily on an assessment of indirect evidence and will have a more or less precarious status.

The kinds of indirect evidence we can draw upon are varied. Consider, for example, the claim that it is in our interests as citizens to have a legal system that provides punishment for crimes committed by responsible agents, and against our interests to treat every criminal as a victim of circumstances who needs therapy. Assume also that the therapy and punishment models of coping with criminals are equally effective as deterrents, so the issue will have to be settled on other grounds. A line of inquiry pursued by J. D. Mabbot, P. F. Strawson and Herbert Morris into the tacit commitments built into our use of such terms as responsibility, guilt, love, and resentment suggests that the application of these concepts to people treats them, under appropriate conditions, as persons having a capacity to form intentions, deliberate, enter into relations of trust, and so on.[37] If we were to expunge these concepts from our language (provided that were possible), we would indeed strip ourselves of the ability to view each other as members of a moral community; we

[37] J. D. Mabbot, "Punishment," in *Justice and Social Policy,* ed. F. A. Olafson (Englewood Cliffs, N.J.: Prentice-Hall, 1961), pp. 39–54; Herbert Morris, "Persons and Punishment," in *Justice and Social Policy,* ed. Olafson; and P. F. Strawson, "Freedom and Resentment," in *Studies in the Philosophy of Thought and Action,* ed. Strawson (New York: Oxford University Press, 1968), pp. 71–96.

would impoverish our lives by restricting the variety of shared experiences within our reach. Since the "preparedness to acquiesce in that infliction of suffering on the offender which is an essential part of punishment is all of a piece with this whole range of attitudes," our operating commitment to treat each other as persons tends to support the institution of punishment.[38] And once we peer into these conceptual connections carefully, we are both more likely to choose a *system* (not necessarily individual acts) of punishment as in our interests as social beings and likely to choose "respect for persons" as a standard relevant to appraisals of their interests. I am not trying to argue for this particular conclusion here, though I find arguments in support of it persuasive. The point is that conceptual clarification can inform the choices we make about interests by helping us to see more profoundly what turns on each alternative.[39]

A second line of inquiry involves one's vicarious and actual immersion in alternative modes of social life, in variable "life styles." A participant study of kibbutzim, various tribal forms, feudal communities, and alternative styles in industrial society provides the materials from which comparative judgments can be made about possible interests not actively sustained by prevailing social arrangements.

These lines of inquiry surely help to bring suppressed presuppositions to the point of more conscious deliberation and choice. But to what extent does such a choice, once made, suffice to determine that the object of choice is really in the agent's interest? The problem is not only that investigators must ask what the result would be if a particular practice or institution were introduced into an alien setting; nor is it merely that the persons who undertake these lines of inquiry are likely to have a deep investment in protecting a certain interpretation.

The near paradox is this: The very process of preparing oneself to make the most reflective choice about his interests affects the evidential status of the choice he makes. Consider the judgment of the girl radicalized by her experiences in the anti-war movement of the middle sixties. It was not only her obligation to join the movement, she now believes, but her involvement generated results which were, in a profound sense, in her own interests.

> Now that I look back on that job, if I had known what I was accepting, I probably would not have done it, because of the insecurities and what seemed so many threatening things . . . (Kenneth Keniston: Was it a rough time then?) No, it was great. I was totally absorbed in the work. (K.K.: You mean that now you would do it again, but at the time,

[38] Strawson, "Freedom and Resentment," p. 93.

[39] The ways in which conceptual clarification can inform choices of the sort discussed here are explored with some care by Richard Flathman, "From Therapy to Theorizing: Conceptual Analysis and Political Philosophy," paper delivered to annual meeting of the American Political Science Association, Los Angeles, California, September 8–12, 1970.

if you had known, you wouldn't have done it?) Yes, that is what I am saying. I think that one of the valuable things was that I was open. I was looking . . .[40]

In one sense this judgment, made *after* having experienced two styles of life, is impressive evidence in favor of the latter alternative. But, in another sense, the fact that a different person is making the choice affects its status as evidence. For her recent experience is mediated through new orientations, expectations, and investments that themselves are supposed to be part of the conditions to be appraised. Even under ideal conditions of choice, then, elements of conjecture and speculation will enter into our assessment of the extent to which alternative modes of social life are more or less in our interests.[41] This incorrigible feature of efforts to appraise "higher level" interests should be reflected in the way we hold and defend views about these matters and in the kind of action we are willing to sanction in support of those who understand their own interests differently than we do.

CONCLUSION

Clarity about what "interest" means does not ensure that disputes about what is in our interests can be neatly resolved. But it does help to sharpen the issues implicated in these disputes and to point towards kinds of evidence most fruitfully pertinent to the core issues. That is the best, I think, we can expect. To promise more, to offer to "translate" these issues into a series of neat hypotheses amenable to precise and impersonal test, is inevitably to corrupt the enterprise undertaken. The outcome, as suggested by past performance, would join surface precision to profound obscurity.

[40] Quoted by Kenneth Keniston, *Young Radicals: Notes on Committed Youth* (New York: Harcourt, Brace and World, Inc., 1968), p. 121.

[41] To focus the problem more sharply, consider the case of a rather contented person who is convicted of a crime, and several years later, comes to prefer the security and routine of prison life to freedom in the larger society. Many of us would want to ask if that choice could be explained away as the result of the prison's constricting influence on the convict's perception and understanding. Stephen Lukes explores problems inherent in making such judgments in the context of deciding between a Marxist and Durkheimian view of human development. "Alienation and Anomie," in this volume. The comparison is particularly pertinent, since I suspect that Marx and Durkheim tacitly share the *notion* of interest I have elucidated, but diverge significantly as to what is most in our interests as social beings.

15

Interpretations of Class Structure in Historical Perspective

Stanislaw Ossowski

TYPES OF INTERPRETATION OF THE SOCIAL STRUCTURE—AN ATTEMPT AT CLASSIFICATION

Ordering Relations and Relations of Dependence in Class Systems

The relations of which we can make use when we speak of a class system are, as we have seen, of a two-fold nature: ordering relations and relations of dependence. This distinction emerged in the opening chapter, when I was discussing the concept of structure in its most general meaning.

Two basic interpretations of social class correspond to these two kinds of relations. We have to do with the first interpretation when the class division is conceived of as a division into groups differentiated according to the degree in which they possess the characteristic which constitutes the criterion of division, as, for instance, income level. Since these groups are arranged in a system of superior and inferior classes according to the degree in which they display the particular characteristic, class structure carries or has the same meaning here as class stratification. As T. H. Marshall pointed out in his study of class conflict: "We are discussing a particular kind of group whose nature is indicated by the phrase 'social stratification.' The groups, that is to say, lie one above the other in layers." [1]

In the second interpretation social classes form a system according to their

Source: Stanislaw Ossowski, *Class Structure in the Social Consciousness,* trans. Sheila Patterson (New York: The Free Press, 1963). Reprinted by permission of the Macmillan Company and Routledge and Kegan Paul Limited.

[1] "The Nature of Class Conflict" in *Class Conflict and Social Stratification,* ed. T. H. Marshall (London: Le Play House, 1938).

one-sided or mutual dependence, dependence being understood in both cases as a dependence based on causal relationships. . . .

Early in the first chapter I drew the reader's attention to the wider connections between the two kinds of relations. Later, these questions reemerged during my analysis of the Marxian conception, in connection with the coincidence between class functions and degree of wealth. Although the categories of capitalist, petit bourgeois and proletarian are differentiated on the basis of their differing relations to the means of production, they can at the same time be ranked on a general scale according to income level. Statistically, there is a correlation between income and the type of relation to the means of production. This correlation is brought out in the Marxian theory of classes in a manner beyond any doubt.

The relation of superiority and inferiority between classes differentiated according to functional criteria can of course be based on something other than the degree of wealth. One instance of this is found in the Hindu caste gradations; another might be in the supremacy of the "working class" amongst the "nonantagonistic classes" of the Soviet conception, where classes are distinguished according to the type of ownership of the means of production and the source of income.[2]

In all such cases we can regard the system of dependence and the system of gradation not only as two different aspects of the same reality but as two different aspects of the same division of the same reality.

Two Interpretations of Mutual Dependence

In describing the second way of understanding class systems, I spoke of relations of one-sided or mutual dependence. An asymmetric relation of dependence in social relationships is usually conceived as a relation of subjection to another's power. In conceptions of class structure mutual dependence may have two meanings. The first is that of an "organic" dependence. Groups are mutually necessary to one another since each performs different functions. The second meaning refers to a negative correlation of interests—the advances of one class are the setbacks of the other.

We encountered the first meaning in the class system of Adam Smith, in the views of the physiocrats which were criticized by Mably, and in Spencer's conception of the social organism. One may also recall at this point the medieval interpretation of society as consisting of three estates which are essential to one another: those who pray, those who defend the country and those who work. We have come across the second meaning in all cases where the conception of class involves class antagonism: e.g., in Madison, Babeuf, Marx and his disciples, and also in some contemporary writers who

[2] T. Gubariev, "O priodolenii klassovykh razlichii v SSSR" (About the overcoming of class differences in the U.S.S.R.), *Bolshevik,* 1951, No. 5.

are far removed from Marxism, like Sorokin. The view of classes as essentially antagonistic groups is also found in Touraine's report of 1953.[3]

Criteria of Internal Cohesion

The distinction between two basic types of understanding class systems is not dependent on the type of criterion taken as determining class affiliations, such as class consciousness or purely "objective" criteria. Nor does it depend on whether cultural criteria or the criterion of social intercourse between classes are applied in determining class boundaries.

We noted that some sociologists use the criterion of social intercourse between classes in their definitions of social class. For Davis and Dollard a social class is the largest group of people between whom intimate social contact can exist, whereas relations between the classes are characterized by an absence of "intimate participation" between members of different classes. For Schumpter the boundaries of a social class are coextensive with the range within which socially permissible marriages may be contracted. These writers regard classes as groupings whose members are linked to one another by virtue of an internal social bond, and inter-class relations as relations characterized by strangeness, social distance or antagonism.

If we accept the assumption that classes are groups which constitute a system of groups in a social structure, we must remember that "social bond," "esprit de corps," "social intercourse," "absence of intimate participation" are insufficient criteria to permit one to recognize a class system in the groups thus differentiated. A system—understood as an arrangement in which each component has its position fixed by its relations to other components—can be constructed only by means of ordering relations or relations of dependence.

On the other hand, esprit de corps, social consciousness, social intercourse, and "class" culture are characteristics whose coincidence with class boundaries in a system established in another manner is very important in the "class" character of a society. I discussed this [earlier], where I considered in what respects the "class" character of a society might admit of gradation. Amongst other concepts this involved the Marxian distinction between a "class in itself," and a "class for itself."

In systems based on ordering relations, that is to say systems of gradations of social classes, the characteristics that determine the internal cohesion of social groups are usually treated as a criterion in determining inter-class boundaries: for instance, between the lower, middle and upper classes or between the lower, middle, upper-middle and upper classes. . . . As we noted, all the American sociologists who consider classes in American society as something more than statistical categories have referred to the phenomenon of

[3] Alain Touraine, Rapport sur la préparation en France de l'enquête internationale sur la stratification et la mobilité sociale (Association Internationale de Sociologie, Congrès de Liège, 1953). Cf. pp. 53–54.

social consciousness and have often treated the range of social contacts or cultural differences as a verifying test of whether the division into classes in a system of gradation is not merely a conventional division, or whether it has a genuine foundation in social reality.

Class Attributes and Types of Dependence in the Dichotomic and the Functional Schemes

. . . Earlier . . . we considered three basic schemes of class structure and also the conception of a classless, nonegalitarian society. Two of these schemes, the dichotomic and the functional, present the social structure as a system of dependence; the third as a system of gradation. In schemes based on relations of dependence the various terms in the system are characterized by different attributes; in a scheme of gradation they are characterized by a differing degree of the same characteristic.[4]

We distinguish the dichotomic scheme not because it consists of two components but because we describe the components of this system in terms of opposite attributes: working class and non-working class; exploiters and exploited; rulers and ruled; propertied and nonpropertied classes. This means that classes in a dichotomic scheme are terms of an asymmetric relation, this relation being described as a one-sided dependence, involving authority or an overwhelming influence over the destinies of others. The slave lives under the rule of his master and the peasant under the rule of his landlord, while at a time of unemployment the worker is at the mercy of the capitalist. This does not however exclude a mutual functional dependence between the components involved in this asymmetric relation.

This sort of mutual dependence is brought about above all by antagonism: conflict of interests is of course a symmetrical relation.[5] But mutual dependence between classes with opposite attributes is sometimes regarded in a different way: as a dependence based on cooperation and the division of functions. It may be recalled that both in Aristotle and in Theodoret we encountered the view that the servants need the masters as much as the masters need the servants. In arguments of this kind, we have to do with an attempt to assimilate the dichotomy of opposed classes to the scheme of mutual dependence, which we have called a functional scheme and which usually has three or more components.

The belief that the dependence of the exploited on the exploiters is a one-sided one has also been undermined in a different way and with a different purpose: that is to say, in the interest not of the ruling class but of the oppressed class. In his parable about the two cities, St. John Chrysostom strove

[4] Cf. Llewellyn Gross. "An *attribute* refers to a quality which has an all-or-none existence. A *variable* refers to a quality which exists in varying degrees." ("The Use of the Class Concept in Social Research," *A.J.S.*, March 1949.)

[5] The co-presence of a one-sided and a mutual dependence between the worker and the industrialists is brought out by, inter alia, Adam Smith.

to persuade his readers that the fortunes of the rich depend on the working class to a far greater extent than the fortunes of those who work depend on the rich. Shelley also stressed the same dependence in a more poetic vein, and it is on this assumption that contemporary advocates of the general strike base their arguments. But the symmetrical relations which we come across in functional schemes are not involved in these cases. Nobody doubts that where there is a stable social order the dependence of the manufacturer on the worker is only a potential one. Those who, like Shelley, try to make the worker conscious of this potential dependence do so with the object of arousing him to liberate himself from the existing one-sided dependence, which runs in quite the opposite direction.

The terms in which the dichotomic scheme is usually formulated (rulers and ruled, exploiters and exploited, and so on) presume a one-sided dependence. Thus we regard the name "dichotomic scheme" as an abbreviation of the expression "dichotomic scheme of one-sided dependence" or "dichotomic scheme with opposite attributes."

Class attributes in a multiple functional scheme suggest mutual dependence, and are particularly suitable for emphasizing dependence based on collaboration and the division of functions. Those who live by rent, those who live by profit and those who live by wages in Adam Smith's scheme are mutually essential to one another.

But this division into three classes in terms of functions in the process of production is simultaneously a division in terms of the source of income (rents, profits, wages), while differences in the source of income combined with reciprocal dependencies lead to conflict of interests. Thus we find mutual dependence in both its aspects in Adam Smith's functional scheme. The second aspect—dependence through antagonism—emerges still more strongly in Madison. With Pareto too a negative correlation of interests applies not only between workers and capitalists but also between the two classes of capitalists which he distinguishes as *rentiers* and *entrepreneurs*, who cooperate with each other.[6]

Thus the two aspects of mutual dependence can be involved in conceptions both of dichotomic and multiple class systems conceived of as a system of dependence, although a dichotomic scheme with opposite attributes is particularly suitable for emphasizing dependence based on cooperation.

Two Interpretations of Dichotomy in the Marxian Scheme

In considering the classic Marxian scheme . . . , I treated it as the result of the intersection of three dichotomies. In view, however, of the prospects of social development outlined by Marx, one should perhaps see in his conception of class structure rather one single dichotomy based on three criteria of

[6] "En réalité, ces deux catégories des 'capitalistes' ont des intérêts souvent différents parfois opposés. Ils s'opposent même plus que ceux des classes dites des 'capitalistes' et des 'proletaires.' " (*Traité de sociologie générale,* Paris, 1919, p. 1427.)

division. In this interpretation the two basic classes are opposed to each other in respect of three pairs of opposite attributes. The class of people who possess the means of production, employ hired labor and do not work themselves[7] is contrasted with the class of those who do not possess the means of production, do not employ hired labor, but themselves work as hired labor.

This ideal type of dichotomic structure of a capitalist society has never had any real existence in the world about which Marx and his followers have written because the attributes have never been fully satisfied. The correspondence of these attributes with reality increases with increasing economic polarization of the society and decreases when the number of moderately prosperous individuals grows larger. But between the two classes which fulfil all three conditions of the ideal dichotomy there is the group of those who fail to fulfil one or two of the conditions for inclusion in one of the two classes. . . .

SEMANTIC CONVENTIONS CONSIDERED AS SOCIAL FACTS

Definitions and Propositions[8]

My analysis of the various ways of interpreting social structure . . . makes it clear that different concepts of social class correspond to different schemes of class system. The differences of opinion were concerned with the type of relations which should determine a class system. In treating these differences of opinion as differences in the meaning of the term "class," we assume that the definition of a social class takes into account not only this class's inclusion in a system of basic groups, but also the type of relations on which this inclusion is to depend: that is to say, that the definition of social class in its more general sense should indicate whether the classes are components of a system of gradation, whether they are antagonistic groups, or, finally, whether they are groups differentiated in respect of their functions in the process of production. . . .

Terminological differences occur when we are employing the same concepts but refer to them by means of different and translatable terms. For instance, Adam Smith called his three basic groups in the social structure "orders," while Marx, when he accepted Adam Smith's division in the third volume of *Das Kapital,* called the same groups the three basic "classes." Here we are dealing with a difference of terminology only. I would also include in the category of terminological differences the sort of case in which the same term designates different concepts, so long as the conceptual contents are sufficiently distinct for the term by which they are referred to in common not to constitute any link between them. In such cases we realize that the common term is not due to the intersection of the extension of the respective concepts,

[7] We should remember that in this context work does not include executive activities.

[8] The term "proposition" as used in this study means "declarative sentence formulated in some particular language." I shall be using "proposition" and "statement" as synonymous terms.

but has its origin in chance. Such an example is the differing use of the identical term "social stratum" by Marxist writers and Centers.

A second and far more important category of the differences we are considering is to be found in situations where the same term refers to different concepts with similar but not identical extensions. Here the use of the same term is accounted for by the fact that the most representative designata of the one and the other concept are common to both.

The majority of social anthropologists and students of the psychology of religion define religion, in line with everyday notions, as a set of rituals and beliefs concerning relations to supernatural beings. For Durkheim and his school, however, religion is a set of practices and beliefs, which are obligatory in a given community under the sanction of universal condemnation. Here the extensions of the two concepts designated by the same term "religion" are not identical. Durkheim's concept would embrace "atheistic religion" as well as others, while from the other viewpoint "atheistic religion" is a *contradictio in adjecto*. On the other hand the Durkheimian definition would not apply to individual religious beliefs, because in this case religion always requires a church, an assembly of the faithful. Thus the extensions of the two concepts designated by the term "religion" do not coincide; nevertheless all religions par excellence (par excellence from one and from the other viewpoint) fall within the two extensions.

Moreover, it was these most typical kinds of religion that provided the material whose analysis produced both these definitions. The reason why Durkheim included "atheistic religions" in the extension of his concept and excluded uninstitutionalized religions from it was because, in his analysis of these religions par excellence, he recognized the significance of other factors than did Leuba or Malinowski; this inclined him to correct the traditional boundaries of the designata accordingly. The particular characteristics of the typical religions which the Durkheimian school considered as most socially significant made it necessary for them to include in the same category certain systems of practices and beliefs which are not connected with the worship of any divine being. Freud, on the other hand, regarded personal relations and the transference of relations characteristic of the family as the most important element in religious beliefs, and he would not have regarded such an extension of the concept of religion as appropriate. Thus by extending or narrowing down the scope of the phenomena falling under a common category we change the manner in which they are perceived.

The Background of Conceptual Differences

Durkheim's concept of religion—to return to this example—is undoubtedly an expression of the French sociologists' interest in the problems of the social bond. On the other hand, a psychologist—who is interested in the influence of belief in a supernatural world on the psychological attitudes of the individual—or a student of the history of religious myths and their role in artistic creativeness would conceive of the phenomena under investigation in terms of different conceptual categories. Here we should also be dealing with different views about the origin of religions, and thus with different views about reality, and finally with different social tendencies. Durkheim's concept of religion can also be associated with the efforts to strengthen the social bond in the atomized France of his day, and with the endeavor to oppose simultaneously the extreme individualism of that period and the claims of the Catholic Church, which itself wished to provide the social cement for the French nation. In all this Durkheim's concept of religion afforded the prospect of finding a "secular" bond which could fulfil "religious functions."

During this study we have frequently encountered the striking fact that different concepts of social class reveal different theories of social life, distinct ideologies and differing codes of conduct. But when we came across different concepts of class in the work of one writer, we attributed this either to the variety of the problems involved or to the way in which practical problems change in different circumstances. For instance, when, in considering the Stalinist concept of the "nonantagonistic class" we maintained that the term "social class" as used in the Soviet Union had changed its meaning in relation to Lenin's definition, we were interested not so much in the terminology and conceptual apparatus applied by Soviet writers as in the images of the country's social structure and the ideological standpoint that was reflected in these conceptual changes.

The relationship between the choice of conceptual apparatus and the choice of problems is perfectly clear and in general arouses no doubts. Less obvious, however, is the relationship between the choice of concepts and statements about reality. The conceptual apparatus to a certain extent predetermines the scope of the problems. On the other hand, one or another way of framing concepts does not predetermine the statements which can be formulated by means of these concepts; the same concepts could be employed for contradictory propositions. In this respect the conventionalists are correct in saying that concepts are neutral with respect to incompatible statements.

But a deliberate formation of concepts or a deliberate acceptance of some and rejection of others is a purposeful activity—we can ask about its aims. To fix the boundaries of the application of concepts in a particular way can be the result of a passive submission to tradition, but it can also be the result of choice. Disputes over the boundaries of concepts are—provided one does not assume a prelogical standpoint—disputes about the relative importance of particular boundaries. This is the case with differences of opinion concerned with the extension of the concepts of social class or religion. Methodological controversies concerned with the extension of concepts of history since Dilthey's time can serve as another example.

If both opposing parties are concerned with the same sort of importance, a difference in their viewpoints may be the result of a disagreement of opinion about certain causal relationships. For example, they may disagree as to which is the more important factor in the social bond: to take a rural population in an as yet unurbanized environment, is it the way of life and cultural traditions or the uniform relation to the means of production? The first instance would involve recognizing the existence of a peasant class; in the second, the collectivity of peasants would be divided up by class boundaries determined according to different criteria. But if—as is usually the case—one of the disputants has in mind a different kind of importance from the other, the differences of viewpoints originate in differing value-scales and practical directives; this does not of course exclude the possibility of a disagreement of opinions as to causal relationships as well.

The Motives of Disputes over Terms

. . . Everyone realizes how important the selection of words is for political speeches or writing. Particular words have a particular sphere of associations and some have acquired a formidable emotional charge, whether positive or negative. In view of practical requirements and consequences it is not a matter of indifference to which designata these emotional values and associations are attributed. The emotional value of words was discussed by Charles Stevenson in connection with his concept of "persuasive definitions." [9] He distinguished between the "descriptive meaning" and the "emotive meaning" of words.[10] I should however prefer to use the term "meaning" in a narrower sense and to distinguish between the "meaning" of words and their "emotional charge," or the emotional quality connected with the expressive function of words.

The use of the term "religion" in Durkheim's sense has been strongly opposed by both the Catholics and the Marxists—but for different reasons. For the Catholics, as for other religious groups, the word "religion" is a term of respect referring to the supreme values, and they do not wish to share it with atheistic groups. Nor do they wish to admit that in the concept of religion emphasis should be put on pressure by the church and the intolerance of believers. For the Marxists, on the other hand, the term "religion" has a negative quality. The Durkheimian use of the term would allow Marxism to be included in the concept of a religion, which in the Marxist milieu is conceived of as an opiate for the masses. Clearly Marxists would not wish to be associated in any way with such a concept, nor to be classified in the same category as the religious churches, which they regard as instruments of the exploiting classes and survivals from the dark past of superstition. The idea of performing a "religious function" would be much easier for Marxists to accept if it were differently named.

An emotional charge of another kind is connected with the word "class."

[9] Charles L. Stevenson: *Ethics and Language* (New Haven: Yale University Press, 1953), Chapter IX.

[10] Ibid., Chs. III and IV.

In the conventional sense it would be possible to substitute the term "stratum" for the term "class." But as a signal for conditioned reflexes the term "stratal enemy" would hardly take the place of "class enemy." The social functions of the term "nation" have also made the Communist Party anxious to confer this name on the Negroes in the United States, although this attribution does not accord with the Stalinist definition of a nation as generally accepted by the Communist Party. . . .

The choice of a particular term, even when it is made with full awareness that this is a matter of convention, may be the expression of certain views about reality, while a terminological difference may reflect incompatible statements. Certain words which have been associated in a special way with important matters have acquired a significance which other words lack. The concept to which such a word refers achieves a higher position in the hierarchy of conceptual importance ("importance" is not here understood in terms of the level of abstraction of concepts). And it is for this reason that when controversies arise about the boundaries of application of the concepts which are to be designated by such terms as "religion," "art," "scientific law" and "social class," it is impossible to separate terminological differences from conceptual ones.

In a controversy about the denotation of the term "religion" involving the designation of two different concepts by the same name, there is from a theoretical standpoint nothing to stop the opponents from reaching an agreement on terminology, whereby this term will be reserved for one of the two competing concepts and the other concept will be referred to by another arbitrarily chosen term. But the term which has already acquired significance will enhance the importance of the scope of application of the concept which is to be designated by this term. And this—apart from propaganda considerations—can exert some influence on the construction and interpretation of a theory even after the various terminological misunderstandings have been clarified. The belief that a particular logical distinction is an essential distinction is responsible for the fact that the terms which are applied to it assume particular importance for us. But the association between the importance of the distinction and the importance of the term works in the opposite direction as well. The belief that we are dealing with an important term usually suggests that the distinction which corresponds to this term is a fundamental distinction, and that the characteristics of the phenomena and the causal relationships thus distinguished in this way are especially significant. In accordance with this assumption, the adoption of such terms as "religion" or "art" in a particular manner constitutes an expression of a particular view about cultural phenomena. One such view might be that which holds that problems concerned with the pressure of any socially sanctioned dogmas of any kind are more important than problems concerned with differences in the social functions of theism and atheism; and that the first set of problems therefore deserve precedence in certain areas of theory construction.[11]

For the purpose of theory construction as well as for propaganda considerations, it is not immaterial whether we agree on a convention to refer to the different *strata* of the peasant *class,* or to speak of the different *classes* of the peasant *stratum.* Long-established associations have given the term "class" a different value for us in theory construction than the term "stratum," and have caused the boundaries between classes to be drawn with a heavier line than the boundaries of strata. This function of certain terms is not exclusively confined to the domain of the humanities and social sciences, and it would be possible to find analogies in the terminology of the natural sciences. . . .

As we have seen, it is possible to apply the majority, if not all, of the schemes we have been considering to almost every class society. Different conceptual categories correspond to different problems. By conceiving a social structure in terms of a particular scheme, we confer a particular aspect on the social structure. Depending on the kind of problem in which one is interested, one can interpret the same society in terms of a dichotomic scheme, of a scheme of gradation, or of a functional scheme; or, alternately, one can apply the same scheme to it in a different manner, for example by introducing different criteria of gradation or of functional divisions.

But particular schemes which are applied, to some extent arbitrarily, to a a specific reality correspond to certain ideal types. Thus when we compare different societies we can indicate objective criteria in respect of which we perceive a greater or lesser distance between particular social structures and a particular ideal type, and thereby assert that a certain scheme is more suited to the one society than another. For instance, there need be no doubt that a dichotomic scheme is more suitable for describing prewar Rumanian society than that of Norway, or for describing Tsarist Russia than the Western capitalist societies of our own times.[12] An interpretation of an estate society as a social-status continuum would seem infinitely more paradoxical than such an interpretation of contemporary British society. . . .

The Ideological Superstructure of Class Structures

In this study I have often noted the striking persistence of the fundamental ways of interpreting the social structure and of certain views of the existing system of human relations. We have come across the same views of class structure in folklore, in religious myths, in the philosophic works of the ancient world, in the writings of the Fathers of the Church, in the trends of

[11] The reference in this passage is to Durkheim's theory of religion.

[12] Cf. Togliatti's statement of May 1, 1956.

social thought in the Middle Ages, in the works of sociological pioneers of more recent centuries, in the social consciousness of the working masses in capitalist countries and in the new socialist republics, where the image of social relations that is in process of formation in different milieux, among peasants, workers and the intelligentsia, is not always in accordance with the interpretation suggested by the authorities.

The persistence over thousands of years of certain ways of interpreting class structure, through changes of social system, of forms of production and of the distribution of wealth, indicates that in the schemes analyzed we are dealing with interpretations of a class society which are concerned with problems whose topicality is not restricted to any single social order; that is to say with interpretations of a class society in the broadest sense. This testifies to the fact that we are here dealing with questions which have been of considerable importance over a long span of generations. There can be no doubt that what is involved here are enduring social ideals, with which the defenders of the existing order also have to reckon. For the underprivileged, these enduring interpretations of class structure emphasize the conflict between the existing state of affairs and the values to which they aspire.

On the other hand, approval of the existing order has somehow, always developed into apologetics. There is no need to look as late as the modern bourgeois democracies for instances of this process. Such apologetic functions were being performed many centuries earlier by the myth of Ham, the myth of the origin of the four Indian castes, or the commonsense arguments of Aristotle or Lactantius.[13] In the middle of the nineteenth century, George Fitzhugh, the defender of the slave system in the Southern states, even appealed in his sruggle against the Northern abolitionists to the principles of Communism; he tried to demonstrate the superiority of a system of slavery from the viewpoint of Communist ideals ("to everyone according to his needs") and attacked class oppression in the "free" states of the industrial North.[14] Equally striking in this respect have been the arguments used since the end of the nineteenth century by defenders of racial discrimination in the United States, or in the former British Empire.

Approval of the existing order, even when expressed in the most ruthless and brutal forms, has become a defensive argument in face of an ideal—an ideal which over the centuries has been extinguished and reborn, aroused people to action, taken the form of unrealizable dreams or glimmered in the mists of an afterworld, but which has always managed to emerge from the recesses of the social consciousness to disturb the existing state of affairs. The defenders of the existing order have even been forced to reckon with this ideal's invasion of the privileged ranks, whence the leaders of revolutionary

[13] Lactantius Firmianus (c. 260–c. 340 A.D.), called the "Christian Cicero," author of *Divinarum Institutionum Libri Septem* and some treatises.

[14] *Sociology for the South or the Failure of Free Society*, Richmond, 1854.

movements have been recruited on more than one occasion. The content of this ideal was codified as the threefold slogan of the French Revolution—*Liberté, Egalité, Fraternité*—and was later neutralized by an appropriate interpretation. But this content is probably more ancient than the legend of the age of Saturn and the extravagances of Antisthenes' followers. It was adopted by the proletarian revolutionaries in the nineteenth century, and it was then that the revolutionary camp accepted the term "classless society" to aid the final realization of these slogans in their full and original meaning.

This three-fold ideal confers special importance on the interpretations of social structure which have recurred for thousands of years. The scheme of gradation emphasizes the conflict of the existing order with the ideal of equality. The dichotomic scheme stresses its conflict with all three ideals of the classless society. Despite its utilitarian justifications, the functional scheme in its negative aspect (conflict of class interests combined with mutual dependence between classes), shows an inevitable conflict between the existing social mechanism and the ideal of fraternity. In its positive aspect (the cooperation of classes through their distinctive functions) the functional scheme, and also the scheme of a social-status continuum, as expressed by the defenders of the status quo, pay indirect tribute to those ideals, because they present such aspects of the existing order as do not arouse sharp opposition from those who accept the principles linked with this triple formula and the revolutionary ideal of the classless society.

In this study we have had an opportunity of observing not only the persistence of certain schemes of class structure but also the persistence, despite cultural changes, of fundamentally opposite ways of interpreting class structure and the persistence of methods of defending the existing order. These methods have been aimed either at demonstrating that the attainment of a society of free and equal men is impossible or at presenting the existing state of affairs in the least offensive way from the viewpoint of the oppressed classes.

These conflicts and these methods have recurred in societies with social orders as far removed from one another as the Roman Republic in the days of the legendary Agrippa, or those in which Lactantius or St. Augustine lived, were from the capitalist society as seen by Spencer and as reflected in the Papal encyclical *Rerum Novarum.* And in our own period the methods of justifying the combating of *uravnilovka* [wage leveling] in the socialist republics are very reminiscent of the arguments advanced on the other side of the Atlantic to justify inequality of economic status on the grounds of the need to increase production. These arguments again have an early precedent in the writings of the Church Fathers in the third and fourth centuries.

Marxism formulated the problem of the ideological superstructure of particular formations. Study of the conceptions of class structure over centuries has shown that class systems have an enduring ideological superstructure independent of their particular social order.

The Modern Model of Social Class and Recent Transformations

. . . The dependence of social status on the relations to the means of production has probably existed and continues to exist in all social systems which have gone beyond a primitive form of economy. But it has never been so important a factor in the system of human relations as in the legitimate countries of free-enterprise capitalism. Marx's theory of class grasped this factor of the social structure that was fundamental for this period. And Marx's criterion of the class division proved immensely fertile in the development of social theory, by helping to draw attention to hitherto unperceived facts and by encouraging profounder investigation of social processes that were taking place all the time.

In our own world the relations of ownership to the means of production are still a factor of immense significance in the formation of human relations; without the Marxian insight into social life it would be virtually impossible to conduct an incisive analysis of the changes which are taking place in the modern world. But the scope of the applicability of the Marxian criterion has undergone important changes. . . .

The Marxian criterion of social class has [also] lost some of its adequacy in relation to the capitalist countries. Here I am not by any means referring only to the Fascist countries, where the large-scale application of the means of compulsion structure of countries in which the principles of economic liberalism are respected. Such changes are seen at their most effective in the United States.

According to Marx and Engels the development of capitalism was to be accompanied by a rapid process of economic polarization and by the disappearance of the middle class. The envisaged polarization did not occur, but it is by no means easy to say whether the process of disappearance of the middle class predicted by Marx is actually occurring in the world's most advanced capitalist country. The old American middle class which formed so large a part of the United States population in de Tocqueville's period, and which in his view was the guarantee of American democracy, was that of the property owners who work in their own establishments. This class has in fact shrunk rapidly, in line with Marx's prediction, although not so rapidly as might have been expected in view of the violent rate of the accumulation of capital. Simultaneously, however, a new middle class has been rising, a class of civil servants, trade union officials, local government officers, a class of technicians, white-collar workers and minor executives in the large industrial establishments.

The rapid rise of this new class shows up strikingly in statistical returns and is changing the whole social structure of the United States. In the time of de Tocqueville and Marx it was too insignificant to be differentiated as a separate class, and it was not included in the framework of the classical Marxian division. It was a marginal group. Now this marginal group among the classes of the Marxian scheme has so increased in size in contemporary America that it is impossible not to regard it as a class, especially when we consider general trends of development in the United States.[15] This new class, which has a corresponding group in the "stratum" of nonmanual white-collar workers in state and local government and in party offices in the U.S.S.R., is, it would seem, even characterized by its own social attitudes and its own subculture.[16]

Thus the answer to the question whether the Marxian forecast about the fate of the middle class is being fulfilled in the United States depends on the interpretation of the term "middle class"; in Marx's day this term did not involve such difficulties.

The well-known conflicts between medium and large property owners which occurred in the United States in the Rooseveltian era, also suggest certain new reflections about the criterion of social class. The owners of medium-sized property whom Roosevelt's legislation was intended to defend against the large property owners were in fact businessmen or firms disposing of hundreds of thousands of dollars, or even "small millionaires" threatened by the great concerns and the multi-millionaires. This bitter "class struggle" which so absorbed American society—and was of great significance for the American social structure—can be presented only within the framework of a scheme of gradation, and not of a scheme of intersecting dichotomies.

There are other reasons why the nineteenth-century conception of social class, in both the liberal and the Marxian interpretations, has lost much of its applicability in the modern world. In situations where changes of social structure are to a greater or lesser degree governed by the decision of the political authorities, we are a long way from social classes as interpreted by Marx, Ward, Veblen or Weber, from classes conceived of as groups determined by their relations to the means of production or, as others would say, by their relations to the market. We are a long way from classes conceived of as groups arising out of the spontaneous activities of individuals or at the

15 Some sociologists have estimated that the percentage of people who owned their own means of livelihood in the decade between 1820 and 1830 was as much as 80 percent of the free population of the United States. Cf. K. Mayer, "Changes in the Social Structure of the United States," *Transactions of the Third World Congress of Sociology,* Vol. III, London 1956, p. 69. The same study gives statistical data to illustrate the reduction of the former middle class and the rise of the new one in the period 1870–1954. According to Mayer the percentage of self-employed persons among the working population of the United States fell from 40.4 percent in1870 to 13.3 percent in 1954, while the percentage decrease of farmers was from 27.1 percent to 5.9 percent. The percentage of wage-workers, including farm laborers, underwent little change—from 52.8 percent in 1870 to 55.8 percent in 1954. On the other hand the percentage of salaried employees (in contrast to wage-workers) grew from 6.6 percent in 1870 to 30.8 percent in 1954: within this group the percentage of civil servants and clerical workers rose from 0.6 percent in 1870 to 13.1 percent in 1954 ("Changes in Social Structure," p. 70).

16 Cf. L. Corey: *The Middle Class* in *Class, Status and Power,* ed. R. Bendix and S. M. Lipset, Glencoe, Illinois, 1953, pp. 372–373, 378, 380, 693.

most of spontaneously created class organizations. In situations where the political authorities can overtly and effectively change the class structure; where the privileges that are most essential for social status, including that of a higher share in the national income, are conferred by a decision of the political authorities; where a large part or even the majority of the population is included in a stratification of the type to be found in a bureaucratic hierarchy—the nineteenth-century concept of class becomes more or less an anachronism, and class conflicts give way to other forms of social antagonism.[17]

[17] Cf. the predictions made by Arturo Labrioli in the early years of the present century: *Karl Marx—L'économiste—Le socialiste,* Paris 1909, pp. 254, 256, 260.

BIBLIOGRAPHY

Part I—The Challenge of Competing Perspectives

Benn, Stanley. "Nature of Political Philosophy." *The Encyclopedia of Philosophy,* Volume 6. New York: Macmillan, 1967, pp. 387–392.

Connolly, William E. *Political Science and Ideology.* New York: Atherton Press, 1967.

Dahrendorf, Ralf. "Out of Utopia: Toward a Re-orientation of Sociological Analysis." *American Journal of Sociology* 54 (September 1958), 115–127.

Hampshire, Stuart. *Thought and Action.* New York: Viking Press, 1959.

Horton, John. "Order and Conflict Theories of Social Problems as Competing Ideologies." *American Journal of Sociology* (May 1966), 701–713.

Johnson, Chalmers. *Revolutionary Change.* Boston: Little, Brown and Company, 1966. See especially Chapters 2, 3, and 4.

Kateb, George. *Political Theory: Its Nature and Uses.* New York: St. Martin's Press, 1968.

Kettler, David. "Political Science and Political Rationality." In *Political Theory and Social Change,* edited by David Spitz. New York: Atherton Press, 1967.

MacIntyre, Alasdair. *Against the Self-Images of the Age.* New York: Schocken Books, 1971.

Mannheim, Karl. *Ideology and Utopia.* New York: Harcourt, Brace, 1936.

Taylor, Charles. "Interpretation and the Sciences of Man." *Review of Metaphysics* (Fall 1971), 4–51.

Part II—Political Man: Some Classical Images

Arendt, Hannah. *The Human Condition.* Garden City: Anchor Books, 1959.

Avineri, Shlomo. *The Social and Political Thought of Karl Marx.* New York: Cambridge University Press, 1968.

Bottomore, T. B., ed. *Karl Marx: Selected Writings in Sociology and Social Philosophy.* New York: McGraw-Hill, 1964.

Durkheim, Emile. *The Division of Labor in Society.* Glencoe: The Free Press, 1947.

Giddens, Anthony. *Capitalism and Modern Social Theory: An Analysis of the*

Writings of Marx, Durkheim and Max Weber. New York: Cambridge University Press, 1971.

Kaufman, Arnold. "On Alienation." *Inquiry* (Summer 1964), 1–25.

Lukes, Steven. *Individualism.* New York: Oxford University Press, 1973.

MacPherson, C. B. *The Political Theory of Possessive Individualism.* Oxford: Clarendon Press, 1962.

Merton, Robert K. "Social Structure and Anomie." *American Sociological Review* (October 1938), 672–682.

Nisbet, Robert. *The Sociological Tradition.* New York: Basic Books, Inc., 1966.

Winch, Peter. "Human Nature." In *The Proper Study,* edited by G. N. A. Vesey, pp. 1–13. London: Macmillan Press, 1971.

Part III—Contemporary Models of Society and Politics

Dahrendorf, Ralf. *Class and Class Conflict in Industrial Society.* Stanford: Stanford University Press, 1959.

Edwards, Richard C., Reich, Michael, and Weisskopf, Thomas, eds. *The Capitalist System: A Radical Analysis of American Society.* Englewood Cliffs: Prentice Hall, 1972.

Kolko, Gabriel. *Wealth and Power in America.* New York: Praeger, 1962.

Mann, Michael. "The Social Cohesion of Liberal Democracy." *American Sociological Review* (June 1970), 423–439.

Mills, C. Wright. *The Power Elite.* New York: Oxford University Press, 1956.

Parkin, Frank. *Class Inequality and Political Order.* New York: Praeger, 1971.

Parsons, Talcott. *Essays in Sociological Theory.* Glencoe: The Free Press, 1954.

Sennett, Richard, and Cobb, Jonathan. *The Hidden Injuries of Class.* New York: Alfred Knopf, 1972.

Tumin, Melvin. "Some Principles of Stratification: A Critical Analysis." *American Sociological Review* (August 1953), 387–394.

Part IV—Theoretical Conflict and Critical Choice

Bachrach, Peter and Baratz, Morton. "The Two Faces of Power." *American Political Science Review* (December 1962), 947–952.

Balbus, Isaac P. "The Concept of Interest in Pluralist and Marxian Analysis." *Politics and Society* (Summer 1971), 151–177.

Champlin, John. "On the Study of Power." *Politics and Society* (November 1970), 91–112.

Dahrendorf, Ralf. "On the Origin of Inequality Among Men." *Essays in the Theory of Society,* pp. 151–178. Stanford: Stanford University Press, 1968.

Gallie, W. B. "Essentially Contested Concepts." In *The Importance of Language,* edited by Max Black, pp. 121–146. Englewood Cliffs: Prentice Hall, 1962.

Oppenheim, Felix. "Egalitarianism as a Descriptive Concept." *American Philosophical Quarterly* (1970), 43–52.

Runciman, W. G. *Relative Deprivation and Social Justice.* Berkeley: University of California Press, 1969.

Schaar, John. "Equality of Opportunity and Beyond." In *Equality: Nomos IX,* edited by J. R. Pennock and J. W. Chapman, pp. 228–249. New York: Atherton Press, 1967.

Williams, Bernard. "The Idea of Equality." In *Philosophy, Politics and Society* (second series), edited by P. Laslett and W. G. Runciman, pp. 129–130. New York: Oxford University Press, 1962.

Wolff, Robert Paul. "Community." *The Poverty of Liberalism,* pp. 162–195. Boston: Beacon Press, 1968.

1 2 3 4 5 6 7 8 9 10